MRS. ABRAHAM LINCOLN

Mary Todd Lincoln

Mrs. Abraham Lincoln

A STUDY OF HER PERSONALITY
AND HER INFLUENCE ON LINCOLN

by

W. A. EVANS

M.S., M.D.

With a Foreword by Jason Emerson

Southern Illinois University Press
Carbondale and Edwardsville

First edition published 1932 by Alfred A. Knopf

Printed in the United States of America

13 12 11 10 4 3 2 1

Library of Congress Cataloging-in-Publication Data
Evans, W. A. (William Augustus), 1865–1948.
Mrs. Abraham Lincoln : a study of her personality and her influence on Lincoln / by W. A. Evans.
p. cm.
"First edition published 1932 by Alfred A. Knopf."
Includes bibliographical references and index.
ISBN-13: 978-0-8093-2971-7 (alk. paper)
ISBN-10: 0-8093-2971-9 (alk. paper)
1. Lincoln, Mary Todd, 1818–1882. 2. Lincoln, Abraham, 1809–1865—Marriage. 3. Presidents' spouses—United States—Biography. I. Title.
E457.25.E94 2010
973.7092—dc22
[B] 2009041823

Printed on recycled paper. ♻
The paper used in this publication meets the minimum requirements of American National Standard for Information Sciences—Permanence of Paper for Printed Library Materials, ANSI Z39.48-1992. ∞

CONTENTS

FOREWORD xiii

PREFACE xviii

INTRODUCTION 3

I. THE GIFTS OF THE ANCESTORS 31

II. CHILDHOOD 65

III. YOUTH BUILDS HER UP 77

IV. THE TRAINING OF MATURITY 113

V. ROUNDING OUT 137

VI. THE PEAK AND A DECLINE 163

VII. TAKING TOLL 193

VIII. MENDING HER FENCES 221

IX. FINANCIAL SECURITY AND INSECURITY 233

X. THE HELP AND HARM OF POLITICS 251

XI. RELIGION 263

XII. THE INFLUENCE OF SOCIETY 269

XIII. THE PHYSICAL PHASES OF HER PERSONALITY 275

XIV. HER MENTAL AND PERSONALITY QUALITIES 287

XV. ON THE ROCKS 305

XVI. MUTUAL INFLUENCE 323

XVII. HEALTH 337

XVIII. JUSTICE 349

BIBLIOGRAPHY 355

INDEX *follows p.* 364

ILLUSTRATIONS

MARY TODD LINCOLN *Frontispiece*

ROBERT S. TODD *following p.* 158

From a portrait owned by Mrs. Emilie Helm

GENEALOGICAL CHART OF MARY TODD LINCOLN

ROBERT TODD LINCOLN

From a photograph in the Frederick H. Meserve collection

WILLIAM WALLACE LINCOLN

From a photograph in the Frederick H. Meserve collection

"TAD" LINCOLN

From a photograph in the Frederick H. Meserve collection

THE MAIN STREET HOUSE OF ROBERT S. TODD, LEXINGTON, AS IT APPEARS TODAY

ONE OF THE BUILDINGS OCCUPIED BY TRANSYLVANIA UNIVERSITY WHEN MARY TODD LIVED IN LEXINGTON

MORRISON HALL, TRANSYLVANIA COLLEGE

ONE OF THE FIRST DAGUERREOTYPE CAMERAS BROUGHT TO AMERICA, NOW IN SAYRE INSTITUTE, LEXINGTON

PLANETARIUM MADE AND MOUNTED BY THOMAS HARRIS BARLOW, OF LEXINGTON

THE NINIAN W. EDWARDS RESIDENCE, SPRINGFIELD

PARLOR OF THE EDWARDS RESIDENCE

THE GLOBE TAVERN, SPRINGFIELD

THE MONROE STREET COTTAGE, SPRINGFIELD

From a drawing

THE LINCOLN RESIDENCE, SPRINGFIELD

THE YOUTHFUL LINCOLN
From a photograph taken in Princeton, Illinois, July 4, 1856

THE YOUTHFUL MRS. LINCOLN
From a photograph owned by Oliver R. Barrett

THE ANDERSON BUILDING, UNITED STATES SOLDIERS' HOME, WASHINGTON

ABRAHAM LINCOLN WHILE PRESIDENT
From a photograph owned by S. R. Cameron

THE WHITE HOUSE DURING LINCOLN'S ADMINISTRATION
From a photograph in the Frederick H. Meserve collection

THE CLIFTON HOUSE, CHICAGO
From a picture owned by the Chicago Historical Society

THE HOUSE ON WASHINGTON STREET, CHICAGO, OWNED BY MRS. LINCOLN

BELLEVUE PLACE SANATORIUM, BATAVIA, ILLINOIS

EAR-RINGS OWNED BY MRS. LINCOLN, NOW IN THE POSSESSION OF HOMER SWEET

MARY TODD WHEN ABOUT TWENTY YEARS OLD
From a portrait, now owned by William H. Townsend, painted by Katherine Helm

MRS. LINCOLN
From a photograph owned by S. R. Cameron

SIGNATURE FROM A BOOK OWNED BY OLIVER R. BARRETT

SIGNATURE FROM A PHOTOGRAPH OWNED BY OLIVER R. BARRETT

MRS. LINCOLN'S SIGNATURE FROM A LETTER IN THE JOHN HAY LIBRARY, BROWN UNIVERSITY

MRS. LINCOLN
From a photograph owned by Oliver R. Barrett

MRS. LINCOLN

Foreword

Jason Emerson

Biographical studies of Abraham Lincoln began immediately after his assassination in April 1865; the life and influence of his wife, Mary Lincoln, was obscured and ignored until the early twentieth century. And still, more than eighty years after the first full biography about her was published, Mary Lincoln remains a misunderstood and maligned woman.

Scholarship on her life and her contributions to her husband's life has increased over the past twenty years, but the articles on her are by necessity limited to specific topics, and the recent books about her fall far short of achieving any lasting success in illuminating her life in a fair, balanced, and comprehensive way. Most of the books published about Mary over the past half century have tended toward egregious apology and overt political revisionism, casting her as a mythic feminist icon that Mary herself would never have recognized, nor accepted. Many of the articles about her over the same time period tend toward vilifying her as a terrible wife, a reprehensible First Lady, and an embarrassing widow—likewise descriptions alien to those who knew Mary.

Of course, the real Mary Lincoln lies somewhere in between those two conflicting versions. I don't know why finding an objective balance about Mary Lincoln's life has been so elusive for writers and historians for so long, but whichever way the interpretation tends, it seems always to overreach and ultimately corrupt whatever new facts may have been discovered.

Interestingly, it is one of the first biographies of Mary Lincoln published that remains probably the best book about her: *Mrs. Abraham Lincoln: A Study of Her Personality and Her Influence on Lincoln* by W. A. Evans, published in 1932. The book has been out of print and overlooked for decades, and its absence has left a huge gap in current Mary Lincoln research and understanding. A reprint edition is long overdue, and hopefully this volume by

Southern Illinois University Press will foster a new appreciation of Evans's outstanding scholarship by a new generation of readers.

William Augustus Evans was born on August 5, 1865, in Marion, Alabama, where his father had been head of that town's Confederate Army Hospital. Evans grew up in Monroe County, Mississippi, both in his family's house in Aberdeen and at their plantation near Prairie. He graduated from Aberdeen High School and completed his B.S. at the Mississippi Agricultural College in 1883. He earned his M.D. from Tulane University in New Orleans in 1885 and completed his postgraduate studies at the Pasteur Institute in Paris, France.

Evans moved to Chicago in 1891 and, for the next forty-three years, had a distinguished career as a physician, public health authority, newspaper columnist, and historian. He was on the staff of Cook County and Alexian Brothers hospitals and also taught pathology at the University of Chicago and Northwestern Medical School. He was president of the Chicago Medical Society in 1902 and 1903 and became Chicago's first Public Health Commissioner in 1907. During his four years as commissioner, Evans established new methods for the city to fight tuberculosis, initiated the study of the problems of air hygiene, improved public health education, and was a strong proponent of the pasteurization and refrigeration of milk. Of his advocacy of the latter, the *Chicago Tribune* later wrote, "It is no exaggeration to say that many thousands of people who are walking the streets today owe their lives to the plans he formulated and the rules he enforced for combating infant mortality thru safeguarding a city's milk supply."[1]

Evans seems never to have been comfortable unless moving forward. In 1910, he received his LL.D. from Tulane, and in 1911, he received his doctorate in public health from the University of Michigan. When he resigned as city health commissioner in 1911, Evans became the health editor for the *Chicago Tribune.* He wrote his medical advice column "How to Keep Well" for twenty-three years, during which time he received more than one million letters from readers.[2]

After Evans retired in 1934, he left Chicago to prospect for gold in New Mexico, then traveled through Central and South America, Asia, and Africa. He returned to his hometown of Aberdeen, Mississippi, where his main interest became researching and recording the history of Monroe County. In 1939, he gave the city of Aberdeen $10,000 for a new library in honor of his family—the Evans Memorial Library. He also assisted in the renovation of Beauvoir, Jefferson Davis's home in Biloxi, Mississippi, as a historical shrine. Evans died in 1948 at the age of 83.[3]

In the midst of his numerous medical and journalistic responsibilities, sometime in 1926 Evans became fascinated by Mary Todd Lincoln—specifically, how her mind and her personality affected and influenced her husband. This idea, as Evans explains in his introduction to this book, sprung from the suggestion of noted Lincoln scholar William E. Barton that Evans should make a study of Mary's personality. The more Evans looked into the topic, the more interested he became; and instead of simply gathering some information and maturing some opinions on the topic as he originally intended, Evans ultimately decided to pursue a complete and thorough study of Mrs. Lincoln.

Evans was an assiduous researcher, as an examination of the bibliography at the end of this book will show. He not only read all available books, journal articles, and newspaper articles about Mary Lincoln, but he also consulted with numerous Lincoln scholars and collectors, Todd family members and friends, and medical experts. He recruited his sister to travel to Lexington, Kentucky, where she interviewed Mary Lincoln's half-sister, Emilie Todd Helm; Helm's daughters; and several other Todd relatives. Evans's sister also found the financial records of the Parker and Todd families and searched "all the newspaper files of the period during which Mary Todd lived as a young girl in Lexington."[4] Evans himself traveled to Springfield, Illinois, among other places, where he consulted with president of the Abraham Lincoln Association and noted Lincoln scholar Paul M. Angle, and also interviewed Mary's nieces Mrs. Edward D. Keys and Mary Edwards Brown.

Mrs. Keys allowed Evans to copy entries from the family bible, and Mrs. Brown showed him numerous family items and directed him toward additional sources.[5] Evans also tried to gain access to the Abraham Lincoln papers stored by Robert Lincoln in the Library of Congress in 1919; but Robert's widow, Mary Harlan Lincoln, would not allow it. The papers were embargoed from public viewing until 1947 under the terms of Robert's will, and his wife would not grant Evans an exception. She did, however, tell him that there were no papers regarding Mary Todd Lincoln—the reason for his request—in the collection. This had been determined by Katherine Helm, Mrs. Abraham Lincoln's niece and author of the family-authorized biography of the former First Lady, when she was allowed to look through the Lincoln papers in preparation of her book.[6]

When researching Mary's mental health, Evans consulted with five mental health experts; he wrote to Mary Lincoln's niece Katherine Helm and asked for her opinions and assistance on the subject; he also sought out Myra Pritchard, who had owned a series of correspondence between her grandmother Myra Bradwell and Mary Lincoln, most of which was written while Mary was in Bellevue Place sanitarium.[7]

In early 1930, Evans was so struck by the lack of historical understanding concerning the cause of Mary Lincoln's death in 1882 that he wrote about the subject in his weekly *Chicago Tribune* column. Evans declared—in what appears to be the first public diagnosis of her death by a historian—that Mary Lincoln died of diabetic coma. He wrote this in order to set the record straight after finding nothing but misunderstanding about diabetes in general and in regards to Mary Lincoln in particular. His diagnosis was based on the medical evidence on Mary's death as reported in the contemporary major Chicago and Springfield newspapers, as well as on the statement of her physician, Dr. Thomas W. Dresser.[8]

By April 1931, Evans had completed his book and was in the editing and revising stage. "The two chapters that are least satisfactory to me are those dealing with the influence of politics and the influence of husband and wife on each other," Evans wrote to historian Paul Angle. "I have been working on this now for five years and I am getting tired."[9] He may have been tired, but Evans clearly was enthusiastic about his subject and his research and was eager to make it public. Many of his conclusions about Mary Lincoln flew in the face of conventional wisdom about her, especially the stories written by William Herndon in 1889 and perpetuated ever after: that Ann Rutledge was the love of Lincoln's life and he therefore never loved any other woman; that Lincoln left Mary standing on the altar during their first wedding ceremony on Jan. 1, 1841; and that Mary Lincoln was fully aware and mentally capable when committing the numerous bizarre acts she undertook during her life. As Evans wrote to Lincoln collector and attorney Henry Horner, "I may need your services as a judge to restrain certain people after the book comes out. I agree with the *Tribune* in thinking the Ann Rutledge myth, the wedding from which Lincoln defaulted, etc., were 'idle tales' and per this some may want to kick me in the pants. I do not think Mrs. Lincoln should be held responsible for what she did and said when she was insane, any more than we hold other insane people responsible, and for that I may need an injunction."[10]

Once *Mrs. Abraham Lincoln: A Study of Her Personality and Her Influence on Lincoln* was released in March 1932, it was highly acclaimed. The *Mississippi Valley Historical Review* declared, "The student of history can only feel grateful for this study of Lincoln's spouse in the light of modern medical science."[11] The *New York Times* review declared:

> No one should pick up this book with the expectation of finding either a jazzy biography over which to lick his lips or, on the other hand, any purple literary passages. It is simply an honest and intelligent study of a subject that should have been looked into long ago. It ought to stand on every shelf which holds a biography of Abraham Lincoln, for his great heart would not have wanted adoration for himself without at least justice for Mary.[12]

For decades, Evans's book was considered the essential biography of Mary Lincoln, and nearly every historian since 1932 has referenced it, although not all agree with Evans's conclusions.[13]

The most vocal praise of Evans's work has come from Ruth Painter Randall, who, in her 1953 biography of Mary Lincoln, declared *Mrs. Abraham Lincoln* a valuable book in general, and more specifically, an "invaluable study of Mrs. Lincoln's impaired personality," and an "excellent a study of the insanity subject."[14] Conversely, noted biographer Fawn M. Brodie, in her introduction to *Mary Todd Lincoln: Her Life and Letters* by Justin and Linda Turner, called Evans's work "disorganized and thin" and declared "there has never been a good clinical study of Mary Lincoln and the etiology of her illness."[15]

I believe *Mrs. Abraham Lincoln* is one of the best books on Mary Lincoln yet written despite its age. While it certainly lacks much primary evidence available today, but which was neither known nor accessible to Evans in 1932, it includes source materials long ago forgotten by current historians as well as original interviews with friends and family of Mary Lincoln available in no other works. It is certainly the most objective book in its interpretations of Mary Lincoln. The impressive impartiality and sheer historical value of this book comes from the fact that Evans did not simply want to write a book about daily events in Mary Lincoln's life, he wanted to *understand* her personality, her life, and her influence on her husband. This result he certainly achieved in what is an incomparable book, and essential reading for any Mary Lincoln scholar and enthusiast.

Notes

1. "Dr. W. A. Evans," *Chicago Tribune,* Nov. 11, 1948, 26.

2. His columns were published in a book of more than 1,300 pages titled *How to Keep Well: A Health Book for the Home* (New York: D. Appleton & Co., 1917). The book was reprinted in 1924 for Sears, Roebuck & Co., and its page count reduced to 1,012.

3. Sources on the details of Evans's life include: *Who's Who in America,* vol. 7, 1912–1913 (Chicago: A. N. Marquis & Co., 1912), 661; "Dr. Evans, 83, Health Editor 23 Years, Dies," *Chicago Tribune,* Nov. 9, 1948, 22; "Mississippi Funeral to Be Held Thursday for Dr. W. A. Evans," *Chicago Tribune,* Nov. 10, 1948, B6; "Dr. W.

A. Evans," *Chicago Tribune,* Nov. 11, 1948, 26; "William A. Evans," *American Journal of Public Health* 39 (Aug. 1949): 1039–40; "Dr. William Augustus Evans," Evans Memorial Library website, http://www.tombigbee.lib.ms.us/evans/history/DrEvans.html.

4. W. A. Evans to Henry Horner, Chicago, June 1, 1929, Personal Correspondence Folder, El-Ev, Box 3, Henry Horner Lincoln Collection papers, Manuscripts Division, Abraham Lincoln Presidential Library, Springfield, Ill.

5. W. A. Evans to Paul Angle, Chicago, Mar. 16, 1931, Correspondence 1931 Folder, Letters D-E, Box 7, Abraham Lincoln Association Papers, Manuscripts Division, Abraham Lincoln Presidential Library, Springfield, Ill. For personal reminiscences of these two women, see also Beulah Gordon, "Mrs. Keys Recalls Stories of Her Aunt Mary Lincoln," *Illinois State Journal & Register,* Aug. 23, 1942, clipping in Mary Lincoln Folder, Sangamon Valley Collection, Lincoln Public Library, Springfield, Ill.; "Abraham Lincoln Married 78 Years Ago Today; Mrs. Mary Edwards Brown Tells Story of Hasty Wedding Plans," *Illinois State Journal,* Nov. 4, 1920; Dorothy Meserve Kunhardt, "An Old Lady's Lincoln Memories," *Life* 46, no. 6 (Feb. 9, 1959): 57, 59–60.

6. W. A. Evans to Mary Harlan Lincoln, Chicago, Apr. 16, 1930, and Frederic N. Towers (for Mary Harlan Lincoln) to W. A. Evans, Apr. 21, 1930, File 75, Container 4, Series 2, Robert Todd Lincoln Family Papers, Manuscripts Division, Library of Congress. Katherine Helm, *The True Story of Mary, Wife of Lincoln: Containing the Recollections of Mary Lincoln's Sister Emilie (Mrs. Ben Hardin Helm), Extracts from Her War-Time Diary, Numerous Letters and Other Documents Now First Published.* (New York: Harper & Brothers, 1928).

7. The names of Evans's medical experts are listed in his preface to the first edition; W. A. Evans to Katherine Helm, Chicago, Oct. 13, 1928, and Katherine Helm to W. A. Evans, n.d., (draft response handwritten on back of Evans's letter to Helm, unclear if it was ever sent), Correspondence Folder, 1926–1927, F Box 2, Todd-Helm Family Items, William H. Townsend Collection, University of Kentucky Libraries, Lexington, Ky.; W. A. Evans

to Myra Pritchard, Nov. 24, 1928, and Myra Pritchard to Frederic Towers, Nov. 28, 1928, and Frederic Towers to Myra Pritchard, Dec. 4, 1928, Folder 4, Cont. 8, Part 2, Robert Todd Lincoln Family Papers, Manuscripts Division, Library of Congress. Pritchard had sold her Mary Lincoln letters to the widow of Robert Todd Lincoln some ten months prior to Evans's inquiry, so he never saw them. The Lincoln family suppressed the correspondence, and it was considered "lost" to history until its discovery in 2005. For the story of the discovery and the contents of the letters, see Jason Emerson, *The Madness of Mary Lincoln* (Carbondale: Southern Illinois University Press, 2007), 140–150, 159–183.

8. Thomas W. Dresser to William Herndon, Springfield, Ill., Jan. 3, 1889, in Douglas L. Wilson and Rodney O. Davis, eds., *Herndon's Informants: Letters, Interviews, and Statements about Abraham Lincoln* (Urbana: University of Chicago Press, 1998), 671; "Mary Todd Lincoln: Her Death in This City at 8 O'Clock Sunday Evening," *Illinois State Journal*, July 17, 1882, 6; "Death of Mrs. Lincoln," *New York Times*, July 17, 1882, 1; "Obituary: Death at Springfield, Illinois, of the Widow of Abraham Lincoln," *Chicago Tribune*, July 17, 1882, 2.

9. W. A. Evans to Paul Angle, Chicago, April 1, 1931, Correspondence 1931 Folder, Letters D-E, Box 7, Abraham Lincoln Association Papers, Manuscripts Division, Abraham Lincoln Presidential Library, Springfield, Ill.

10. W. A. Evans to Henry Horner, n.d., Personal Correspondence Folder, El-Ev, Box 3, Henry Horner Lincoln Collection papers, Manuscripts Division, Abraham Lincoln Presidential Library, Springfield, Ill.

11. A.C.C., "Mary Lincoln: Wife and Widow, Part I; Mary Lincoln: Wife and Widow, Part II. Letters Documents and Appendix; Mrs. Abraham Lincoln," *Mississippi Valley Historical Review* 21, no. 1 (June 1934): 99.

12. R. L. Duffus, "Justice Done to Mary Todd, the Wife of Lincoln," *New York Times*, Mar. 6, 1932, BR3.

13. The sole biographer of Mary Lincoln not to utilize and reference Evans's work has been Jean Baker in her 1987 book *Mary*

Todd Lincoln: A Biography.

14. Ruth Painter Randall, *Mary Lincoln: Biography of a Marriage* (Boston: Little, Brown and Company, 1953), 22, 192, 432.

15. Fawn M. Brodie, introduction to Justin G. Turner and Linda Levitt Turner, *Mary Todd Lincoln: Her Life and Letters* (New York: Alfred A. Knopf, 1972), xv.

Preface

WHEN ONE UNDERTAKES A STUDY OF THE LIFE OF A public man or woman, one can expect to find something of a printed record. If the study is based on the subject's connection with high lights of history, the sources of information are easily accessible. Nor is there a dearth of material when one delves somewhat more into the private life of a person who is very much under public observation. Free access to a few good libraries generally suffices to make available as much material as can be used. But when one undertakes a study of a wife and mother who lived over fifty years ago, even though her husband was President of the United States, the task is not so easy. If the undertaking includes an investigation of her behavior — private as well as public — the difficulties are greater. To attempt to explain that behavior in the light of more modern views of personality adds to the difficulties.

There are many Abraham Lincoln collectors and a large Lincoln literature, but there are no Mrs. Lincoln collectors, and no collection of Mrs. Lincoln literature. It is true that much has been written about the wife of the first president to be assassinated, but it is not assembled. The material must be sought for in many places.

It is a pleasure for me to acknowledge the help I have had, and to express my appreciation thereof and gratitude therefor to:

Mrs. J. O. Wynn, my sister, who visited Lexington, Kentucky, three times and there interviewed Mrs. Emilie Todd Helm, her three children, and others — relatives of Mrs. Lincoln and descendants of friends of her family. Mrs. Wynn read the files of the Lexington papers from 1817 to 1840 and other documents in the Lexington Public Library and in the library of Transylvania College. She read the Draper Collection in the State Historical Society of Wisconsin, and the Durrett Collection in the University of Chicago.

Mrs. I. D. Rawlings, wife of my long-time associate in the Chicago and the Illinois Departments of Health, who read the files of the Springfield papers, and other documents and books, in the Illinois State Historical Society, Springfield.

The following libraries for access to their Lincoln material and newspaper files — given either to me personally or to someone helping with the investigation: those of the Chicago *Tribune,* the Chicago Historical Society, and the Illinois State Historical Society, the Newberry Library, the library of the University of Chicago, the Chicago Public Library, the library of the State Historical Society of Wisconsin, that of Transylvania College, the Lexington Public Library, the John Hay Library of Brown University, the Congressional Library, the New York Public Library, the Huntington Library, the library of the Union League Club of Chicago, and that of the Lincoln Historical Research Foundation; to the librarians and their assistants for intelligent guidance and help, especially Mildred Burke, of the Chicago *Tribune* Library, Mrs. Harriet Taylor, of the Newberry Library, and Mrs. Charles F. Norton, of Transylvania College Library.

Dr. B. J. Cigrand, of Batavia, Illinois, who undertook to find what medical record the Bellevue Place Sanatorium had of Mrs. Lincoln. When he found that the sanatorium had not saved any of Dr. R. J. Patterson's notes or the history sheets of Mrs. Lincoln's mental illness, Dr. Cigrand put at my disposal his collection of newspaper references to Mrs. Lincoln, consisting principally of items appearing in the Fox River Valley papers, and those of Chicago in 1875.

Oliver R. Barrett and Judge Henry Horner of Chicago, who gave me access to their Lincoln material, permitted me to use part of their collections, and helped me to get court records.

William H. Townsend, of Lexington, Kentucky, who also helped me to get court records, and assisted in many other ways.

John G. Oglesby and David Davis, of Illinois, for their kindness; and Dean Harry E. Pratt, of Blackburn College, Illinois, who made known to me some sources.

Dr. Louis A. Warren, of the Lincoln Historical Research Foundation, Fort Wayne, Indiana; and Paul M. Angle, of the Abraham Lincoln Association, Springfield, Illinois; M. L. Houser, Peoria, Illinois, and George F. Hambrecht, Madison, Wisconsin.

All those who permitted the use of their material, and to whom I hope I have given credit in each instance.

The relatives of Mrs. Lincoln wherever they have helped. Much of the material of interest is not of a nature that easily gets into print. An extensive correspondence with descendants of Mrs. Lincoln's nearer relatives was undertaken. Several were visited and interviewed. The courtesy and forbearance of these ladies and gentlemen, in spite of the fact that they were asked direct and often intimate questions, some of which were not pleasant to either party, is gratefully acknowledged.

A group of physicians who specialize in mental diseases — Drs. C. A. Neymann, Charles F. Read, David B. Rotman, Meyer Solomon, W. G. Stearns. It would not have been possible for me to interpret Mrs. Lincoln's behavior, to understand her personality, or to form opinions as to her responsibility in different relations and at different times, had it not been for their help. In a few instances I submitted statements of facts to them for their explanation. More frequently the points in question were the subject of extended discussions in person. Neither individually nor collectively are they responsible for what I have written, but I hope they will accept my acknowledgment of their guidance.

Dr. L. J. Mitchell, of Chicago, and Marion Carey and Anne Vinton Barnes, of the How to Keep Well Department, the Chicago *Tribune,* for helping with the editing and preparation of the study for the publisher.

The courtesy of Alfred A. Knopf and his competent staff.

The many unmentioned who gave aid along the way as occasion offered.

I would not end without paying tribute to the memory of Dr. William E. Barton for the suggestion that we try to understand Mrs. Lincoln and be just to her; and for the kindly, patient help and wise advice he gave.

Introduction

Truth is generally the best vindication against slander.

— Abraham Lincoln

So very difficult a matter is it to trace and find out the truth of anything by history.

— Pericles

Introduction

SEVERAL YEARS AGO THE LATE DR. WILLIAM E. BARTON and I were discussing Abraham Lincoln, particularly the quality of his mind. The subject was intriguing, for Lincoln's mind presents more than one phase that is not understood. Many of his moods cannot be measured by ordinary standards.

To explain him requires considerable knowledge of the laws of inheritance; no small understanding of biology, physiology, and anatomy, and of psychology and psychoanalysis, and behavior in relation to these sciences. To know the politics, the customs, and the habits of his period, and the episodes and incidents of his life, is not enough.

Presently the influence of Mrs. Lincoln on her husband became the theme of discussion. In his short autobiographical sketch [1] written in December 1859, Lincoln said in substance that when he came of age (which was about when he arrived in Illinois), he could read and write, and cipher to the rule of three, and that was about all. It is given to few men to grow as much as Lincoln did between 1830 and 1865, or even as much as he did between 1840 and 1865. How much of the transformation was due to the influence of Mrs. Lincoln? We had no answer. We were compelled to admit that however little one really knew about Lincoln's mind, our knowledge of Mrs. Lincoln's was less. It was not possible to discuss intelligently the influence of the wife on the husband without a better understanding than we had of her.

Dr. Barton said (rather than asked): "Why don't you make a study of Mrs. Lincoln?" He had in mind a study

[1] Bibliography, No. 57.

of her personality rather than one dealing with the incidents of her life.

The primary reason for this present study lay in a wish to comply with Dr. Barton's suggestion, principally because he had made it. The intent did not carry beyond a wish to gather some information and to mature some opinions that he might make use of should he write a book on the mind of Lincoln. I knew he was contemplating a book on this subject, to be one of his group dealing with different aspects of the life of Abraham Lincoln.

Other interests, as well as other Lincoln books, engaged the time of Dr. Barton, and he died before he had set down his opinions of Lincoln's mentality. Meanwhile I was becoming more interested in the subject assigned me. I found myself asking how much Mrs. Lincoln's mind influenced that of her husband. In how far was she responsible for decisions he made and positions he held that shaped the history of the country in crucial times? Gradually the wish to find an answer to these questions for myself was added to the wish to help Dr. Barton — in fact, was overshadowing that primary purpose if not eclipsing it.

At about this time a third reason for this work came into existence. One day I went to a library and asked the attendant to give me what she had dealing with Mrs. Lincoln. When the material was produced, it dealt principally with Mr. Lincoln; there was little about his wife. I turned most of it back, saying: "I am not looking for material on Mr. Lincoln now. I am making a study of Mrs. Lincoln." The librarian's comment was: "The poor woman lived a life of trouble. She was censured bitterly. She had many enemies. Her reputation is an unhappy one. She died in trouble. She was buried in peace. Why dig her up? Why not let the world forget?" Since then I have heard the same statements made by a number of other people.

Very few people think of Mrs. Lincoln at all, or have any real opinion about her. This does not prevent many of them from repeating, somewhat superficially, what they have read or heard about her. Ay, and sometimes with some show of emotion. If such expressions can be called a prevailing opinion, then one may say that it is generally accepted that Mrs. Lincoln was and is not deserving of the goodwill of her fellow-countrymen.

I gave thought to the question whether I should stop or go on. There were a few relatives, including some descendants. If Mrs. Lincoln deserved the reputation that most people said she bore, it would be considerate of the feelings of these relatives to stop, as I was advised to do. But perhaps she did not deserve her reputation. Shakspere wrote: "The evil that men do lives after them; the good is oft interred with their bones." The possibility that Mrs. Lincoln's good had been interred with her bones was sufficient to warrant study.

I learned that one of the White House staff, W. O. Stoddard, suspected that something was wrong with her, soon after he commenced having opportunities to observe her. He was nonplussed, whereupon — wise beyond the times — he consulted a medical man who — also wise beyond the times — explained it to him. In the light of that explanation he saw that she was irresponsible. He had told this in a book that was widely read in the latter part of the last century.[1] I found abundant evidence that Mrs. Lincoln was not responsible for many things she did and said, and that in addition she was the victim of much slander and libel. Many false charges were made against her, first and last. If she was condemned unfairly, held responsible when she was not, and lied about as well, was it fair to leave her reputation as it stood? Desire to uncover the truth and, by telling it, to secure justice for her became a third reason for the study.

At this stage of the investigation it was plain that a simple recital of facts was not enough. Conclusions as to

[1] Bibliography, No. 167.

Mrs. Lincoln could not be based solely on what she did and what she said — and what people said of her — without doing her injustice. If the evidence was to stop there, many might honestly think she was "guilty as accused," to borrow a phrase from the courts; or that her reputation was justified, to use a street verdict. It was evident that to form a proper opinion one must try to understand Mrs. Lincoln's personality, to fathom her type of mind.

By "mentality" or "intellect" we mean the combined qualities and capacities of the mind. "Personality" includes mentality and much else. It embraces personal appearance, facial expression, features, stature, figure, bodily grace or lack of it, posture, manners and mannerisms, social attitudes, social grace and charm or lack of it, likes and dislikes, prejudices, emotions, personal magnetism, and many other attributes, in addition to those we call intellectual or mental.

It was not possible to understand Mrs. Lincoln without going back to the reasons for her actions. If she was blamed for things she did and said, the first question was whether she did do and say them. This was followed by the second: In how far was she responsible? Justice and fairness required that Mrs. Lincoln's degree of responsibility be considered, as well as her actions.

This necessity determined the trend of investigation. What was Mrs. Lincoln's type of mind? What were her personality traits? How did she come by these traits and how did she acquire her mental qualities? How much of them did she inherit? What experiences and influences of her childhood contributed to her personality? What in her make-up is explained by the experiences of her life as a girl in Kentucky, and as a marriageable young woman in Springfield society? What were the effects of her experiences as a married woman and a mother in Springfield? As the wife of a president? What influences did health, religion, politics, financial problems, society, have on her?

Was she altered by successes and failures in any of these fields? Did she change radically as she went along the highway of life? Was she more responsible for what she did at one time than another? Answers must be found for these questions before it would be possible to say what is justice to Mrs. Lincoln.

The quest of a basis for understanding in personality and mentality led so far beyond the primary plans that it brought about new motives. The desire to understand her became a motive in itself — the fourth reason for the study.

I became interested in secondary questions growing out of the main question. What are the relations of intellect to personality? When do intellectual and personality disintegrations become insanity? Up to what point should a person be held responsible? When does irresponsibility begin? Can a person control his conduct in some ways, have objectives and accomplish them, manage his finances successfully, and be irresponsible? And then arose some even more intricate and difficult questions. Physicians now recognize diseased personalities. Among such is the introvert personality. Should there be a revision of our rules of responsibility so as to make them include personality pathology, along with mind pathology, in a grouping that marks a person as irresponsible? Behavior is more influenced by personality and by emotional reactions than it is by intellectual processes pure and simple. Should we not recognize irresponsibility for behavior where that behavior is the result of pathologic personality, even though intellectuality is within the bounds of normalcy? These queries added to my interest in the search.

As the investigation continued, it was discovered that some part of Mrs. Lincoln's reputation was due to things over which she had no control. For example, she was the victim of at least one myth, the influence of which has been far-reaching. The fascination of running down this myth became a fifth reason for the study. I confess that this search was in some measure a branching off from the main stem of the inquiry. But how often men suffer because of things beyond their control! And is the effect less real?

And, finally, there is a reason that will appeal to others more than it did to me, though it was one that actuated me somewhat. The reference is to the truth or falsity of charges that were made against Mrs. Lincoln. If a charge is proved false, our major interest is transferred to the personality of the accuser. And yet, in a study of personality, we must consider false charges as well as true, for the false ones also hurt. How much of what was said against Mrs. Lincoln was true; how much untrue? How much was her personality injured by this gossip, true or untrue?

SOURCES

It is said that more has been written about Abraham Lincoln than about any other man in history, Jesus Christ alone excepted. The number of books and magazine articles dealing with Napoleon does not equal those devoted to the martyred President. In comparison with her husband, Mrs. Lincoln appears to have been neglected; not so when she is compared with the wives of other presidents, however.

While people condemned her and jeered at her, she was an enigma to them. Curiosity, and interest in the mysterious and unexplainable, have made people anxious to read of Mrs. Lincoln, and writers, sensing the demand, have attempted to respond as they have not done in the case of other White House ladies—at least, not to the same degree. What was written has been reasonably adequate in so far as it has supplied biographical facts and details. But all the while there has been a craving for the reason why, and that has not been satisfied.

The biographies of Abraham Lincoln are uneven in their treatment of Mrs. Lincoln. Some do not mention her and others barely do; while, at the other extreme, the biographies of Herndon and those based on Herndon furnish the corner-stone on which rests the present-day opinion of Mrs. Lincoln.

LINCOLN BIOGRAPHIES

Dr. Barton's paper before the Illinois Historical Society in 1929[1] is a valuable analysis of Lincoln biographies. It should be read as a part of every study of Lincoln literature.

When Lincoln entered Congress, he wrote that famous and often quoted biographical sketch for the *Congressional Directory,* which is so revealing as to the character of its author, but is thoroughly unsatisfactory as a source of biographical data. In this statement he did not mention his wife. The next biographical sketch of any importance was that written for Jesse Fell,[2] to be used in a Pennsylvania newspaper. This was a factual document, written by Lincoln himself, after the Lincoln-Douglas debates and before the ensuing presidential election. It was written for political purposes, and no mention is made of Mrs. Lincoln. This is the earliest genuine source of first-hand Lincoln biographical material. It was the only source on which the general run of campaign political writers drew in 1860.

Among the campaign lives which appeared in 1860, there was one, the John L. Scripps *Life,*[3] of which M. L. Houser, in a foreword in the 1931 edition, writes: ". . . is the only biography of himself that Mr. Lincoln ever authorized, revised, and endorsed. . . . Lincoln insisted that every statement, however unimportant, should be meticulously accurate. To insure that, he requested that the manuscript be submitted to him before publication." In this Scripps *Life* there is one paragraph about Mrs. Lincoln, in which this is found: " Mrs. Lincoln is a lady of charming presence, of superior intelligence, of accomplished manners,

[1] Bibliography, No. 12, p. 58.
[2] Bibliography, No. 57.
[3] Bibliography, No. 156, pp. 55 and 36.

and in every respect well fitted to adorn the position in which the election of her husband to the presidency will place her. The courtesies of the White House have never been more appropriately and gracefully dispensed than they will be during the administration of Mr. Lincoln." This statement has the flavor of a campaign document, but it has the merit of having been scrutinized by the man who knew the facts better than anyone else in the world.

After the election of 1860, there were no Lincoln biographies until 1864, and those of that year had no merit except from the political standpoint.

Following the assassination of the President there came a flood of studies of the man, his career, and his personality. The first biography of this type and group to appear was that of Holland.[1] On May 23, 1865 the Chicago *Tribune* published a telegram from Springfield which read: "Dr. J. G. Holland is in the city collecting statistics and items for his forthcoming life of Abraham Lincoln." This work was finished in the autumn of 1865 and appeared the following year. It was one of the considerable group of Lincoln biographies which supply almost no information about the President's wife or his domestic affairs. If he heard of Ann Rutledge while in Springfield, or central Illinois, Holland was not impressed by what he heard.

The defect of these biographies — if omission of references to the martyred President's wife, his domestic affairs, and even his personality is to be so considered — was soon to be remedied.

Dr. Holland's visit stirred into activity a long-cherished ambition of William H. Herndon. On June 3 another telegram from Springfield to the Chicago *Tribune* announced: "Mr. W. H. Herndon, his old law partner, is preparing to write a life of Abraham Lincoln." "Mr. Herndon," the telegram added, "is well qualified for the task, having been a partner of Mr. Lincoln since soon after his coming to

[1] Bibliography, No. 79.

Springfield. The partnership had not terminated when Mr. Lincoln became President. It continued, at least nominally, while Mr. Lincoln was in the White House, and did not end until Mr. Lincoln died."

This statement as to Herndon's opportunities for knowing Lincoln intimately was well within the facts. From 1841 to 1861 no other man saw so much of Lincoln or was so intimately associated with him. It is said that Herndon attracted Lincoln's interest because of his outspoken opposition to slavery, when he was a student at Illinois College. Since his father was said to be in favor of slavery, young Herndon was expected to take sides with the pro-slavery group. It was at a time when the feeling between two Jacksonville factions — those from New England and those from Southern antecedents — was hottest. At a meeting discussing the support given Lovejoy by President Beecher of Illinois College, young Herndon made a telling speech against slavery. This brought down on him the wrath of the stronger local faction, as well as the violent anger of his father.

In 1842 Mr. Lincoln had served two legal apprenticeships as a junior partner in law firms. The first was with Judge John T. Stuart. The second was with an even abler lawyer, Judge Stephen T. Logan. Feeling that the need of apprenticeship had been met, he was planning to organize a firm in which he would be the senior member. It was commonly accepted that office detail was not to his liking. He needed a junior partner who would relieve him of some of the burden that both Stuart and Logan had expected him to carry.

Mrs. Lincoln wrote Judge David Davis that her husband regarded Herndon merely " as an office drudge," and intimated that he was not regarded as an equal, or even as a meritorious subordinate. But this she wrote in the white heat of her resentment of the Herndon stories about Lincoln and Ann Rutledge and herself. She knew better.

Herndon was a good law partner for Abraham Lincoln. He was reasonably good in the detail work of the office, on both the business and the legal sides. He was not studious, but he was more so than his partner. He had read much — enough law and more than enough history and literature. The art of drawing a good brief and preparing a good legal paper was his. Lincoln learned much law from Herndon, and the latter learned still more from Lincoln. Each liked to talk. They discussed politics, religion, history, and maybe family affairs. As these two exceptionally good talkers sat together, there were few subjects that escaped their attention. The firm of Lincoln and Herndon lasted more than twenty years, enduring longer than any other association of Lincoln's life with two exceptions. These exceptions were: Abraham and Mary Lincoln, husband and wife, father and mother; and Thomas and Abraham Lincoln, father and son. Assuming that Herndon's experience and wide reading had qualified him as a writer, he should have made good as a Lincoln biographer.

Horace White [1] wrote: "The world owes more to William H. Herndon for this particular knowledge than to all other persons taken together." In this opinion most, if not all, Lincoln students concur. The world owes him an everlasting debt, not only for the persistence and intelligence with which he gathered information at first hand, but also for the fact that he set down what he gathered honestly, resisting that pressure which, as he said, would have made of him a Weems, and his subject a Weems's Washington.[2]

Herndon's biography was very slow in appearing, for reasons not necessary to discuss here, but in spite of that his views became widely known in a few months. J. F. Newton [3] says: "He delivered a series of lectures on Lincoln during the winter of 1865. Besides, he wrote articles for the Chicago *Tribune*. These articles, with excerpts from

[1] Bibliography, No. 75b, p. xxvi.
[2] Bibliography, No. 127, p. 291.
[3] Ibid., p. 290.

his lectures, went the rounds of the press and he was severely censured by many." It was through these lectures and articles that the Herndon point of view, as well as information, became incorporated into Lincoln literature before the appearance of the biography. In 1869 Herndon sold a copy of his Lincoln material to Ward H. Lamon,[1] who, in conjunction with Black, wrote a biography which appeared in 1872. It thus happened that the first "Herndon" Lincoln biography in fact appeared seventeen years prior to the issuance of the Lincoln biography written by Herndon himself.

The first issue of the Herndon biography, appearing under the name of Lincoln's law partner, was issued about 1889.[2] It was written jointly by Herndon and J. W. Weik, or possibly it would be more accurate to say that most of the facts and opinions were supplied by Herndon, and most of the writing was done by Weik. In 1884 Weik had come to Springfield, and for four years had helped Herndon in gathering material and in writing the life. This work, very well illustrated, was issued by Belford, Clarke and Company, in 1888 or 1889. A second printing [3] of the same text was made by Herndon's Lincoln Publishing Company in 1922. It was an exact reproduction of the Belford, Clarke printing, as far as the text was concerned.[4]

In 1892 White [5] prepared a second edition of the Herndon-Weik Lincoln, supplying an introduction and two new chapters, and altering some of the Herndon-Weik statements.

Almost every Lincoln biography dealing with the personality of the subject and with his domestic affairs follows Herndon, and in most instances merely reflects him.

---

[1] Bibliography, No. 98.
[2] Bibliography, No. 75.
[3] Bibliography, No. 75a.
[4] A third printing of this first edition was issued by A. & C. Boni in 1930; Bibliography, No. 75c.
[5] Bibliography, No. 75b.

However, there are three outstanding exceptions: W. O. Stoddard, I. N. Arnold, and H. B. Rankin.

Stoddard[1] writes of the Washington life in the present tense, making his statements appear to have been written before 1865. His book was not published, however, until 1884 and he doubtless read Lamon's work and some of the lectures and newspaper articles by Herndon before he finished writing. Nevertheless, he writes of what he saw and heard, and gives little or no evidence of having been influenced by Herndon.

Arnold began gathering material for his biography prior to the assassination of the President. In 1867 he finished his *History of Abraham Lincoln and the Emancipation of the Slaves.*[2] E. B. Washburne tells us that Arnold was not satisfied with this as a life of Lincoln, and in 1882 he began writing the *Life,* which he finished in 1884.[3] This work tells of Lincoln's personality, his domestic affairs, and his wife, making less use of the Herndon material than did any of the biographers writing of the more personal side of the subject.

Rankin,[4] who wrote many years later, was well aware of what Herndon had written as well as said about Mrs. Lincoln, but, far from following him, he undertook to refute him.

These are about the only Lincoln biographers dealing with Mrs. Lincoln that do not follow the Herndon material. However, Barton, Carl Sandburg, and, in her later writings, Ida M. Tarbell often disagree with Herndon. When Tarbell began, she followed the Herndon material and did not question his story of the projected wedding and all its embroidery, the Ann Rutledge myth, and the opinions he expressed of Mrs. Lincoln. Some twenty-five years later, as the result of independent investigation consisting largely in interviews with Mrs. Lincoln's family and others having

[1] Bibliography, No. 167.
[2] Bibliography, No. 3.
[3] Bibliography, No. 4.
[4] Bibliography, No. 149.

intimate knowledge of the subject, she changed her opinion, coming to the conclusion that the story of the planned marriage was " the work of a morbid imagination building on flimsy, indirect evidence." [1]

Herndon loved Lincoln, even though he chastened him; but he had no liking for Lincoln's wife. This is his own story of how the cruel war began: It was in 1839. Miss Todd had but recently arrived in Springfield. She was at a dance and had just finished waltzing with Herndon. " A few moments later, as we were promenading through the hall, I thought to compliment her graceful dancing by telling her that while I was conscious of my own awkward movements, she seemed to glide through the waltz with the ease of a serpent. Her eyes flashed as she replied: ' Mr. Herndon, comparison to a serpent is rather severe irony, especially to a newcomer.' " [2] Since the garden of Eden the Eves have resented reptilian comparisons.

The ill will between Mrs. Lincoln and Herndon smoldered through all the Springfield years. It burned high when Herndon lectured and when he wrote the Lincoln biographies.

He conceived the theory that Mrs. Lincoln married for revenge. In his discussion of Mrs. Lincoln he first mentions her antecedents, family connections, and education and training. Then he tells of her Springfield history and covers the failure of Lincoln to marry Mary Todd in January 1841. To this theme he devotes several pages. After that he considers the events that led up to the wedding, and the wedding itself. This is the background for an exposition of Mrs. Lincoln's attitude toward Mr. Lincoln. He says: [3] " Miss Todd first loved Abraham Lincoln but the failure to marry her, in January 1841, changed that emotion to the one which animated her until 1865. . . . But the disappointment

[1] Bibliography, No. 170, p. 237.
[2] Bibliography, No. 75a, Vol. II, p. 209.
[3] Bibliography, No. 75a, Vol. II, pp. 230, 433, 434.

had crushed her proud, womanly spirit. She felt degraded in the eyes of the world. Love fled at the approach of revenge. . . . Whether Mrs. Lincoln really was moved by the spirit of revenge or not, she acted along the lines of human conduct. She led her husband a wild and merry dance. If, in time, she became soured at the world, it was not without provocation; and if, in her later years, she unchained the bitterness of a disappointed and outraged nature, it followed as logically as an effect does the cause." Later he wrote: " Besides, who knows but she may have acted out in her conduct toward her husband the laws of human revenge?"

Herndon conveys the impression that revenge, or its equivalent, was the key to those acts of Mrs. Lincoln that puzzled so many people. In order to support the thesis he exaggerates what happened or did not happen in January 1841. In furtherance of his thesis, too, he made use of things he knew and things he learned from Springfield gossip; and doubtless he again exaggerated.

Commenting on this theory, Newton[1] said: " While Herndon was right as to his facts, his inference from them was nothing short of absurd. That the proud, high-spirited Mary Todd held fast to so forlorn a lover for revenge is hardly less believable than the legend that she foresaw his future distinction."

Doubtless a considerable part of Mrs. Lincoln's reputation is due to the myth for which Herndon was responsible.

THE ANN RUTLEDGE MYTH

In constructing a story that would give him his revenge against Mrs. Lincoln, Herndon developed the Ann Rutledge romance. Since the public needed a romance to round out the Lincoln they wanted to believe in, they accepted this story even though they did not care for the author's work as a

[1] Bibliography, No. 127, p. 322.

whole. When Herndon went to New Salem to talk with the old Lincoln friends, he heard something of a possible love-affair with Miss Rutledge, the daughter of the hotel-keeper with whom Lincoln had once boarded. Out of the little neighborhood gossip drawn from dim memories, he developed the Ann Rutledge myth.

Herndon returned to Springfield and began work on the lectures out of which he was to build a book. He wrote to Mrs. Lincoln and asked for an interview. On September 6, 1866 she went to Springfield to visit her husband's grave, and on that occasion she met Herndon and they had a long and intimate conversation about Mr. Lincoln. She gave him much information that he wanted, but he made no reference to the marriage for revenge, the disappointed bride, the Ann Rutledge story, or to his intention to give lectures on the domestic life of the Lincolns.

Newton [1] wrote: "The lecture on the domestic affairs of the Lincoln family, on Mrs. Lincoln, and in which he brought out the Ann Rutledge affair, was delivered in 1866. Parts of it appeared in the papers at the time and created a flurry of comment." It came to the attention of Mrs. Lincoln and Robert, and it also doubtless came to that of many persons who were to write Lincoln biographies within the next quarter-century.

At the time Herndon created the Ann Rutledge myth, Ann had been dead thirty years. Decades after that lecture Barton found a letter to Ann, written by her brother in school at Jacksonville and received after she was attacked with her fatal illness. This letter was inferentially supportive of the statement that Ann had some plans for college. A part of the story is that Lincoln had persuaded her to try to get an education at Jacksonville. Barton also heard from some of the young woman's relatives that there was a family rumor that Ann and Abraham Lincoln had been

[1] Bibliography, No. 127, p. 295.

sweethearts. When Barton heard of this family tradition, it was more than eighty years after Ann Rutledge's death, and more than fifty years after Herndon had started the ball rolling, and it is not certain whether these relatives had heard the legend from without or from within the family circle. It may have been that they heard it directly or indirectly from Herndon. Since not even Herndon found as much basis for the story as did Barton, it is important that the latter was firm in his conviction that the story was a myth.

I have run across two letters from Mrs. Lincoln, and one from Robert, in which they gave their reaction to it. These letters were written in protest against the Herndon lecture and particularly against the alleged early romance and the attack on Mrs. Lincoln.[1] Mrs. Lincoln wrote that Mr. Lincoln regarded Herndon " as an office drudge," and as such treated him. His habits made him impossible. In what he wrote about Ann Rutledge he was untruthful and worse. One who reads these letters understands that the members of the Lincoln family resented the attacks on Mrs. Lincoln and rejected in all of its essentials the romantic phases of the Ann Rutledge story.

I am convinced that there was no adequate basis for the story. The theory that this love-affair was a major factor in shaping Abraham Lincoln's life is founded on emotion and is without logic, sense, or foundation in fact. But, however much of a myth it was, it served Herndon's purpose well. Having demolished Mrs. Lincoln's reputation, he was left under the necessity of finding a romance for Abraham Lincoln.[2]

---

[1] These letters are in a privately owned collection. Robert Lincoln's letter indicates that Herndon gave his lecture more than once. He was emphatic in his condemnation of Herndon, and Mrs. Lincoln was even more so.

[2] After the above had been written, Dr. G. Koehler called my attention to the Editor's Preface by P. M. Angle, in a recent printing of the Herndon-Weik *Abraham Lincoln*, issued by A. & C. Boni (Bibliography, No. 75c, pp. xxix, xli, xliii, xliv). I am in accord with Mr. Angle's opinions of Herndon as a biographer. His distinc-

After the Herndon lectures and his writings covering Mrs. Lincoln and Ann Rutledge, that vague something—public opinion—had no great difficulty in loving and lauding Lincoln and at the same time berating and condemning his wife, particularly as Mrs. Lincoln's acts made it so easy to blame her.

SOURCES OF INFORMATION OTHER THAN THE LINCOLN BIOGRAPHIES

There is but one Mary Lincoln biographer in a real sense, and that is Katherine Helm, though Honoré Willsie Morrow's fiction is based on quite comprehensive investigation and use of factual material. Miss Helm had her mother's magazine article about Mrs. Lincoln in her possession, as well as a great deal of family data obtained by her mother. This included the Elizabeth Humphreys Norris letter.

Other stories dealing with Mrs. Lincoln in certain periods are valuable sources of information. These several sources, supplying biographical data about Mrs. Lincoln, are best discussed by periods.

---

tion between Herndon as a reporter of what he saw and as a psychologist and analyzer is interesting and valuable.

I am sure that Herndon always intended to tell the truth, the whole truth, and nothing but the truth; and when he is telling what he knew, his record should not be questioned. His explanations and interpretations are not so dependable, since they contain too much of what the newspapers call editorial view-point. Especially was this true in those fields in which there was controversy about his statements. The reader will see that my interpretation of the value of Herndon's report of the Ann Rutledge story and the proposed wedding of January 1841 are almost identical with those of Angle.

The following are some of his views as to the Ann Rutledge affair: "The possibility of error must be reckoned with. . . . It is difficult to accept at face value Herndon's account of the cataclysmic effect of Ann's death on Lincoln. . . . The enduring effect is, of course, pure inference. No better example can be found of the absurdities to which Herndon's propensity for drawing inferences led him." (The last sentence refers to the revenge theory.) Angle quotes the Chicago *Tribune* as terming the Ann Rutledge episode "an idle tale."

MRS. LINCOLN'S ANCESTORS

The best source of information is a genealogy of the Todd-Parker-Porter family, written by Emilie Todd Helm, for the *Kittochtinny Magazine*.[1] Mrs. Helm also covered the story in her magazine article on Mrs. Lincoln,[2] as did Miss Helm [3] and William H. Townsend [4] in their books. Some additional facts are found in publications of the Pennsylvania, Kentucky, and Illinois Historical Societies. The Columbia, Missouri, branch of the Todd family wrote some informing letters that are found in the Draper Collection, Wisconsin Historical Society.

1818 TO 1826

There is no source of information for this period. The biographers of Mrs. Lincoln dismiss it with a few chance sentences.

1826 TO 1839

What we really know about Mary Todd after 1826 and until she reached Springfield is nearly limited to what is found in the letter written to Mrs. Helm by her cousin Mrs. Norris, years after the occurrence of the events recorded. Mrs. Norris was a Miss Humphreys, a niece of Mrs. Betsy Humphreys Todd, who lived with her aunt in the Lexington home for several years and roomed with Mary Todd during some of this time. Both went to the Ward School and were in the same classes. After 1832, when Mary was in Mentelle's, Miss Humphreys continued to live in the Todd home for a few years and saw Mary on week-ends and at school parties. During vacations they visited Frankfort and went together to parties and other social affairs.

[1] Bibliography, No. 7.
[2] Bibliography, No. 72.
[3] Bibliography, No. 73.
[4] Bibliography, No. 176.

The text of this long letter indicates that after Mrs. Lincoln had come into public notice, Mrs. Helm, remembering her cousin's companionship with her half-sister, asked Mrs. Norris for her opinions and observations. This letter came in reply. In writing of Mary Todd's Lexington life Mrs. Helm[1] did not have much printed or written material except Mrs. Norris's letter. Miss Helm[2] made extensive use of it also. Both mother and daughter drew on family recollection and tradition to supplement this letter.

The sources of information about the social and political life of Lexington were found in the Transylvania Library and the City Library of Lexington, and in those of the University of Chicago and the Wisconsin Historical Society.

1839 TO 1851

A valuable source of information about Mrs. Lincoln in the forties is what may be termed the "Springfield tradition." This consists principally in what is commonly called "back-fence gossip." Some of it has found its way into books; part of it one hears by talking with old residents of Springfield. As a source it needs to be carefully weighed. Much of it has the usual faults of ordinary gossip. Much of it has been flavored by political considerations, by the backwash of the myths, by personal animosities, and by the natural tendency of all gossip to grow.

Mrs. Lincoln wrote few letters during this period. She was too busy with her babies and her household cares. A few that she did write have been preserved and are available. Among them are the Peoria letters, and correspondence between Mr. and Mrs. Lincoln while he was in Congress. These tell us something about her.

The expressions of her sisters Mrs. N. W. Edwards and Mrs. William Wallace, while written years later and being general estimates, are of great value, but they are far too

[1] Bibliography, No. 72.

[2] Bibliography, No. 73.

brief. Mrs. Helm's article, Miss Helm's book, and Townsend's books give incidents that are helpful sources of information.

For Springfield lore the files of the Springfield *Register* and the *Illinois State Journal,* J. C. Power's *History of Springfield, Illinois,*[1] Joseph Wallace's *Past and Present of the City of Springfield and Sangamon County,*[2] and C. M. Eames's *Historic Morgan and Classic Jacksonville*[3] supply material. Data about Springfield are also found in Knox's[4] and in Williams's[5] Springfield city directories; in the library of the Illinois Historical Society, Springfield; and in the Newberry Library and the library of the Chicago Historical Society in Chicago.

1851 TO 1861

In the second half of Mrs. Lincoln's life in Springfield more of the family history was going into the record books than in the immediately preceding years. Lincoln was becoming a success and in some degree a national character, and there was a little more notice of his wife. Mrs. Helm visited Springfield, and she told and wrote of the life there. Miss Helm used several letters written to her mother by her aunt. Arnold was visiting the Lincoln home and later wrote of his visits; and the same was true of O. H. Browning. Rankin was gaining the impressions which he was later to record. There was that same neighborhood gossip which later mingled with the Herndon lecture material to make the "Springfield tradition." The Lincoln statement to Fell, and the Lincoln-censored Scripps biography appeared in these years. What Mrs. Edwards and Mrs. Wallace wrote of their sister was based on what they saw of her in this decade, as well as before and after it. Some of Mrs. Lincoln's letters written in the fifties have been preserved.

[1] Bibliography, No. 144.
[2] Bibliography, No. 180.
[3] Bibliography, No. 51.
[4] Bibliography, No. 95.
[5] Bibliography, No. 192.

1861 TO 1865

The sources of information about the Washington period are ample. Mrs. Lincoln wrote numerous letters, and many were kept. The lure of the White House stationery is great; few people destroy letters with the imprint of the White House, however trivial they may be and however unimportant the subject. Mrs Lincoln's letters written in this period throw light on her qualities as well as on her activities. A preponderance of her letters related to politics and particularly to political appointments. Members of her family were recipients of a goodly number of the letters, and a few went to old Springfield friends.

A valuable source is the story of the White House life written by Mrs. Elizabeth Keckley,[1] Mrs. Lincoln's seamstress, who had an opportunity to see " behind the scenes " in the Lincoln life during the White House period and for several years thereafter. Mrs. Helm spent a week or more with her half-sister after General Helm's death, and she kept a diary. Her story is of value.[2] Miss Helm used some of her mother's recollections and experiences in her book,[3] and therefore it can be regarded as source material.

Another valuable source is an article written by Mrs. Lincoln's first cousin Mrs. Elizabeth Todd Grimsley.[4] Mrs. Grimsley was one of the several members of the Springfield Todd family who attended the inaugural. She lived in the White House family circle for several months.

For a view of social life in Washington, with some reference to Mrs. Lincoln and her day, we get information from Ben Perley Poore,[5] Mrs. E. F. Ellett,[6] Mary Ames Clemmer,[7] Esther Singleton,[8] Genevieve Forbes Herrick,[9] Laura C. Holloway,[10] Edna M. Colman.[11]

[1] Bibliography, No. 85.
[2] Bibliography, No. 72.
[3] Bibliography, No. 73.
[4] Bibliography, No. 67.
[5] Bibliography, No. 141.
[6] Bibliography, No. 53.
[7] Bibliography, No. 41.
[8] Bibliography, No. 160.
[9] Bibliography, No. 77.
[10] Bibliography, No. 80.
[11] Bibliography, No. 44.

Of those who wrote about the Lincoln family in the White House, Stoddard[1] was the clearest-headed and had the deepest insight. He was almost the only one who knew the reason for the vagaries of Mrs. Lincoln's conduct. Those who would understand Mrs. Lincoln would do well to begin their reading with Stoddard's book. How unfortunate that Herndon did not include a talk with him in his work of investigation!

For the first year of the Washington life Julia Taft Bayne[2] supplies valuable factual material about the Lincoln family.

The majority of the newspaper stories and political accounts that mention Mrs. Lincoln lose some value because of their partisan bias. This was an era of great political emotion, and Washington was the storm-center. That vague mass of mixed information and misinformation, of likes and dislikes, that elsewhere has been referred to as the "Lexington tradition" or the "Springfield tradition" was in operation in Washington as it was in the other places. More of the "Washington tradition," however, ultimately found its way into public print.

1865 TO 1875

Mrs. Keckley's narrative covers the time between 1861 and 1870 and is our best source of information on one of the three outstanding episodes in the life of Mrs. Lincoln in these years.

Mrs. Lincoln was a busy letter-writer. We do not know whether she was always so, but that she was when her bill for a pension was pending before Congress is proved by the number of letters written by her then that are still in existence. That many of these were from Europe is one reason for their preservation; their coming from the widow of President Lincoln is another. I have read, and in some

[1] Bibliography, No. 168.

[2] Bibliography, No. 17.

measure studied, many of them. I have been permitted to see one considerable collection written by Mrs. Lincoln and her son Robert.

The *Congressional Globe* (*Record*) is a valuable source, as we should expect when we recall that Mrs. Lincoln's pension bill was hotly contested in two Congresses.

The newspapers supply much source material. The controversy over the proposed sale of Mrs. Lincoln's wardrobe was almost exclusively newspaper agitation, and Mrs. Lincoln and her affairs came in for notice during the pension fight. Again, the newspapers gave space to Tad's death.

The court records are valuable sources of information. When President Lincoln died, his estate went into court and remained there until after the death of Tad, a minor. Judge David Davis, the administrator, made periodic reports. Some of these referred to Mrs. Lincoln and the whereabouts and expenditures of both mother and son. The court records of the trial of Mrs. Lincoln for sanity supply information. In his testimony at Mrs. Lincoln's trial Dr. Willis Danforth told of his patient's mental and physical health subsequent to the death of Tad.

We may say that there is none of the vague collection of opinions and data that we call local tradition about Mrs. Lincoln in this period. She lived in Chicago most of the time, and that city paid very little attention to her. She went to Europe, but there she was almost unknown. She traveled elsewhere, but she did not remain long in any place visited. Her restlessness and mania for travel, manifested between 1865 and 1875, were in part responsible for the lack of a tradition then. However, they were responsible for many letters now found in Mrs. Lincoln collections.

The paucity of any record or source material for the years 1872 to 1874, inclusive, is remarkable. To a degree it was evidence that her aloofness had become pathologic.

1875 TO 1882

The most impersonal, least biased, and, therefore, most dependable sources of information for the last period are the court records. Abraham Lincoln's estate was in court for several years after 1865; that of Tad from the date of his father's death until his own death in 1871. When Mrs. Lincoln was declared insane, in 1875, her estate went under the control of the court and there remained until late in 1876. Upon her death, in 1882, the court again took charge.

Neither Lincoln nor his wife made a will. In fact, will-making was never a habit in the Lincoln family. The Kentucky Abraham left no will, and the estate was settled by Kentucky law, greatly to the disadvantage of Thomas, a younger son. Thomas left no will. Robert T. Lincoln's will, filed a few years ago, was the first will of one of his Lincoln succession in certainly more than a hundred years. There may never have been a Lincoln will in this line prior to his.

Since Tad Lincoln's estate was in charge of the court, it was the duty of Judge Davis, the administrator and Tad's guardian, to know where he was and what was happening to him. When Mrs. Lincoln was in charge of the court, it had a right to know, through the administrator and Dr. R. J. Patterson, the physician in charge of the sanatorium to which she was committed, what was happening to her.

The next best sources of information are the files of the newspapers. The Chicago dailies carried comprehensive accounts of her two sanity trials. The comment was dignified and kindly, in marked contrast with that given the wardrobe and the pension episodes. At the time of her death the papers gave place to humane news stories and editorials.

A search of the records of Bellevue Place Sanatorium discloses almost nothing relative to Mrs. Lincoln, but a moderate amount of information can be gleaned from letters and newspaper files. The principal sources of newspaper information for this time are the files of the Aurora *News-Beacon.*[1]

When the letters between Mrs. Lincoln and her friends Judge and Mrs. J. B. Bradwell were being exchanged, some of the reverberation reached the newspapers. At least one Chicago paper sent a reporter to Aurora, to write an article about Mrs. Lincoln and the sanatorium and provide a setting for it by telling of the attractions of the Fox River country.

There has been access to a letter written by Dr. Patterson to a newspaper — a letter stimulated by the Bradwell correspondence. Much about Mrs. Lincoln, published principally at the time of her death, was found in the files of the *Journal* and the *Register* of Springfield, and in those of the Chicago papers.

It is to be regretted that we have nothing of the Bradwell correspondence except the tradition. It was said that Mrs. Lincoln, writing from the sanatorium, charged her son with putting her there — which was true — and for improper motives — which was not true. The world accepts these untrue charges as the natural attitude of a mentally disturbed person, particularly if the bent of the patient tends to be paranoid,[2] as was Mrs. Lincoln's. Insane people are generally obsessed with the urge to write letters, and in doing so they frequently make accusations. Well-informed people recognize this and are able to evaluate such charges.

There is a dearth of letters written by Mrs. Lincoln in the latter part of this period. Her aloofness was increasingly pathologic.

Several members of Mrs. Lincoln's family who knew her in Springfield during her last years are alive. Mrs. Edward

[1] Dr. B. J. Cigrand of Batavia, an industrious Lincoln student, has gathered all of the available information as to Mrs. Lincoln's stay in Batavia. He wrote several of the articles which appeared in the Aurora *News-Beacon.* This material he kindly made available for the purposes of this study.

[2] Paranoia is "a form of insanity characterized by systematized delusions; insanity with delusions of persecution." Bibliography, No. 48.

D. Keys, her niece, was married and living in Springfield at the time of Mrs. Lincoln's death and for several years before. Mrs. Mary Edwards Brown, her grand-niece, was a young woman when her grand-aunt died. They have been kind enough to tell their impressions of their aunt, her mode of life, her habits, and some of her conversation. A few friends, some of them friends of her children, are still living in Springfield, and they have told what they remember.

The only contacts of others were in the stores or on the street. The " Springfield tradition " of this period, if it may be called such, relates principally to Mrs. Lincoln's life of seclusion, her miserliness, and her shopping practices.

CHAPTER ONE

The Gifts of the Ancestors

How can I call my life my own
When the scheming dead try to live through me?
How can I know what I really am
With their wishes hounding me greedily?

— ESTHER PINCH: "Heredity,"
Century Magazine, Spring 1930

CHAPTER ONE

The Gifts of the Ancestors

A HUMAN PERSONALITY IS A MOSAIC, THE PICTURE BEING made by the combination of many stones. Some of these are contributed by heredity, the constitutions of ancestors — the experiences of their lives as well as their inheritances — being passed on to succeeding links of the chain of which they are a part.

When Mrs. Lincoln was fifty-six years old, a jury of her peers, adjudging her insane, gave it as their opinion that "the disease is not with her hereditary." This statement was technically true, at least in the sense in which it was made. No such statement is ever true in the scientific sense, provided the word "disease" is changed to "personality," or "constitution," or whatever we choose to call it. Inheritance contributed to Mrs. Lincoln's constitution — physical, mental, and moral. In the stream which flowed from her ancestors into Mrs. Lincoln and, through her, into her descendants, there was much of superiority, and something of that which is not admirable.

In her family tree were many superior men and women — superior intellectually, some of them; others, physically. Many occupied commanding positions. From them she must have inherited some degree of intellectual ability. Some of them were dominating persons. They must have transmitted drive and desire to dominate, as well as ambition. And then among them we find some difficult, if not diseased, personalities. Some of the waters were crystal-clear; some were muddy. 'Tis always so.

REMOTE INFLUENCES

THE TODDS

The Todds were people of substance in Scotland and Ireland before they migrated to America. As a stock they were superior to most of the immigrants. They settled in Pennsylvania and were good citizens, remaining there for several generations. Some of them were men of authority in that state. In Pennsylvania there was begun a close association between the Todds, the Porters, and the Parkers, with an occasional marriage between young people of the three families. They held together in migrating from Pennsylvania to central Kentucky, and in their new home continued the old neighborly relations.

One of the Pennsylvania Todds, David, sent three of his four sons to his brother, Rev. John Todd of Louisa, Virginia, to be educated. This brother was a man of great ability, an outstanding educator and a forceful preacher. The three boys, Levi, John, and Robert Todd, never returned to live in Pennsylvania, for their uncle had political influence, and this he used with his friend Governor Patrick Henry to secure jobs for his nephews. We can well understand Governor Henry soliloquizing: "These boys are made of the right stuff. They have been educated and trained by my friend the Rev. John Todd. I know that their training has been good. Virginia cannot afford to lose the services of these boys. I will make John Lieutenant Commander of Illinois County, Virginia; I will commission Levi and Robert as officers in the army of George Rogers Clark, Commander of Illinois County." And so he did.

John, Levi, and Robert Todd began their life-work as officers in the army of Clark, serving Virginia in its Illinois country. In the wars which held the Illinois territory for

Virginia and later for the new states carved out of it, two of these Todd boys won their spurs as fighters; the other discharged the civil duties of administration and was generally known as Governor Todd. After peace and security had been attained for the territory north of the Ohio and east of the Mississippi, the three Todds transferred their activities to the still insecure Kentucky region. They fought the Indians in Kentucky, and each rose to the rank of general in the Kentucky militia. John was killed in the Battle of the Blue Licks.

In Kentucky the Todds matched their usefulness as defenders in war by their service as citizens. They were among the founders of Lexington, and in the early days no citizens of that city were more influential than they. To them came a shipment of books from their uncle and preceptor in Virginia. It was to be a gift to their city, and as such they accepted it. It became the nucleus of the library of Transylvania University. For more than one hundred years this library has been held to be good in most particulars and in some without an equal on the continent. It was the Todds and their relatives, associates, and friends who laid the foundation of the first university "in the wilderness that lay beyond the mountains." There were few of the catalogues of Transylvania in its earlier years that did not carry the name of one or more of the Todds or the near-Todd relatives in some list of trustees, faculties, or students.

This statement, found in the Shane collection,[1] shows how extensive were the landholdings of this family in Kentucky after the country began to fill up with settlers: "The Todds at one time owned from Lexington all the way to and beyond Walnut Hills, on each side of the road, except the Overton place. Robert Todd, uncle of Robert S. Todd, lived off to the right of the road."

Levi Todd, one of the three brothers, was Mrs. Lincoln's grandfather. The following statements, written by

[1] Bibliography, No. 157, p. 83.

one of his sons, David Todd, not only supply a pen picture of Levi Todd, but give a reason for his leaving Virginia that differs from the one usually given:[1]

"In 1775, Levi Todd was defeated in an election in Virginia for ensign, as lieutenant of a company; then concluded to go to Kentucky and went, in early 1776, with his brother, Robert Todd."

"I am aware my father was not in the Virginia line. He was not of the standing corps, but he ranked as lieutenant, being the aid of Clark. Clark sent him as a spy from Kaskaskia to Louisiana to examine the Spanish force and disposition to the American cause."

"Gen. Levi Todd was five feet eight inches high, well proportioned, inclined to corpulence at forty and after. Received when with his father a good education. Was brought up on a farm. Had opportunity in reading and in science with General Robert Porter, with whom he stayed occasionally. He visited Col. Preston in Fincastle County, then embracing the wilds of Kentucky, deriving from him some information of the county. Set out and in March 1776 reached Boonesboro. Shortly after, located at Harrodsburg and appointed Clerk through influence of his older brother. Upon division of the counties he removed to Fayette, about 1780. He married Jane Briggs, daughter of [Capt.] Samuel Briggs, Logan's Fort, she being niece of the Logan family. He left a handsome estate and bestowed liberal education on his children. He rose to the station of major general. Was a patron of young men. His general deportment was polite and agreeable. Had a fund of information which was interesting; of good mind. Had most general acquaintance, commanding the respect of all."

Mrs. Lincoln's father, Robert S. Todd, was of the second Lexington generation. He was a member of the legislature, and holder of some other offices, and was several times considered for higher offices than those he held. He was a

[1] Bibliography, No. 49, November 15, 1851.

banker, a manufacturer, a farmer, a merchant of financial worth, and one of the local political group, in close personal contact with Henry Clay, which strove ever and always, for more than two decades, to elevate that great statesman to the presidency. It scarcely need be added that he and his family stood high in the social circles of Lexington.

While all this is true, it must be said that the Todds of the second and the third Lexington generations were not so outstanding in Lexington affairs as were their parents and grandparents. They were men and women of ability, but they did not have the capacity for leadership that their forbears had. In the newer generations the Breckinridges and their contemporaries were forging ahead of the Todds, as the earlier Todds had forged ahead of rivals in theirs.

There are two statements about Robert S. Todd which should be borne in mind in a discussion of Mrs. Lincoln's inheritance. One is that he was "impetuous, high-strung, and nervous."[1] So were Mrs. Lincoln and her sons Robert and Tad. Another[2] is that Mrs. Lincoln inherited from him her love of fine dress, jewelry, and personal adornment.[3]

THE PORTERS

Among Mrs. Lincoln's Todd ancestors who achieved distinction were her father, Robert S.; her grandfather, General Levi, and his two brothers, known as General Robert and Governor John; and her great-grand-uncle, Reverend John. This was a goodly company and one of which any "best family" might be proud.

But the record of the Porters, another of Mrs. Lincoln's lines, was even better.

[1] Bibliography, No. 176, p. 46.

[2] Bibliography, No. 121, p. 60.

[3] At the time Levi, Robert, and John Todd (Pennsylvania Todds), and their descendants to the third generation, were living in the blue-grass region, a branch of the Virginia Todds lived in Lexington and Frankfort. Some of them occupied positions of prominence. Occasionally these Virginia Todds have been confused with the Todd family to which Mrs. Lincoln belonged.

General Andrew Porter, of the second American generation of Porters, was the first of his family to achieve distinction. He was a general in the Revolutionary Army, and for a time was in command of all Pennsylvania troops. He was one of General Washington's supporters and counselors. His first wife was a McDowell, and it was from her that Mrs. Lincoln descended directly. This made her a kinswoman of another distinguished American family. Andrew Porter married as a second wife Eliza Parker, a member of the Pennsylvania Parker-Todd family to which Mrs. Lincoln belonged.

The records of one hundred years ago ignored the women of the family almost without exception. Every now and then there was a woman so capable in some way that not even the most orthodox of historians dared fail to mention her. Eliza Parker Porter, wife of Andrew and a relative of Mrs. Lincoln's, was one of these exceptions. W. A. Porter, the family historian, devoted several lines to extolling the good qualities of this mother of the tribe of Porter.[1]

Three sons of Andrew and Eliza Parker Porter were men of great prominence: Governor G. B. Porter, of Michigan; Governor David Rittenhouse Porter, of Pennsylvania; James Madison Porter, a great lawyer who was appointed Secretary of War by President Tyler. While Lincoln was struggling to get on politically in Springfield, his young wife had two cousins in a President's cabinet. When her husband was President of the United States, he signed the commissions of two Porter cousins to high positions in the Army of the Potomac under General McClellan.

Among the children of the Andrew Porter-Parker family, in addition to those mentioned, there was another son, John Ewing Porter. This son was a man of education and capacity, but he appears to have been hard to get along with. He was a promising young lawyer in Pennsylvania when he married a young woman of whom his father did not approve.

[1] Bibliography, No. 143.

Father and son quarreled. The quarrel was so violent that John Ewing Porter became embittered against his father. The breach was never healed. The son changed his name to John Ewing Parker, changed his profession to medicine, and went to South Carolina to live.

The career of this Dr. John Ewing Porter, or Parker, bears some resemblance to that of Mrs. Lincoln's full brother, Dr. George Rogers Clark Todd, of whom the reader will learn later. His personality is suggestive of that of Mrs. Lincoln, a type which came to her from the Parker-Porter inheritance more than from the Todds. Lest we overstress this family relationship, let us recall that Mrs. Lincoln and her full brothers and sisters descended from the McDowell wife of Andrew Porter, and while there was kinship to the Parker wife, it was not close.

THE PARKERS

The family tree shows that the last of Mrs. Lincoln's Todd forbears to live in Europe married a Miss Parker. It is not known that this woman was of the Parker family that in later years was frequently intertwined with the Todds and the Porters in Pennsylvania and Kentucky. There is some likelihood that she was, since the two families were so closely associated and for so many years.

The Parker family must have been an excellent one. The family historians never fail to say so. At the same time, we do not find among them many men or women who were of great prominence. It was the cross between a Parker and a Porter, or a Parker and a Todd, or both, that seemed to produce a superior individual.

The Robert Parker who was Mrs. Lincoln's maternal grandfather was a man of wealth and social position, but the member of his family of whom we read most is his widow, Eliza Parker, and she was born a Porter — the daughter of Andrew. The day after her marriage she and her husband left Pennsylvania and rode horseback through the wilderness to Kentucky. It was she, as the "Widow" Parker, who dominated her grandchildren and did so much to make them dissatisfied with their stepmother. The accounts agree that the "Widow" Parker lived in a fine house, had a high social position, and was esteemed a superior woman. However, it was her grandchildren who quarreled amongst themselves and engaged in family lawsuits — something new in the Todd-Porter-Parker family.

We know nothing of the Eliza Parker who married Robert S. Todd in 1812, except it be such statements as these by William H. Townsend:[1] "Eliza was a sprightly, attractive girl with a placid, sunny disposition"; and: "Plucky Eliza Parker was willing that he should go" (referring to her husband's going to war in 1812).[2]

---

[1] Bibliography, No. 176, pp. 46, 48.

[2] No picture of Eliza Parker Todd has ever been found. There is no letter written by her that anyone knows of. The following is part of a letter written by one Eliza Todd, and found in the Kentucky Manuscript, Shane Collection, Wisconsin Historical Society. It was hoped that this letter might prove to have been written by Eliza Parker Todd, but that theory had to be abandoned. In the futile search for an author it was found that twenty-five women bore the name "Eliza Todd," through either birth or marriage, in this family connection in the first half of the nineteenth century.

Lexington, Kentucky, Feb. 9, 1804.

Dear Nancy,

You wished me to give a description of Mr. Todd myself. That I don't think I can do but shall only say that he is . . . clever fellow and one that will make me happy the remainder of my days. I have been housekeeping about four months, and find it a very troublesome business, but the pleasure and satisfaction of an affectionate husband makes up for all other difficulties. We are now living in Lexington, which is not altogether agreeable to me, but Mr. Todd's business is such I must submit to it for a few years. My acquaintance in this place is not extensive, owing to its being selected off in large parties, which is the case more or less in every large place.

Your ever affectionate friend,

Eliza Todd

My love to your mama and papa. I shall expect a letter from you by post. Direct them to Mr. Todd.

E. T.

OTHER FAMILY STRAINS

In addition to these, there were several other families that married into the connection and made their contribution to the stock. Among them were the Briggs, the Owens, the Smith, and the Hamilton families; and through them, in one way or another, the Todds were also related to the Bodleys, the McFarlands, the Findleys, and the Majors, and, less closely, to the Wickliffes.

When Mrs. Lincoln died, Mayor Crooks of Springfield issued a proclamation in which he officially did honor to the widow of Abraham Lincoln.[1] He asked Springfield to suspend business out of respect to her. The citizens of Springfield, said their Mayor, should honor Mrs. Lincoln because of her husband and on her own account. And, recalling her ancestry, he adds: "It will be seen that Mrs. Lincoln sprang from no humble origin. She traces her ancestry beyond the Revolution. Her family assisted in the growth and development of the nation from its incipiency, and her immediate ancestry was closely identified with the early history of Illinois."

MILITARY ANCESTORS

Relatives of Mrs. Lincoln participated in both the Revolutionary War and that of 1812. One of the heroes of the Revolution was General Andrew Porter. Major Robert Parker was an officer in that war, with a record for distinguished gallantry. In the Indian wars of Illinois and Kentucky, Generals Levi, John, and Robert Todd won reputations, and John was killed. In August 1812 Robert S. Todd joined the Fifth Kentucky Regiment, and served until the latter part of 1813, in the campaigns against Indians allied with the British. He fought in the bloody River Raisin battle, in which his brothers, Sam and John, were captured

[1] Bibliography, No. 32, July 19, 1882.

by the Indians. It was one of these brothers who lived among the Indians for many years and finally went back to the whites and settled in Columbia, Missouri, where he became a judge.[1]

Robert S. Todd went home on furlough during the War of 1812, was married, and went back to his regiment immediately. Perhaps that was the reason he came home two years before the war ended, instead of staying through and possibly winning his father's rank of general.[2]

So far as we know, Colonel John J. Hardin, a distant cousin, was the only Todd kinsman who fought in the Mexican War. Levi may have considered himself a little too old at the time, and George, a little too young. The prowess of families in war oftentimes hinges on the ages of their menfolk and whether or not they were married at the time of the wars. In the Civil War Mrs. Lincoln had a fine array of kinsmen fighting, some on one side, some on the other.

There are several American patriotic societies in which one test for membership is proved descent from a soldier in an American war. Mrs. Lincoln would have been eligible for membership in every such society for which a woman of her day could have qualified.

ANCESTORS IN BUSINESS AND IN THE PROFESSIONS

The members of Mrs. Lincoln's family were not professionally minded.

In her entire accumulation of ancestors the only physicians were the quite remote Porter relative who quarreled with his father, Andrew; and her father's brother, Dr. John Todd of Springfield. Her youngest full brother, George,

[1] The Draper Collection contains contributions from the Columbia branch of the Todd family that are especially valuable sources of information.

[2] Bibliography, No. 176, p. 48.

took up medicine, but that was not the only manifestation of his lack of harmony with the rest of the family.

Likewise, it is necessary to go some distance up the family tree — or down — and then up other limbs to find any lawyers among Mrs. Lincoln's forbears. One of the sons of Andrew Porter was a great lawyer, but that was a long way off and out on another limb. The grand-uncle John, known as Governor Todd, might be claimed by the lawyers, but the claim could not be conclusively proved. Her father, Robert S. Todd, studied law and even arranged to practice — with a relative, an ex-cabinet member; but he never went beyond the stage of preparation. There were several lawyers among the Parkers, but they were in collateral lines. The Lexington papers, 1800 to 1840, contain several references to Parkers who were lawyers.

Nor were there any clergymen. Her Grandfather Levi Todd's Uncle John was the Rev. John Todd of Virginia who had the reputation of being a great preacher. And that exhausts the list. The stepmother, Betsy Humphreys Todd, came of a clerical family, and her Grandfather Brown was a great minister in Rhode Island. But the only way this could have borne on Mrs. Lincoln's life was that it may have caused the family to be more regular in attendance at church and Sunday school when Mary was a child, a girl, and a budding woman.

The only teacher among her ancestors was that same distant relative — the great-grand-uncle, Rev. John Todd of Virginia — who educated her grandfather and his two brothers.

The Kentucky Todds seem to have remained under the influence of the Reverend John. Two of the nephews had to do with the founding of Transylvania University and its library. The family saw to it that the young people were well educated. Among the connections were several teachers in Transylvania. Of these was Dr. Samuel Brown, a physician, one of the professors who left their mark on Transylvania.

But Dr. Brown was Betsy Humphreys Todd's uncle, not a blood relative of Mrs. Lincoln.

As it happened, the Todd family atmosphere in Springfield, Illinois, was distinctly professional — but that is beside the case. There was her uncle Dr. John Todd, the physician; her cousins Judges John T. Stuart and Stephen T. Logan were lawyers; and of the brothers-in-law only one was in business.

Nevertheless, the Todd type of mind and personality fitted the male members of the family for business. Levi O. Todd, Mrs. Lincoln's full brother, was a business man. Robert S. Todd, her father, studied law, but quit it for merchandising, manufacturing, banking, farming, and politics. Levi and Robert, grandfather and grand-uncle, began as soldiers, but when they were ready to settle down, they became pioneers, farmers, and dealers in real estate; the third brother, John, who was killed in one of the battles against the Indians, had started, in the new country, as Governor and judge and owned the land on which Lexington was located. David Todd, another son of Levi, was a farmer and merchant. Most of the Parkers and Porters of Mrs. Lincoln's close ancestry were also merchants and farmers.

These facts bear on Mrs. Lincoln's mental make-up. In their light we should expect her mind to run to business and business matters, to finance and affairs of barter and trade, to salesmanship, to the making and saving of money, to acquiring, to competition. For this reason we should not expect her thoughts to follow the channels that the minds of clergymen and physicians run in. That such expectations are not always realized is true; but, according to the laws of averages and of heredity, people with Mrs. Lincoln's inheritance can be expected to succeed best and be most satisfied when they follow business careers.

THE PARKER-TODD FAMILY

Robert S. Todd was married twice. His first wife, Eliza Parker, bore six children who reached maturity. There were four girls — Mary (Mrs. Abraham Lincoln), Elizabeth (Mrs. N. W. Edwards), Frances (Mrs. William Wallace), Ann (Mrs. C. M. Smith); and two boys — Levi O., and George R. C.

MRS. ELIZABETH EDWARDS

Mrs. Lincoln wrote of Mrs. Edwards from the White House, September 29, 1861:[1]

"I received a letter from Elizabeth E. [Mrs. Edwards] the other day. Very kind and affectionate, yet very characteristic. Said if rents and means permitted, she would like to make us a visit, I believe for a season. I am weary of intrigue. When she is by herself she can be very agreeable, especially when her mind is not dwelling on the merits of [her] fair daughters and a talented son-in-law. Such personages always speak for themselves. I often regret E. P. E.'s little weaknesses. After all, since the election she is the only one of my sisters who has appeared to be pleased with our advancement. You know this to be so."

We can readily believe that Mrs. Edwards was a matchmaker for her daughters and for many others besides. Match-making was the chief indoor sport of matrons in that day, and Elizabeth Edwards had early begun the game. She was little more than a child when she met and married Ninian Wirt Edwards and left the brood of Parker-Todd children she had been mothering to preside over a home in Illinois. As soon as she felt sure of her ground, she sent for her sister Frances to come to her home in Springfield and "make it her home." Well did both of them understand that

[1] Bibliography, No. 108.

the Edwards home was to be her home until she and her able, intriguing sister could make a suitable match for her. Soon Frances married the most eligible physician in town, Dr. William Wallace.

This meant that Elizabeth Edwards was now ready to undertake match-making for another sister. As soon as Mary arrived, in 1837, Mrs. Edwards gathered around her Stephen A. Douglas and all other eligibles available. Somewhat tardily, because of more than one consideration, Abraham Lincoln was added to the number. In the course of a little time Mary was married in her sister's parlor, as Frances had been. She married a promising lawyer and politician and a future president.

Whereupon Mrs. Elizabeth Edwards sent for her youngest sister Ann. She again exercised her great talent as a match-maker, and " landed " C. M. Smith, the most promising eligible merchant in the city of Springfield, as the husband of Ann, though Ann failed to follow the example of her sisters and marry in the Edwards parlor; she returned to Lexington for that function. Mrs. Edwards's mind dwelt on the merits of fair daughters and fair sisters as well, and on brothers-in-law, in addition to sons-in-law.

Ninian W. Edwards was the son of a governor who was a man of wealth and political power, and Elizabeth Edwards presided over the home of her widowed father-in-law.[1] Her husband was a lawyer and a politician of no mean ability. For him she was ambitious. She gave parties, entertained, and did whatever she could to promote her husband's interests. Had he been as ambitious and aggressive for himself as she was for him, two of the Todd sisters might have gone down in history as the wives of great leaders. It is

[1] This is the commonly accepted statement, but it may not be correct. Ninian Edwards's term as Governor terminated one year before the marriage of Ninian W. Edwards. The son took his bride to Illinois in the spring of 1833, and the father died in Belleville in the July following. If the bride went to Belleville to preside over the home of her father-in-law, she did not remain there long. A few months later Ninian W. Edwards and his wife were living in Springfield.

altogether possible that she was somewhat envious of her sister in the White House, when she thought of the start her husband had had and the short distance he had traveled. We could forgive her some envy. But Mrs. Lincoln wrote that she "appeared to be pleased with our advancement." And she was.

Mrs. Edwards was a worthy woman with a great heart. She mothered her sisters and her brothers, her husband and children. No one who knew her said unkind things about Mrs. Edwards. I am sure she was normal, and so are her descendants so far as I could learn. Whatever blight there was in the family, Mrs. Edwards and her children and their children escaped it.

MRS. FRANCES WALLACE

Of the second sister, Frances (Mrs. Wallace), Mrs. Lincoln wrote:[1] "Notwithstanding Dr. Wallace has received his portion in life from the Administration, yet Frances always remains quiet. E. [Mrs. Edwards] in her letter said Frances often spoke of Mr. L's. [Lincoln's] kindness in giving him his place. She little knew what a hard battle I had for it, and how near he came getting nothing."

Except this sentence in Mrs. Lincoln's letter, there is nothing in the record that reflects on Mrs. Wallace or any members of her family. Nor was there anything abnormal in her personality.

MRS. ANN SMITH

Of Mrs. Smith, Mrs. Lincoln wrote:[2]

"Poor, unfortunate Ann, inasmuch as she possesses such a miserable disposition and so false a tongue. How far, dear Lizzie, are we removed from such a person. Even if Smith succeeds in being a rich man, what advantage will it be to

[1] Bibliography, No. 108.

[2] Ibid.

him who has gained it in some cases most unjustly, and with such a woman, whom no one respects, whose tongue for so many years has been considered 'no slander,' and who, as a child and young girl, could not be outdone in falsehood. 'Truly the leopard cannot change his spots.' She is so seldom in my thoughts. I have so much more that is attractive, both in bodily presence and my mind's eye, to interest me. I grieve for those who have to come in contact with her malice, yet even that is so well understood the object of her wrath generally rises, with good people, in proportion to her vindictiveness.

"What will you name the hill on which I must be placed? Her putting it on that ground with Mrs. Brown was only to hide her envious feeling toward you. Tell Ann for me — to quote her own expression — she is becoming still farther removed from 'Queen Victoria's Court.'

"How foolish between us to be discussing such a person. Yet really it is amusing in how many forms human nature can appear before us."

It is easy to surmise that Mrs. Elizabeth Todd Grimsley, her first cousin, had written Mrs. Lincoln some of the Springfield gossip. She had repeated something unkind that Mrs. Ann Smith had said of her sister and her White House pretensions. Mrs. Lincoln flared up in anger and wrote back in kind, or worse.

When one makes inquiry in Springfield, one hears much to confirm Mrs. Lincoln's opinion of her sister Ann. If we strip from this characterization so much as may be attributed to Mrs. Lincoln's anger, we are left with a description that can be matched in the Springfield gossip. Jessie Palmer Weber wrote Senator A. J. Beveridge:[1] "I remember her [Ann Smith] well. She was the most quick tempered and vituperative woman (if I can use such a word) of all the sisters."

---

[1] Bibliography, No. 18, p. 307 (Letter from Mrs. Jessie Palmer Weber, dated March 23, 1925).

After all proper allowances have been made, we must conclude that Mrs. Smith had a difficult personality; one of a type that did not differ much from that of Mrs. Lincoln herself. In fact, one very old resident of a town in which Mrs. Lincoln lived — with rather good opportunities of forming a correct opinion — when shown this statement of Mrs. Lincoln's about her sister, flashed back: "Mary was writing about herself."

Mrs. Smith left a considerable family. There is very good evidence that part of her difficult and peculiar personality was inherited by some of her descendants. Though the evidence consists in nothing more than gossip and "clothes-line stories," there is enough to justify the conclusion.

LEVI O. TODD

In this first group of Todd children — the Parker group — there were two boys who grew to maturity. Levi was less than two years older than Mrs. Lincoln. There is no question that he had an abnormal personality. He became City Treasurer of Lexington and manager of some of his father's businesses and seemed to fit in fairly well for a while; but after his father's death his abnormality became more apparent.

In 1852 he backed his brother, George R. C. Todd, in objecting to their father's will. In 1853 he had Oldham and Hemingway, in which his father's estate held partnership, sue Abraham Lincoln.[1] In this suit allegations reflecting on Lincoln's honor were made. Townsend says:[2] "Evidently Lincoln was aware that his brother-in-law, Levi Todd, was responsible for this suit against him." Levi never was on good terms thereafter with Abraham Lincoln or with many of the family. In a suit for divorce filed against Levi O. Todd by his wife, Louisa Todd, in 1859,[3] these allegations

[1] Bibliography, No. 175.

[2] Bibliography, No. 176.

[3] Louisa Todd, Plaintiff, against Levi O. Todd, Defendant, Fayette County (Kentucky) Circuit Court, 1859. Secured through the kindness of W. H. Townsend.

are made: "He has a confirmed habit of drunkenness. . . . Wasting of his estate. . . . No suitable provision for the maintenance of his wife and children. . . . Cruel and inhuman manner. . . . Wholly unfit to have the charge of any of these children, he has no estate and for some time past has made little or no provision for the maintenance of his family." The divorce was granted. In 1860 Levi was a Union man, but he did not vote for his brother-in-law Abraham Lincoln. The probability is that he voted for Bell. He was too infirm to enter either army during the Civil War, and there is no reason for thinking he cared to do so.

He seems to have fallen out with everyone. He used whisky to excess, and possibly other drugs. Abandoned by his former friends, at enmity with his stepmother, he moved away from Lexington and died, in 1865, in Franklin County; whereupon his stepmother claimed the remains of the almost friendless man, brought them to Lexington, and had them buried by the side of his father. Townsend says:[1] "Years later, when her eldest stepson, Levi — a victim of unfortunate habits — had become estranged from his wife and children, it was Betsy Todd who vainly sought to reclaim him, and when he died brought his body back to the old home and buried him by the side of his father and her own children in the Lexington cemetery."[2]

[1] Bibliography, No. 176, p. 74.

[2] In the Todd family lot in Lexington, there are stones which mark the graves of Robert S. Todd, Eliza Parker Todd, Betsy Humphreys Todd, Mrs. Kellogg, Mrs. White, Mrs. Herr, and Mrs. Helm; and several unmarked graves, one of which is that of Levi O. Todd. The others may be the graves of those who died in childhood. Betsy Humphreys Todd's tombstone bears this inscription on one side: "In memory of my boys, Samuel B. Todd, David H. Todd, Alex. H. Todd, all Confederate soldiers." It is not presumed that these three sons are buried on this lot. David H. was not. The inscription gives evidence of the loyalty to the Confederacy of Mrs. Lincoln's stepmother.

G. R. C. TODD

The story of George Rogers Clark Todd is equally unhappy.[1] He was a baby in arms when his mother died, and he was too young to know when the new mother came into the household. He grew up in association with the second group of children and knew almost nothing of his own sisters except Ann.

When he attained his majority, he moved away from Lexington and the family, took up his residence in Versailles, Kentucky, and thereafter evinced no fondness for any of his relatives. In 1852 he objected to the probating of his father's will and had it rejected on a technicality. He most certainly did not vote for his brother-in-law for president in 1860. In 1861 he entered the Confederate Army, and served through the Civil War as a surgeon with a good record. After the war he settled in Barnwell, South Carolina, and there practiced medicine until his death.

Dr. A. B. Patterson has written me a letter about his former fellow-practitioner of medicine in Barnwell, from which I quote the following:[2]

"Met Dr. Todd quite often, and knew him very well. He said his family regarded him unfavorably. Used the word 'black sheep.' As to the doctor's personality: Would seem very pleasant when he wished to be, but generally not agreeable. Did not get along with people. Was very bright and well informed, very egotistical, and extremely jealous of his professional reputation. Very peculiar and eccentric. Drank whisky to excess. Not on friendly terms with his son. Deeded his property to a friend in town, Joe Porter. Mr. Porter deeded it to George (the son).

"Impression was that he was not on friendly terms with his family in Kentucky. It is said he died from an

---

[1] Bibliography, Nos. 175, 176, 177.

[2] Personal letter from Dr. A. B. Patterson of Barnwell, South Carolina; dated July 1, 1930.

overdose of chloroform taken himself alone in his house. He was buried by the side of his second wife in Camden, South Carolina.

" He was a surgeon in the Confederate Army. I have often said the State ought to erect a monument to his memory because he resisted such temptation from his brother-in-law, preferring to be faithful to his section. He performed, while surgeon in the Confederate Army, the first successful amputation at hip joint, a matter of record in the government archives at Washington, D. C."

H. L. O'Bannon, his attorney, said of Dr. G. R. C. Todd:[1]

" He was of small build, florid of countenance, and inclined to stutter when he talked. He had his peculiarities but was highly esteemed and honored. He was inclined to be abrupt almost to brusqueness in his manner to those whom he did not like. He took no pains to conceal his dislike for those who had incurred his displeasure and he had even been known to withdraw himself from a company when one whom he disliked appeared. The old doctor refused to consort with his own contemporaries to any great extent. After the death of his wife he lived alone and was given to moods of deep melancholy.

" Doctor Todd's only child, a son, was a disappointment to him. This son, evidently afflicted with 'wanderlust,' left Barnwell and went out west. After his father died he returned to Barnwell and recovered the property which his father had willed to others, but who gave it to the lawful heir as his right. He sold this property and again went away, never to be heard of again. Some of his father's old friends think he is still alive."

The evidence is conclusive that Dr. G. R. C. Todd had an abnormal personality.

[1] Bibliography, No. 66, July 5, 1931.

THE HUMPHREYS-TODD FAMILY

Having developed the fact that four of the children of Eliza Parker Todd and Robert S. Todd had abnormal personalities, we turn to the family born to Robert S. Todd and his second wife, Betsy Humphreys Todd. There were nine children in this family, of whom eight reached maturity: Margaret, Martha K., Emilie P., Elodie, and Katherine B.—five daughters; and three sons—Samuel B., David H., and Alexander H.

Margaret married C. H. Kellogg and went to live in Cincinnati, several years before the outbreak of the Civil War. She and her husband were visited by the Lincolns and corresponded with them. The Kelloggs were Union sympathizers, and Mrs. Kellogg visited at the White House. Mr. and Mrs. Kellogg were the parents of four children. Of these, one, Franklin Pierce Kellogg, born in 1853, is living. He writes me[1] that the few peculiarities and idiosyncrasies he has are of no importance. For instance, he will not lick stamps, but moistens the envelope instead (not a bad practice).

Of the children of the Humphreys group, other than Margaret (Mrs. Kellogg), Samuel B. was not married; David H. married a Mrs. Williamson (there was one child born to this couple); Martha K. married Clement White (they had no children); Emilie P. married General B. H. Helm (they had three children); Alexander H. was not married; Elodie married General N. H. R. Dawson (they had two children); Katherine B. married W. W. Herr (they had four children).

With the exception of Mrs. Kellogg, all of the Humphreys group of Todd children, as well as Betsy Humphreys Todd herself, were staunch sympathizers with the Confederacy. Of the three sons, two were killed outright, and

[1] Personal letter from F. P. Kellogg, April 4, 1931.

one died as a result of wounds received in battle. General Helm was serving as a Confederate officer when he was killed on the field. Mr. White and General Dawson were ardent supporters of the South. Yet so honorable and circumspect were they that Mrs. Helm and Mrs. White visited the Lincolns in the White House. Mrs. White violated the hospitality of her host once, the degree of offense being a matter of some dispute. Mrs. Helm was never charged with any violation of good sense or good taste.

I have been at some trouble to find what I could about this family of children and their descendants. I have inquired as to insanity among them; their use of drugs, including alcohol; whether they were ever in disfavor in the communities in which they lived. Did they fit in? Had they abnormal personalities? What idiosyncrasies did they have? I have not found facts or opinions that reflect on any of them.

One letter says that David H. was somewhat impractical and eccentric. One son of Mrs. Dawson, while regarded as a man of outstanding character and a high sense of duty, was somewhat over-sensitive. These were minor blemishes in very good characters. The general reputation of this division of the family as good neighbors ranks well above the average.

The trend toward abnormal personality was far greater in the Todd-Parker group than in the Todd-Humphreys group of children. Some of this difference in the two groups may have resulted from nicking of the Todd and Parker qualities. Some of it was a Parker-Porter inheritance.

THE LINCOLN CHILDREN

There is confirmation of the theory of hereditary transmission, in that some of Mrs. Lincoln's peculiar traits were found in the personalities of two of her children.

ROBERT T. LINCOLN

Robert Todd Lincoln was well educated. The outbreak of the Civil War found him in the final stretch of his college career, and he did not go into the army at first. For this both he and his mother came in for more abuse than the circumstances warranted. After he was graduated, however, his parents found a place on the staff of General Grant for him. This again caused some adverse criticism, as shown by the contemptuous designation "The Prince of Rails." Admitted to the bar in Chicago, February 26, 1867, in a few years he had become a member of one of the strongest law firms in the city. He rose to be a cabinet member, an ambassador to England, a president of the Pullman Car Company, and a rich man.

Measured by the ordinary standards, his life was a success. He fitted into society, he got on with people, and he won position and money. These methods of measurement, however, are too crude for our purposes. Let us look somewhat behind the record of offices held and honors achieved.

In the letters written by Mrs. Lincoln after 1865, there first appears a note of discontent about Robert. We find her complaining of his neglect of her, and of his attitude in general. In at least one letter she compares him with the other children greatly to his disadvantage. After the sanity trial in 1875, she never forgave Robert for his part therein. Once Robert went to Springfield and asked for her forgiveness and love. He took with him his daughter, Mary, and used her in this appeal. His mother said she would forget and forgive—but she did not. On the other hand, there are many letters written by Robert Lincoln,[1] after his father's death in 1865 and before his mother's breakdown in 1875, which portray him as a young man doing his best to meet difficult situations in a manner worthy of his name. These letters show a fine sense of

[1] Privately owned letters seen by me.

responsibility, and a poise and decision unusual in a man of his years.

An article in an encyclopedia [1] contains the following statements: " He was peculiarly sensitive in the matter of gaining reputation or position on account of the name he bore, and this sensitiveness, planted on a nature which in its youth was curiously remarkable for stubbornness and a phlegmatic temperament, made him perhaps more marked than would have otherwise been the case. . . . He was a man of sound sense, good judgment, and integrity of character." At his death, the Chicago *Tribune* said: [2] " He was taciturn and retiring, but to those who knew him well he was a charming conversationalist and a good story teller."

His reaction toward his father's memory was somewhat abnormal. To steer between Scylla and Charybdis was not an easy matter, and in doing so he did not display the same qualities of judgment with which he made other decisions. His peculiarities of personality caused him to steer too far from the rocks on the one side and to hit those on the other.

I had no acquaintance with him. From such evidence as I have found, I hold the opinion that Robert Lincoln was sensitive — in fact, supersensitive; that he was emotional — quite over-emotional under certain influences; and that most of his attitudes on personal and family matters were defense reactions. There was much in life that gave him pain. In his personality he inherited from his mother much more than from his father. He lacked his father's humor, wisdom, and poise. On the other hand, he had some of the good qualities of both President and Mrs. Lincoln. While his personality was somewhat abnormal, the trials to which he was subjected never even threatened to push him beyond the limits of his endurance.

---

[1] Bibliography, No. 1, pp. 243–4.

[2] July 27, 1926.

EDWARD BAKER LINCOLN (EDDIE)

The second son, Edward, died in early childhood and before the Lincoln family was much in the public eye. We know nothing of his personality.

WILLIAM WALLACE LINCOLN (WILLIE)

Julia Taft Bayne said of him:[1] "Willie was the most lovable boy I ever knew, bright, sensible, sweet-tempered and gentle-mannered."

Mrs. Grimsley wrote:[2] "Willie, a noble, beautiful boy of nine years, of great mental activity, unusual intelligence, wonderful memory, methodical, frank, and loving, a counterpart of his father save that he was handsome."

N. P. Willis wrote:[3] "His leading trait was a fearless and kindly frankness. He was willing that everything should be as different as it pleased . . . but resting unmoved in his own conscious single-heartedness." Elizabeth Keckley said that Mrs. Lincoln cut from a newspaper this quotation from Willis and pasted it in a book where it met her eyes daily: "It is an accepted fact that Lincoln's admiration and love for Willie was extraordinary, so much so that he more than once broke down and cried when someone, moved by sympathy, would tell of some incident in Willie's life."

The following letter,[4] written by Willie Lincoln to a playmate of his own age, is typical not only of the letter-writing but of the thinking of a child between eight and nine years old:

Chicago, Ill June the 18, 59

DEAR HENRY

This town is a very beautiful place. Me and father went to two theatres the other night. Me and father have a nice room

[1] Bibliography, No. 17, p. 8.

[2] Bibliography, No. 67, pp. 48–9.

[3] Bibliography, No. 85, p. 106.

[4] The original, written by Willie Lincoln to his playmate, Henry Remann, is in the possession of Mrs. Mary Edwards Brown of Springfield, Illinois.

to ourselves. We have two little pitchers on a washstand. The smallest one for me the largest one for father. We have two little towels on top of both pitchers. The smallest one for me, the largest one for father.

We have two little beds in the room. The smallest one for me, the largest one for father.

We have two little wash basins. The smallest one for me, the largest one for father. The weather is very fine hire. in this town. Was through exhibition on wednesday before last.

Your Truly

WILLIE LINCOLN

Notice that " me " comes first. There is no circumlocution and no pretense. The boy writes about what interests him and about nothing else. He does not dissemble. His mother would have sent the same kind of letter, had she written some child of her age at the time her aunt turned the Todd home over to the new Mrs. Todd.

A second letter [1] to the same playmate, Henry Remann, was written by Willie when he was practically ten years and nine months old:

Washington, D.C., September 30, 1861
Executive Mansion

DEAR HENRY,

The last letter you sent to me arrived in due time, which was on Saturday. My companions and I are raising a battalion. When I came here, I waited until the beginning of June, and then joined another boy in trying to get up a regiment. We failed, however, and I then attempted to muster a Company. That soon broke up. Thereafter a boy stated he commanded a battalion, and my Company and I at once joined, believing that he spoke the truth, but we found out that was not the case. Disappointed in every way we set to work and raised one, which is in a high state of efficiency and discipline.

I am
Dear Henry
Yours sincerely
WILLIAM W. LINCOLN

[1] The original is in the possession of Mrs. Mary Edwards Brown.

In the intervening two years and three months Willie had extended his vocabulary and acquired a letter-writing style. When this letter is compared with that of June 1859, it will be noted that Willie not only had been studying in school, but was being educated by experience and by contacts. One can note the influence of his elders in his choice of words and in his style. The letter is still the product of a child's mind, however. He puts his own interests above all else, and he tells of what happened to himself; what is said of others is incidental. His mother might well have written a similar letter toward the latter part of 1829, or just about the beginning of the period in her life concerning which Elizabeth Norris wrote.

Of the three Lincoln children Willie was the most intelligent and the best poised. All the accessible evidence confirms the opinion that his personality was thoroughly wholesome, that he did not inherit any peculiarities.

THOMAS LINCOLN (TAD)

While many writers refer to Tad as very lovable, they all agree that he was given to great eccentricity. In fact, though the stories about Tad are amusing and diverting, they almost without exception refer to conduct that indicates abnormality of personality. This he had to a marked degree. Had he lived to assume the responsibilities of manhood, he would have broken under a strain much less than that required to break his mother; and had the strain been great, the degree of disaster would have exceeded that which befell her. While he was frequently referred to by his mother and others as a very loving and lovable child, he was highly emotional and most unstable.

Lulu Boone Carpenter described Tad, then sixteen to eighteen years old and living in Chicago, as follows: " He was devoted to his mother, who was quite ill. He neither smoked, drank, nor danced. The imperfection in his speech was slight. . . . People said Tad looked much like the dead President." Lloyd Lewis, who quotes Mrs. Carpenter, says of his speech impediment:[1] "Tad's defective speech — either a cleft palate or a tied tongue — served to endear him all the more to his father." The Chicago *Tribune,* when Tad died, said:[2] "After the death of the late President . . . he accompanied his mother to this city, and studied at the Northwestern University [which seems improbable]. . . . In 1869, he went to Europe, and attended school for six months in Frankfort-on-Main, Germany. He was next in school at Brixton, near London. . . . He was tall and thin and resembled his father in many mental traits and characteristics."

Mrs. Grimsley wrote:[3] ". . . Taddie, a gay, gladsome, merry, spontaneous fellow, bubbling over with innocent fun, whose laugh rang through the house, when not moved to tears. Quick in mind and impulse, like his mother, with her naturally sunny temperament, he was the life, as also the worry, of the household." Speaking of the two little boys when they went to the White House, she called them "irrepressible Tad and observant Willie."

But there are other reports that are not so complimentary. A recent correspondent, writing in the Chicago *Tribune,* said that Tad attended the Elizabeth Street school (now the Tilden), in 1867; that he was very nervous; that he stuttered and was called "Stuttering Tad" by the children. His mother, a woman in black, brought him to school daily. Another correspondent wrote: "Tad did not stutter . . . but had a slight deficiency in speech. . . . The writer . . . sometimes protected him from pests who teased him because of his manner of speech and his timidity. He was a bright boy, slight, and delicate in health — too advanced to have attended a primary school."

These writers differ but slightly, so far as concerns es-

[1] Bibliography, No. 102.
[2] July 16, 1871.
[3] Bibliography, No. 67, pp. 47–8.

sentials. Tad was more than twelve years old when he came to Chicago. He was sixteen, or nearly so, when he and his mother went to Europe to continue his education. He was in schools in different parts of Chicago for four sessions, and, since he lived near Elizabeth Street, on Washington Street, in 1866 and part of 1867, he was probably attending the school named above. He was fourteen years old then. It is also quite possible, as Lewis says on the authority of Mrs. Carpenter, that he had a sweetheart. Before he left for Europe, he is very likely to have had a youthful love-affair.

Mrs. Bayne wrote of him:[1] "Tad had a quick, fiery temper, very affectionate when he chose, but implacable in his dislikes. A slight impediment in his speech made it difficult for strangers to understand him."

There is ample evidence that Tad was painfully backward in his studies. When his father died, Tad was twelve years old. Today a normal child of that age is in the sixth or seventh grade. Mrs. Keckley wrote[2] that Tad did not know how to read in the spring of 1865. She tells of his difficulty in learning to spell words of one syllable and three letters, such as "ape." She quotes Mrs. Lincoln as chiding Tad in her efforts to get him to study, saying: "You would not like to go to school without knowing how to read." In the summer of 1865 Mrs. Lincoln wrote to Judge David Davis, telling him of her plans to put Tad in a school in Racine, Wisconsin, that fall. She was uneasy because he could not read. In letters written later, she expressed pleasure at the progress he was making in school.

That Abraham Lincoln recognized that Tad was backward is apparent from this statement about him, made to N. Brooks:[3] "Let him run. There's time enough yet for him to learn his letters and get poky. Bob was just such a little rascal, and now he is a very decent boy." To this,

---

[1] Bibliography, No. 17, p. 8.
[2] Bibliography, No. 85, pp. 216, 217.
[3] Bibliography, No. 25, p. 281.

Brooks adds his own comments: "Even when he could scarcely read, he knew much about the cost of things, the details of trade, and the habits of animals, all of which showed the activity of his mind and the turn of his thoughts."

In January 1868 Robert made an effort to have Tad's difficulties of speech corrected. He and his mother, with the approval of Tad's guardian, Judge Davis, had Tad take lessons to overcome his speech defects from Dr. McCoy, a man of some reputation. About the same time the need to have Tad's teeth straightened was recognized. He was taken to one dentist, who put springs on his teeth. Wearing them was very uncomfortable and made Tad's speech defect worse. He was much harder to understand. A second dentist was consulted, who did not think much of prosthetic dentistry. He advised that the springs be removed and that the teeth be left to take care of themselves. The family acted on the advice of the second dentist.

Dr. William E. Barton wrote:[1] "Tad, the little tongue-tied lad with the cleft palate and the slow intellectual development, was a lovable, spoiled, undisciplined boy." Elsewhere, he wrote of Tad:[2] "He was a sweet and lovable boy, but with defective speech and retarded development. He grew to be a big tall lad, with a frame that might have become as gigantic as his father's. He was a very religious child, extremely affectionate, but given to outbursts of temper like his mother."

There is not one letter written by Tad in any Lincolniana.

That Tad was either backward or worse is established by the word of his mother and of Mrs. Keckley, and supported by the opinions of Lincoln himself, Barton, and others. His early actions raise the question: Was it backwardness or feeble-mindedness? The evidence is quite con-

[1] Bibliography, No. 10, p. 49.   [2] Bibliography, No. 11.

clusive that backwardness resulting from lack of application and discipline was the cause.

Mrs. Bayne tells us that her brothers shared the services of a half-day tutor employed by the Lincoln family in 1861. Under this tutelage Willie made rapid progress, but to Tad the proceedings were not a matter of serious concern. Brooks, who knew the Lincoln household intimately, wrote:[1] "Tutors came and went like changes of the moon. None stayed long enough to learn much about the boy. He abhorred books and study."

But after his father had died, and his mother had set her mind on Tad's schooling, and Tad had had a chance to see where he stood with other boys, the story was different. He applied himself, and when he did, he learned satisfactorily; before long he was abreast of his comrades.

In May 1871 he was back from Europe and eighteen years of age. Although he was then suffering from the illness which resulted fatally two months later, he talked over with Robert his plans for the future. Robert wrote to Judge Davis of this interview, giving his opinion that Tad was a good boy, and that his progress in education and development was sufficient to make his interest in a life-work natural and about as was to be expected of a boy of eighteen. This indicates that Tad's backwardness in his earlier years was the result of lack of training.

No small part of Mrs. Lincoln's traits of personality were the result of inheritance — some good and some bad. She had ancestors who gave her the right to be dominating and ambitious, to have drive, to be interested in politics, business, and finance, to have no aversion to war. On the other hand, a certain pattern of personality disturbance is noted weaving in and out. She was a link in a chain. At one end she connected with the links of some of her ancestors; at the other, with those of her children; laterally with those

[1] Bibliography, No. 25, p. 281.

of some of her fraternity. Many links were cut from the same pattern.

C. R. Stockard says:[1] "The heroes of history were biologically superior individuals long before they were born." The Cornell professor continues: "It is evident from historical record and the present state of human affairs that the struggle for existence and supremacy in artificial societies does not divide persons into qualitatively different groups, but separates them into definite classes of graded successfulness, in accordance with their degrees of ability in the competitions concerned." It is contended that the unusually large number of outstanding individuals in Mrs. Lincoln's lineage is proof that they were possessed of high "degrees of ability in the competitions" they engaged in, and this gave to Mrs. Lincoln an exceptionally good genetic background. The distinguished biologist further says: "Neither the genetic background nor the developmental environment is sufficient without the other. . . . The influences of the surrounding elements are important factors in determining the nature and success of the final personality."

[1] Bibliography, No. 166, pp. 291, 303.

CHAPTER TWO

Childhood

Train up a child in the way he should go and when he is old he will not depart from it.

— Proverbs xxii, 6

A mother once asked a clergyman when she should begin the education of her child, which she told him was then four years old. The reply was, "Madam, you have lost three years already."

— Whately

INCIDENTS AFFECTING MRS. LINCOLN

1806 to 1826

1806 *June 12,* Thomas Lincoln married Nancy Hanks.

1807 *February 10,* Sarah Lincoln born.

1808 Thomas Lincoln and family moved from Elizabethtown to near Hodgenville, Kentucky.

1809 *February 12,* Abraham Lincoln born.

1812 *November 26,* Robert S. Todd married Eliza Parker, Lexington, Kentucky.
Robert S. Todd in the War of 1812.

1813 *November,* Elizabeth P. Todd (Mrs. N. W. Edwards) born, Lexington, Kentucky.

1815 Frances Todd (Mrs. William Wallace) born.

1816 Thomas Lincoln and family, including Abraham, moved from Kentucky to Indiana.

1817 *June 25,* Levi O. Todd born.

1818 *October 5,* Nancy Hanks Lincoln died.
December 13, Mary Todd (Mrs. Abraham Lincoln) born.

1819 *December 2,* Thomas Lincoln married Sarah Bush Johnson.

1820 Robert Parker Todd born.

1824 Ann Todd (Mrs. C. M. Smith) born.

1825 *July 4,* George Rogers Clark Todd born.
July 5, Eliza Parker Todd died.
Lafayette, in America, visited Lexington; was visited by Porters in Pennsylvania, and Todds in Lexington.

CHAPTER TWO

Childhood

THERE IS NO DIRECT INFORMATION ABOUT MARY TODD'S life or her personality during the lifetime of her mother. There are the bare dates of births and deaths, and that is all. Neither Emilie Todd Helm nor her daughter gives any data other than these. William H. Townsend has found a single item, relating to the deaths of Eliza Parker Todd and her infant son, Robert P. Todd. Such opinions as can be formed of the life of the child Mary Todd prior to 1826 are based on the few facts that we know of Robert S. Todd and his household and the very little that is known of his wife Eliza. The remainder is conclusion based on inference.

Mary Todd was born in Lexington, Kentucky, December 13, 1818, the third daughter and the fourth child of her parents. Her eldest sister was five years old; her next, three; her brother, a year and a half, when Mary was added to the family circle.[1] Two years later a son was born, but he died when less than two years old. When Mary was in her sixth year, another sister joined the flock of young children. On July 4, 1825 still another son was born, and on the next day the mother, Eliza Parker Todd, died.

[1] After this was written, I visited the cemetery at Springfield, and read the inscriptions on the tombstones of Mrs. Lincoln's sisters. These indicate that Mrs. Wallace was born only twenty-one months before Mrs. Lincoln. If this is correct, Levi O. could have been the next child following Mary, and not her immediate predecessor. This is in accordance with the entry in the Levi O. Todd family Bible owned by Mrs. Edward D. Keys.

At Mrs. Todd's death the ages of her living children were, approximately, 11 years, 10 years, 8 years, 6½ years, 1½ years, and 1 day. Mary was the 6½-year-old.

The homes of well-to-do Kentuckians of that day were plentifully supplied with efficient servants. Such was the Todd home. With five children, the eldest only eleven years old, Mrs. Todd could not have managed had there been any lack of trustworthy helpers. When Mary came, there were already three small children, the eldest not old enough to dress herself.

During the first seven years of life a child is egocentric — an individualist. Starting with a world in which there is but one person — and that person himself, with supreme rights — he slowly learns. The experiences of the day gradually teach him that there are others in the world, and that they have rights to be considered.

In this Todd household there were six babies or children of tender age, each being gradually and slowly educated out of selfish individuality and learning to become socially minded.

Mary, doubtless, was the beneficiary of her mother's placid, sunny disposition, even though she did not inherit it. That influence may have thrown a long ray down her life and assisted her to restrain herself at times when she was sorely tempted to yield to emotional storm. It may have helped her to maintain the calm and poise which became the major objective of her life in the period between 1876 and 1882. On the other hand, the influence of her "impetuous, high-strung, sensitive" father probably pulled her in the opposite direction during times of stress and strain.

The impressions made on the soul of a young child by the conduct of the parents are lasting, and persist throughout life. In these early years Mary was in the home school. She learned from her parents. She learned even more from her Negro mammy and the other household servants. But she was indebted most of all to Elizabeth, Frances, Levi, and Ann. Doubtless the children of this Parker-Todd family visited their cousins, as well as the children of neighbors. When children are so young, however, visits are infrequent and contacts are casual. When Mary met the children of other homes, she told them about her own family and her own home. She played with them, but the games had a solo quality. Children of this age play individualistically, even though they are in a group. No child and no adult outside the family group had any particular influence on her. We except from this statement Grandmother Parker and, possibly, Aunt Eliza Todd Carr.

Next followed a little more than a year of a motherless home presided over by the aunt, Mrs. Charles M. Carr, the father's sister. Robert S. Todd's marriage to Elizabeth Humphreys took place when Mary was practically eight years old. The eighth year is a very important one in the socialization of a child. Mary passed through it without a mother's help. What we know of Elizabeth (Mrs. N. W. Edwards) leads us to think that she must have been the best teacher Mary had in this year — and for several years thereafter.

A saying that is frequently heard in religious circles is: "Give me a child until he is seven and you may have him thereafter." The general interpretation of this is that unless a child is well grounded morally and ethically in childhood, it will be difficult to hold him to good morals, ethics, or religion in later life.

Mary Todd's mother was living during the first six and a half years of Mary's childhood. We have no knowledge of Eliza Parker Todd's character that would throw any light upon her ability or disposition to train her large family of children in morals, ethics, and religion. We may assume that she was a good woman, and even that she went to church as regularly as her domestic duties would allow; and that she sent the children to Sunday school when they reached the proper age. But whether she was of a type that undertook definite moral and ethical training of her children we do not know. It is reasonably certain that Mary Todd was taught the Ten Commandments and was made to understand the meaning of about four of them. The Sunday school would have attended to that had the mother failed to find time.

There are four Commandments that deal with the principles of organized religion. These the Todd children were taught to repeat, but practically all they understood about them was that they were not to use bad language, they were to go to church and Sunday school, and they were to deport themselves sedately on the Sabbath day.

Two deal with the establishment of a family and some rules therefor. The Todd children learned these, but they did not understand them.

Three relate to the security of property and life. Not only were the Todd children taught these by rote, but their connotations were explained and emphasized. These were made to register. One prohibits murder, and a second interdicts stealing. A third relates to lying, or dishonesty on another level. Stealing and lying have to do with fairness between individuals. These two are fundamental social laws, as is that relating to security of life. Children in well-ordered homes learn these Commandments both in form and in principle; and Sunday schools are of great service in teaching them.

The Tenth Commandment opens up an entirely different field. It is built around covetousness, a development of wishful thinking plus something else. This Commandment leads into the field of envy, jealousy, and the various emotional reactions which develop in " those who have not " and who are in contact with " those who have." It brings mental hygiene and immediate personal qualities, as distinguished from social and religious, into the purview of religion and ethics. All children of that day learned the Tenth Commandment, but none of them understood its meaning or had any thought of its connotations.

Mary Todd unquestionably knew the Ten Commandments when she acquired a stepmother. Her life indicates that the principles of nine of them had been taught her directly, and indirectly by epigram, precept, and example.

She may not have leaned on religion in her time of trial as much as she should have done for her own good. But never until after 1865 did she fail in her church attendance and affiliations.

Her life also indicates that she not only learned, but took to heart those two Commandments which deal with the family. She was always and ever a family woman. As a young girl that was the aim of her planning. As a wife and mother she was faithful. When her son Robert married, she was most cordial to his wife, writing her many letters and putting in them such pleas for domesticity as this:[1] "Mrs. R. said housekeeping and babies were an uncomfortable state of existence for a young married lady. I think her experience was different from most mothers who consider that in the outset in life a nice home, a loving husband, and a precious child are the happiest stages of life."

The exception to all of this is the Tenth Commandment. Probably she learned the words but not the meaning. It is quite likely that her mother, her Sunday school teacher, and even her preacher did not fully comprehend this Commandment. How, then, could Mary learn it? To the fact that Mary never understood the significance of the Tenth Commandment and never built conformity to it into her personality was due some of the trouble which came to her in later years, particularly between 1842 and 1865.

Julia Taft Bayne, who, as a sixteen-year-old girl, saw much of the Lincoln family in 1861 and the early part of 1862, wrote of the household:[2] "If there was any motto

[1] Bibliography, No. 73, p. 282.

[2] Bibliography, No. 17, p. 107.

or slogan of the White House during the early days of the Lincolns' occupancy it was this: 'Let the children have a good time.' " She heard Mrs. Lincoln say this on many occasions. It typified her notion of the way to bring up children: that is, let them grow up naturally with the least possible amount of restraint, instruction, or guidance; and with the greatest possible liberty to enjoy life in their own way. Mr. Lincoln followed the same policy and took much pleasure in doing so. Mrs. Bayne cites many illustrations of the educational and training influence of Willie, the elder, on Tad, the younger; but she says little of what the mother did in this respect. She remarks:[1] "They [the children] were never accustomed to restraint." This testimony is confirmed by others who were close to the family in either Springfield or Washington. In the absence of better light on the subject we surmise that Mary Todd the child was reared much as were her own children, Willie and Tad.

Mrs. Bayne observes:[2] "Mrs. Lincoln wanted what she wanted when she wanted it." This quality goes by the name of "immediacy." It is an infantile quality. It is most easily recognized in babies, but sometimes carries over into adult life. When it does, it constitutes a flaw in the personality. In Mrs. Lincoln the defect was one of the points at which her personality fractured.

The tendency for infantile characteristics to persist at older age periods is quite marked in particular types of mental abnormality. It is especially prominent in feeble-mindedness, and also in the adolescent-minded. It is an outstanding feature of certain insanities. It is also present in special types of adult mind; and in these, in proper circumstances, improves the quality of the mind. Comparative success in doing specific things is sometimes achieved by people because they have this peculiarity.

C. R. Stockard[3] is of the opinion that a prolonged infantilism is partly responsible for the superiority of man over

[1] Bibliography, No. 17, p. 8. [2] Ibid., p. 49. [3] Bibliography, No. 166.

the lower animals. Thus a persisting infantilism has certain advantages. For the average situation, however, the Biblical saying: " When I was a child, I spake as a child, I understood as a child, I thought as a child; but when I became a man, I put away childish things " [1] represents the normal.

The probability is that Mary Todd inherited this attribute of immediacy, because we find it in some of her full brothers and sisters. But a proper training might have overcome it. This training is usually supplied by association in the family with several older children. In Mary Todd's family there were three such, but — wherever the fault lay — she was not cured.

There is every reason for thinking that Mary Todd as a young child was impatient under restraint. Mrs. Bayne and scores of other witnesses say Tad was, and he inherited it from his mother. " When Tad came in and saw me he threw himself down in the midst of the ladies and kicked and screamed and had to be taken out by the servants." [2]

The foundation for this characteristic begins in the first few days of life. If the nurse pinions the arms of a newly born baby or holds his legs, the restraint is resented, and the resentment is shown by screaming, a red face, and other manifestations. If the quality persists in a somewhat older child, it shows itself as temper tantrums. If years of adolescence have been reached, it appears as hysteria, and often as major hysteria.

In Mrs. Lincoln it took the form of excessive mourning and convulsions of grief; and, in the earlier years of her married life, of unreasonable outbursts of anger. These we read of at Springfield and on a few occasions in the White House, but never with the same violence after that.

It is a pretty good guess that Mary Todd as a child was subject to temper tantrums, and she may have had night-terrors. The children who are fortunate in having brothers and sisters may be cured of these traits through the

[1] I Corinthians xiii, 11.

[2] Bibliography, No. 17, p. 201.

education administered in the nursery and home by those most valuable childhood educators. Mrs. Lincoln's success in controlling her temper during the last half of her adult life shows what little more of educational training in her childhood would have sufficed for the control of this weakness.

The relation between the urge that most children feel to collect things, and a certain outstanding peculiarity developed by Mrs. Lincoln in later life, will be given some attention elsewhere.

Since we have no information from anyone — not even from the Helms — as to Mary Todd's disposition in her first eight years, we can be guided only by her disposition in later years, and by the inference that her youth was somewhat akin to that of her children. All adult qualities have their roots in childhood years, certain of them more than others.

We can be reasonably sure that Mary Todd, with her inherited introvert personality and her drive and force, was much in need of training suited to such a personality, especially in the first eight years. She needed to learn restraint, patience, passivity, and relaxation. Above all, she needed to learn the Tenth Commandment in all its connotations. What we know of her adult life indicates that as a young child she did not receive the training her nature required.

CHAPTER THREE

Youth Builds Her Up

Youth is the time of enterprise and hope; having yet no occasion of comparing our force with any opposing power, we naturally form presumptions in our favor and imagine that obstruction and impediment will give way before us.

—Dr. Samuel Johnson

INCIDENTS AFFECTING MRS. LINCOLN

1826 to Autumn 1839

1826 *August 2,* Sarah, Abraham Lincoln's sister, married Aaron Grigsby.
November 1, Robert S. Todd, Mary's father, married Betsy Humphreys, Frankfort, Kentucky.
Mary Todd started school at Ward's.
1827 Robert S. Todd born; died in infancy.
1828 *January 28,* Sarah Lincoln Grigsby died.
December 14, Margaret Todd (Mrs. Charles H. Kellogg) born.
1830 *February,* Abraham Lincoln moved from Indiana to Illinois.
March 25, Samuel B. Todd born.
1831 Lincoln, living in New Salem, cast his first vote.
1832 *February 29,* marriage of Elizabeth Todd to Ninian W. Edwards.
March 9, Lincoln announced his candidacy for the Illinois legislature.
March 20, David H. Todd born.
April to July, Lincoln in Black Hawk War.
July 10, Lincoln mustered out, Whitewater, Wisconsin.
August 7, Lincoln defeated for the legislature.
Lincoln piloted steamboat to Springfield.
Mary Todd entered Mentelle's.
1833 Mrs. Ninian W. Edwards moved to Illinois.
June 9, Martha Todd (Mrs. Clement White) born.
1836 Frances Todd (Mrs. William Wallace) went to Springfield to live.
November 11, Emilie Todd (Mrs. B. H. Helm) born.

1837 *March,* Lincoln moved to Springfield and studied law.

April, Lincoln became partner of Judge John T. Stuart (Mary Todd's first cousin).

Abraham Lincoln broke with Mary Owens.

Mary Todd visited Springfield for three months.

Autumn, Mary Todd in Ward's school again.

1839 *February 18,* Alexander H. Todd born.

Mary Todd finished at Ward's and went to Springfield to live.

CHAPTER THREE

Youth Builds Her Up

AFTER THE DEATH OF HIS WIFE IN THE SUMMER OF 1825, and until his remarriage in the autumn of the next year, Robert S. Todd managed his household as well as he could. He had help from his sister, Eliza (Mrs. Charles M. Carr), but that lady had her own children to look after. His mother-in-law, Eliza Parker, lived near by, and she helped.

In the autumn of 1826, when Mary was almost eight years old, Robert S. Todd married Elizabeth (or Betsy) Humphreys. This marriage met with the outspoken disapproval of Mrs. Parker. The grandmother did much to foster the somewhat natural or at least often manifested dislike of the Todd children for their stepmother. The children visited in the home of their grandmother, and no doubt when they did, their dislike of the new Mrs. Todd was fanned.

Mrs. John C. Lanphier, a grand-daughter of Mrs. Carr, and Mrs. Mary Edwards Brown, a grand-daughter of Mrs. Edwards, both think they have heard that Mrs. Carr was rather sympathetic with the antagonism of the first family to the stepmother. Members of the family are authority for the statement that during this period the children lived in the home of this aunt, and that after the second marriage of Mr. Todd the children lived there more than half the time.[1]

[1] Personal communications.

I have not been able to verify these statements. It is more likely that such time as the first set of children lived away from the Robert Todd home was spent in the home of Grandmother Parker.

Between 1826 and 1832 Mary Todd lived in her father's home with her stepmother, her three sisters and two brothers, and an increasing number of children of the second family. She was attending the preparatory department of Ward's Academy.

The year 1832 is given some emphasis because it was in that year that two events of some moment occurred. One of these was the marriage of Elizabeth Todd to Ninian W. Edwards.[1] This marriage was destined to influence profoundly the life of Mary Todd. The second event of importance to her in this year was her entering the boarding-school for girls kept by Madame Mentelle. Thereafter she lived for five days a week of the school year away from her stepmother. In 1833 Mrs. Edwards moved from Lexington to Springfield, probably by way of Belleville; and in 1836 she began her policy of inviting her sisters to Springfield.

In June 1837 Mary Todd was graduated from Madame Mentelle's and went almost at once to Springfield to spend the summer with Elizabeth. At the end of her visit she returned to Lexington and again became a student. This time she lived in her father's home and went to school in the academic department of Ward's Academy. In 1839 she finished her studies at Ward's, whereupon she took leave of her father's home and of Lexington and joined her sister's family in Springfield. Once settled in Springfield, she entered society, finding her friends among the members of the Edwards circle.

That autumn she met Abraham Lincoln. In 1840 she was engaged to marry him. In January 1841 the engagement

[1] Mrs. Lanphier and Mrs. Brown think Elizabeth Todd married at Mrs. Carr's home instead of her own. They think Elizabeth's dislike of her stepmother was so great that she had left home and was living with her aunt when she was married. There is some basis for accepting this as true, but there is no way of establishing it.

was broken under circumstances which led to the generally accepted story of the bride waiting at the altar while the groom hung back in a state of distraction. This story is not true, but the engagement was broken. Later in the year the friendship was renewed. In November 1842 they married.

HOME LIFE AND FAMILY RELATIONS

In spite of its charm, the home of Robert S. Todd could not have been a wholesome place for a child during the thirteen years following 1826. Not even a beautifully appointed house, with servants, conveniences, and all else that money can buy and the town can supply was enough to make it so.

For one thing, there were too many children. When Mrs. Betsy Humphreys Todd took charge, there were six children, ranging in age from one year to twelve. In 1827 her own brood commenced arriving, and thereafter new members appeared with regularity until nine had been born. By 1832 the second Mrs. Todd had added four to the original Todd group of children. As one of these had died, the number of children in the home was nine. In this year Elizabeth married, but the subtraction was offset by the addition of Elizabeth Humphreys, Mrs. Todd's niece, who came to live with her aunt and go to school. It is from this Elizabeth Humphreys, later Mrs. Norris, that we get our first authentic pen picture of Mary Todd and her home life.

Between 1832 and 1839 Frances had been the only member of the family to leave, and every year or so there was an addition. In the last months that Mary was in the Robert S. Todd home, that home school and kindergarten had a daily attendance of four children of the first family and six of the second. They ranged in age from Levi O., who was twenty-two years of age, to Alexander H., who was less than six months. The house was commodious and comfortable. There were plenty of competent servants, many of them faithful slaves of the house-servant class.

Mrs. Norris, whose long and helpful letter was quoted at length by both Emilie Todd Helm and Katherine Helm, describes the home as a most desirable one, presided over by the father and his wife, each a worthy head of the household. She tells us of a tutor, or private teacher, who added to the family educational equipment as well as to its personnel. This tutor gave Mary, who did not like him, an opportunity to practice her wit and to exhibit some of the personality traits which, grown out of proportion, made trouble for her in later life.[1] Probably there were other tutors at other times; and special nurses and care-takers for the numerous progeny doubtless served to swell the crowd.

In this home Mary Todd could not have received much parental training. With ten children around the fireside — always one baby in arms and another crawling out of mother's lap to play on the floor with a third — the mother had no energy or time for child-training. However intelligent, conscientious, and willing she may have been, it was inevitable that she should fail in this.

DISCORD

To this overcrowding and inevitable neglect of training — at least, parental training — there was added an element of family discord of far greater consequence in the harm it did. The second marriage of Robert S. Todd was bitterly resented by the mother of the first wife.

It is possible that the interference of Mrs. Parker in her son-in-law's family affairs may not have been as pernicious as it appears, since it is not easy to arrive at a just conclusion of the facts in family quarrels where there are no records and where the truth must be winnowed out of old gossip. This, however, stands out: the first group of children

[1] Bibliography, No. 73, p. 55.

had a persisting ill-feeling for their stepmother, and there is much reason for thinking their grandmother contributed to it. They took part in the quarrel from its beginning and participated in it with various degrees of activity and rancor until well toward Civil War times.

There is some contradiction in the scanty evidence as to the family discord between 1826 and 1832. Elizabeth may or may not have left her father's home; and her marriage may have occurred there or elsewhere. The *Kentucky Reporter,* February 29, 1832, carried this brief notice: "Married in this city, Ninian W. Edwards, of Illinois, to Miss Elizabeth Todd, daughter of Robert S. Todd, Esqr." There is no statement as to who was there or where the wedding occurred. From some source there comes the information that the wedding was performed by Dr. Robert Stuart, a professor in Transylvania University, and the husband of one of Robert S. Todd's sisters, as well as the father of Abraham Lincoln's first law partner in Springfield.

When Elizabeth Todd married young Ninian W. Edwards, the latter was a student at Transylvania. After he was graduated, in 1833, it is said that he took his wife to his father's home to be the mistress thereof. This Ninian Edwards had been the Territorial Governor of Illinois, and then Governor of the state by election. He was much the most influential man in Illinois at the time.

When Abraham Lincoln ran for the legislature the year Ninian W. Edwards married his future sister-in-law, the political parties in the new state to the north were not so much Whig and Democratic as they were "Edwards" and "Anti-Edwards." Governor Edwards was a former Kentuckian, the owner of thousands of broad, fertile, Kentucky acres, and had been a judge in that state.

Mrs. Edwards soon offered a sanctuary, or alternative home, to her sisters. Beginning in 1836, there came successively to Elizabeth's home, at her warm invitation, Frances,

Mary, and Ann, all of whom married and settled down near their hospitable sister and away from the parental home.

It is significant of the depth and fixedness of the ill-feeling between Mrs. Todd and her stepdaughters that all of them left their home when they were old enough to do so; that the younger ones went to live in their sister's home in another state, where they entered society and married; that neither Robert S. Todd nor his wife attended these weddings; that the father rarely visited his married daughters; that the daughters rarely visited Lexington after going to Springfield. These facts stand as barriers hard to explain away when we try to lend a willing ear to the Helm view that Betsy Todd and her stepchildren were on reasonably pleasant terms.

In May 1848 Mrs. Lincoln, visiting in her father's home, wrote to her husband about her stepmother: "She is very obliging and accommodating, but if she thought any of us were on her hands again, she would be worse than ever." [1] Lincoln's correspondence with his wife, especially when she was in Lexington, contains references to the need of caution in view of strained family relations.

In the litigation over the Todd estate, there is evidence in the record of the unfriendly relations existing, especially between Levi O. and George, on the one hand, and the stepmother, on the other.

But there is something of a brighter side to this picture. In 1844 Mrs. Lincoln and her stepmother were in friendly correspondence. Miss Helm's narrative shows that the family did not look on the relations as being so unpleasant as is generally thought. In 1865 and before, Mrs. Todd, the stepmother, showed her kindliness toward Levi O., and her willingness to forgive, by several gracious acts.

[1] Original owned by Oliver R. Barrett, Chicago, Illinois.

SCHOOL EDUCATION

Mary Todd's formal or school education began at Ward's, where she studied in what would now be called the "grades." When she reached almost the level of what might now be called the high school, she went to Mentelle's. She finished there in 1837, and then decided to go to Springfield to visit her sisters and have a try at society. In the fall, however, she was back in Lexington and, what is more, back in school.

Abraham Lincoln once had a peek at a law court in Cincinnati, where he saw big corporation lawyers in action and where he was well snubbed. Someone asked him what he intended doing about the insult. Lincoln's reply was that he was going back home and study law. Somewhat similarly, Mary spent two years in doing what might be termed "postgraduate work." She wanted to be exceptionally well qualified for life, and she was willing to give the necessary time and work to preparation.

Thus when Mary Todd ventured forth for conquest on the high seas of society in 1839, she had had about seven years of high-school and college work and, almost as certainly, another six years of lower, or what might be termed "grade," education. This makes a total of thirteen years of formal schooling. Practically no women and very few men of that period received so much formal education.

An incidental result of these years at school was that Mary was removed largely from close contact with her stepmother for at least five of the thirteen years elapsing between her father's second marriage and her departure for Springfield.

What was the character of the education she received in these schools? It was both basic and cultural.

The building occupied by Ward's school is still standing, near the business center of Lexington and in close proximity to Transylvania College. When Mary Todd went there to school, she had to carry her books only a few blocks. The present building has the appearance of being able to house both boarders and day pupils, and of having been well suited for school purposes in that day.

The impression one gets from reading of the Ward school is that it specialized in the fundamentals — reading, writing, and arithmetic — and in discipline that was puritanical.

William H. Townsend writes of Doctor Ward:[1] "Kindly, scholarly, benevolent, he was, nevertheless, a strict disciplinarian. Far in advance of his time, he believed in co-education, and his school numbered about one hundred boys and girls from the best families in Lexington." G. W. Ranck [2] says of Doctor Ward that he was an Episcopal rector (the second in Lexington), an educator, and the founder of a girls' school.

The Mentelles were natives of France who fled to America to escape persecution. Mr. Mentelle was of some importance in the affairs and politics of Louis XVI; and when his monarch fell, it was necessary for the subject to surrender his property and leave the country. He became a man of affairs and of high standing in Lexington.

In Mentelle's school Mary Todd acquired a proficiency in speaking and reading French that stood her in good stead when she met the representatives of foreign governments in Washington. Whoever wrote of her always had something to say about her fluent use of French. Her reading knowledge of this language made possible a range of literature to which few had access. To be well-read in the polite French literature of 1840 was enough to give a woman social status. Mary was equipping herself to win a husband and to shine in society; this study of French helped her in her second objective and did not harm her in her first.

Madame Mentelle taught the girls society manners; and Mary was an apt pupil. Dancing, singing, conversation,

[1] Bibliography, No. 176, p. 57.

[2] Bibliography, No. 146.

letter-writing — all the social graces — were in the curriculum and made a part of the daily habit, as is the way of finishing-schools today. But this does not convey a proper impression of the character of the Mentelle instruction. In fact, Townsend[1] says that Beveridge was misled into the belief that little else than dancing and French was taught there. The Lexington *Intelligencer,* March 6, 1838, carries an announcement of Mentelle's, stating that it gives ". . . a truly useful and solid English education in all its branches." The school was located on a tract of ground donated for the purpose by Mary Todd's cousin.

Here, then, were two periods of schooling, having two differing objectives and pursuing different methods. Mentelle's had as its objective preparing young women for polite society, teaching them social graces, synchronously with English, French, and other cultural subjects. We are quite prepared to read the statement from her schoolmate Katherine Bodley (Mrs. Owsley):[2] "Of course, we girls at Madame Mentelle's used to discuss our future husbands."

On the other hand, the instruction at Ward's was hard and puritanical. It trained in obedience, dependability, regularity, and duty, while it taught grammar, geography, and arithmetic. The keynote of Ward's was discipline. And that was good for Mary Todd. She had not had much opportunity to learn this in her own home, presided over first by busy Eliza Parker Todd and later by even busier Betsy Humphreys Todd.

We know little about Mary's schooling from 1837 to 1839. She took up additional studies in Ward's, but what they were we do not know. Although there were primary day students, there were also boarders at Ward's, and probably instruction was given to advanced pupils.

Mrs. Elizabeth Edward's statement about Mrs. Lincoln[3]

---

[1] Bibliography, No. 176, p. 61, n.

[2] Bibliography, No. 73, p. 119.

[3] By courtesy of the Huntington Library and Art Gallery, Pasadena, California, Lamon MS.

includes the following: ". . . well educated . . . taught at private school in Lexington, Mrs. —— keeping it." When I read this, I interpreted it as meaning that Mary went back to Lexington and undertook to teach. Had this been so, it would have been highly significant of something—what, we can only speculate. But Dr. William E. Barton[1] cleared up the matter by reference to Herndon's notes of his interview with Mrs. Lincoln in the St. Nicholas Hotel, Springfield, Illinois, September 6, 1866, from which he quoted: "Came to Illinois in 1837; was in Illinois three months; went to school two years after I came to Illinois; returned to Illinois in 1839 or 1840." Barton commented: "This, from Herndon's notes, omits her return to Lexington, which followed the first three months' visit. In another part of the interview she says that her schooling, after Madame Mentelle's, was in 'Mr. Ward's Academy,' where she 'finished.' This would seem to preclude her teaching." Mrs. Edwards probably meant that she *was* taught.

It appears settled that those last two years were spent in Ward's. But we have no information as to the studies or the discipline during this period, or even whether she boarded in the school. We are probably safe in concluding that she pursued cultural subjects.

SOCIAL EDUCATION

Quite as important as the formal education, and even more so in preparation for life as housewives in the middle of the last century, were the social experiences and contacts of the young women.

The Todds were welcome in the best social circles in Lexington and in Frankfort. Mrs. Norris writes of a visit which she and Mary paid to Mrs. Betsy Humphreys Todd's mother in Frankfort. This Mrs. Humphreys was the widow of Dr. Alexander Humphreys and a sister of the famous

[1] Personal letter to me, dated March 28, 1929.

Brown brothers, two of whom were United States Senators and two, outstanding physicians. No professor in Transylvania University Medical School, not even the renowned Dr. B. W. Dudley, was a better servant of his school than was Dr. Samuel Brown, one of these brothers. When Mrs. Humphreys's daughter married Robert S. Todd, the groomsman was John J. Crittenden, later United States Senator.

Miss Mary Todd had access to the best society in the Blue-Grass. Her intimate associates were girls such as the Misses Wickliffe, Preston, Bodley, Stuart, and Trotter and the Breckinridges and Clays. But never once in any list of her friends is there given the name of an eligible bachelor or outstanding beau. Why is it that there is no record of a Kentucky sweetheart for Mary Todd? Why is there no legend of young men whom she might have married, similar to the stories of Lincoln and Ann Rutledge, or Lincoln and Mary Owens, or to that of Mary Todd and Stephen A. Douglas in Springfield?

The answer, I think, is that Mary Todd never had much general social experience in Lexington. She was always a schoolgirl in her home town. Mary went out in company with girls and boys during the week-ends and the summer vacations, but she never molted her girl feathers nor acquired the plumage of a society belle. When in the company of young men, she probably talked and danced with them, but she was never more than a " sub-deb." When the time came to launch her real social career, she headed for Springfield.

It is true that the Lexington papers did not have society columns, and it was not regarded as good form to have notices of social affairs appear in the papers. Mary Day Winn refers [1] to " the old rule that a lady's name should appear only twice in the paper—first, at her marriage, and, second, at her death . . . and the accompanying feeling that if it appeared at any other time her nearest male relative

[1] Bibliography, No. 193.

was under a moral obligation to shoot the editor. . . ." This was the rule in Lexington when Mary Todd lived there. Since she neither married nor died in that city, she escaped newspaper notice. However, that is only a part of the reason that we find so little Kentucky record of Miss Mary Todd's social career.

Though there is such scant evidence of her participation in the social activities of Lexington, and nothing at all to be found in the Lexington papers, the page is not wholly blank. Gustav Koerner attended the Alton Lincoln-Douglas debate. When Lincoln met him in the hotel, he invited him to go to their room to see Mary. Koerner wrote:[1] "I had not seen Mrs. Lincoln, that I recollected, since meeting her at the Lexington parties when she was Miss Todd." In another place he wrote of Lexington society between 1825 and 1840: "Most of the parties were very elegant . . . splendid supper at midnight. . . . At one party at the Todds I met Mary Todd, who became Lincoln's wife."

POLITICAL EDUCATION

Lexington was the home of Henry Clay [2] during his entire political life. This is equivalent to saying that it was a political storm-center for the greater part of fifty years. Clay was in several cabinets, was a United States Senator and a member of the House, and was more than once, if not at all times, a candidate for president. Many of his political supporters, including Robert S. Todd, were always engaged in political strategy to promote the presidential candidacy of their friend, one of America's greatest statesmen. No one disputes the fact that Henry Clay was Lexington's

[1] Bibliography, No. 97, Vol. I, p. 361, and Vol. II, p. 66.

[2] Henry Clay was a member of the Kentucky Constitutional Convention in 1799; Kentucky legislature, 1803 and 1809; U. S. Senate, 1806–7, 1810–11, 1831–42, 1849 to time of death; member of the House and sometimes Speaker, 1811–30; Secretary of State, 1825–9; candidate for president, 1824, 1832, 1840, 1844, 1848.

political sun, or the further fact that during his reign Lexington was the political Mecca for Clay followers.

But Henry Clay was not the only presidential timber that Lexington knew. His bitter political enemy Andrew Jackson rode that way when he was campaigning for re-election in 1832. In 1836 neither Clay, of Kentucky, nor Jackson, of Tennessee, was a candidate for the presidency, but one of the group of candidates selected by the Clay forces to help beat Jackson's candidate was Hugh M. White, a man from the mountains just to the east of Lexington.

Among Lexingtonians of that day there were always some cabinet members, governors or ex-governors, senators or ex-senators. A man walking down the street would greet some neighbor by a high-sounding title before he had gone five blocks, and nearly every rising, ambitious young man looked on himself as a future statesman or, at least, officeholder. One young man of the Lexington days, Breckinridge, was to be a serious contender for the presidency against Lincoln. Napoleon is credited with saying that every soldier of France might carry a marshal's baton in his knapsack. Change a few words, and the epigrammatic statement might have been applied to the youth of Lexington during that period which began with the ending of the Virginia-Massachusetts political era, and itself did not end until the issues of Civil War were joined.

Lexington began to be a political caldron early in its day. Clay made it so when, just as the century began, he, with Webster and Calhoun, shifted the political scene. Lafayette's visit there brought together a group of men who proceeded to brew some political medicine.

Its proximity to Frankfort, the state capital, was another reason for the perpetual heat of politics in Lexington. Not only was Frankfort near; it was the terminus of highways that went through Lexington. People journeyed there to take the boat as well as to make politics. Any place within commuting range of a capital is a place of political intrigue.

One who reads the Lexington papers published between 1830 and 1850 finds no need to speculate. The proof is there that Lexington was a training-school for politicians.

Did this concern Mary Todd, schoolgirl? It did. Her father was a politician, several times an office-holder, and frequently a candidate. He was one of the Clay "guards." He read law in the office of a former cabinet member. He was either an advocate or an opponent in politics of nearly every one of his neighbors and friends. Mrs. Betsy Humphreys Todd also came of a political family, two uncles having been United States Senators. She could have been expected to talk politics with her husband in the home circle. Mrs. Norris supplies some information about her roommate's fondness for politics, her partisanship, and her forthrightness, and Miss Helm supports this story with incidents drawn doubtless from the family tradition. These incidents relate to Mary Todd's contacts with Henry Clay and Andrew Jackson, among others.[1]

Miss Mary Todd was politically minded. There is some proof that she was so in Lexington, and there is much evidence of the effect of that Lexington political training in her history in the Springfield and Washington days.

LEXINGTON

U. B. Phillips quotes [2] Timothy Flint as saying in Boston: "A full century ago they were saying in the Blue-Grass that Heaven could only be another Kentucky."

H. B. Fearon wrote of Lexington in 1815:[3] "It is with delight we notice the great prosperity and rapidly rising importance of the future metropolis of the west; where town lots sell nearly as high as in Boston, New York, Philadelphia, or Baltimore."

E. P. Fordham, writing of Kentucky people in 1818,

---

[1] Bibliography, No. 73, p. 1.

[2] Bibliography, No. 140, p. 12.

[3] Bibliography, No. 56b, p. 245.

said:[1] "The homes have a cleanliness which contrasts strongly with the dirty Ohio homes and the Indiana and Illinois pigsties in which men, women, and children wallow in promiscuous filth. But the Kentuckians have servants and, whatever may be the future consequences of slavery, the present effects are in these respects most agreeable and beneficial. A Kentucky farmer has the manners of a gentleman; he is more or less refined according to his education, but there is generally a grave, severe dignity of deportment in the men of middle age, which prepossesses and commands respect."

Phillips[2] also quotes a writer in the *Cultivator,* testifying as to conditions on farms in the Blue-Grass region in 1845: "In point of comforts, of luxuries, and even elegancies the Kentucky farmer compares well with the English, Irish, and Scotch gentlemen farmers in every respect. Their houses, generally speaking, are of brick, well and tastefully planned, large and roomy, and if any fault is to be found at all, they are too magnificently furnished for a farmer's residence."

An excellent account of society in that section was written by Governor Gustav Koerner,[3] of Belleville, Illinois, who studied law in Lexington: "Lexington is a lively, handsome city, built on wavelike hills surrounded by beautiful villas. No wonder that the inhabitants are very proud of it. My American guidebook calls it perhaps the finest spot on the globe. Of course, I cannot subscribe to this panegyric, but I am quite pleased with the place. It is the richest city in Kentucky and hence there is much show and luxury here. I have been in several homes and must confess that with us — in Frankfort-on-the-Main — the wealthiest do not live as elegantly and comfortably."

Koerner boarded with a Mrs. Boggs, the widow of a Kentucky politician, and the mother of a governor of

[1] Bibliography, No. 59a, p. 216.
[2] Bibliography, No. 140.
[3] Bibliography, No. 97, Chapter xv, p. 346.

Missouri. He gives us this glimpse of society in Lexington, as he observed it in Mrs. Boggs's home and among her friends: "Mrs. Boswell, a rich widow, a daughter of Mrs. Boggs, usually had a large company of young ladies in the drawing-room. Most of the ladies were highly accomplished according to the fashion of the country. Some of them played very well on the piano, and some sang remarkably well. They played for me German melodies and songs translated from the German. . . . I may say that towards the end of the season, when parties followed upon parties —and I had to attend a good many—the waltz mania had spread, and while of course quadrilles were the rule, we generally had two or three round dances every time. Yet, with the exception of one grand ball given on the occasion of the Legislature visiting Lexington in a body, to which the law students were invited, and one concert, there were no other public amusements, for not only did all the fashionable and respectable world go to church twice every Sunday in grand toilet, but there were frequent sermons."

We can get no truer and more graphic picture of the social life of Mary Todd in Lexington than by imagining her as a member of the group about which Koerner wrote. Her family was the oldest in town and had always been prominent. The group of girls and beaux with whom she associated was the highest socially in Lexington, and they occupied their time quite as Koerner describes. So much for Miss Todd's social environment.

Ranck says:[1] "The literary culture and educational advantages of Lexington had become such by 1824 that the city was spoken of far and wide as the 'Athens of the West.' . . . The society of Lexington was noted for its intelligence, its appreciation of literature, its good taste, and eloquence. . . . The city library was the largest in the West and has never been more liberally patronized. [The period is that of Miss Todd's residence there.] A

[1] Bibliography, No. 146.

botanical garden had just been established, the pencil of Jouett had made him famous, and scholars and distinguished men from all over the country visited Lexington. . . . The Lyceum was the successor to the debating society called the 'Lexington Junto,' in which Henry Clay distinguished himself by the first speech he made in Lexington, in the year 1798." (Many of the professors of Transylvania University and many distinguished men from different parts of the world spoke before this Lyceum. Dr. B. W. Dudley, Dr. Samuel Brown, and Dr. Dan Drake were among these.)

One of the powerful cultural influences of Lexington was Transylvania University. There were other institutions of learning there; but none ranked in age, in reputation, or in influence with Transylvania. The period in which we are interested is that of Dr. Holly; and the golden age of Transylvania was that in which he was its president.

Audubon lived for a while in Kentucky, and his influence lay on Lexington as well as elsewhere. A love of birds, of nature, and of beauty flourished by the side of more lettered culture.

In Lexington, one hears much of Rafinesque, a Transylvania professor and the "Lexington Audubon." Professor John Torrey wrote of Rafinesque:[1] "He is the best naturalist I am acquainted with"; David Starr Jordan: "No more remarkable figure has ever appeared in the annals of science."

James Whaler, who wrote *Green River*[2] round some incidents in the career of Rafinesque, says of him: "Today his name is not wholly forgotten on the campus of Transylvania College, where for years he lectured on natural science and where his bones now lie buried. They still speak of him as their eccentric genius. The current college catalogue so refers to him. Open any manual of botany or ichthyology, and here and there 'Raf' still

[1] Bibliography, No. 187, Introduction.

[2] Bibliography, No. 187.

stands beside some genus or species which he first found or classified."

Another of the Transylvania professors was Mary's uncle by marriage, Professor Robert Stuart, the father of Judge John T. Stuart of Springfield. Among the great men in the medical department were: Professor Samuel Brown, uncle of the second Mrs. Todd; Dr. Dan Drake, the best-known physician of his day in the Mississippi Valley, and the only physician Abraham Lincoln is known to have consulted; Dr. B. W. Dudley, the greatest surgeon the Blue-Grass ever produced; and Dr. Ephraim McDowell, renowned for having done the first ovariotomy. Among the students of the period in the university was Jefferson Davis.

In Miss R. Peter's *History of the Medical Department of Transylvania University*,[1] there is this statement about the botanical garden: "A project inaugurated by Rafinesque, while a professor at Transylvania, was called the Botanical Garden of Transylvania University. It was chartered January 7, 1824 — a charming resort for the élite who were expected to stroll at evening perchance through sylvan borders. . . . To benefit farmers by supplying new fruits and flowers and grains. . . . Lectures and practical demonstrations to be given to the students. . . ."

Transylvania sent men to Europe at frequent intervals to gather books and manuscripts for the library and objects of interest for the museum. Among the museum pieces brought back and curiously inspected, even today, is one of the first daguerreotype machines brought to America, if not the very first. This was in Transylvania by 1839. Since Mary Todd did not leave Lexington until the summer of that year, it is quite possible that the daguerreotype from which Miss Helm painted the portraits (a part of one of which is reproduced facing page 277) was taken by this machine while the young lady was preparing to leave her Lexington home.

[1] Bibliography, No. 139.

It is certain that Transylvania University contributed to the cultural training of Miss Todd. It was part of the atmosphere in which she budded.

Among the great men in Lexington referred to by Ranck [1] is Richard H. Menefee, "one of the most wonderful men Kentucky ever produced." Among the artists he mentions Jouett, Oliver Frazier, and Joel T. Hart. Among the lawyers were Thomas A. Marshall, H. Marshall, John Brown, and B. W. Dudley. The politicians and statesmen cited by Ranck had national and, in some instances, international reputations.

One section of Ranck's history is devoted to the inventions made by men of Lexington. Of these, one of the most noted was a planetarium invented by Thomas Harris Barlow in 1825. This planetarium was copied in all parts of the world and finally found its way into the museum of Transylvania University.

Ranck says [2] the Louisville, Cincinnati, and Lexington Railroad, incorporated January 27, 1830, was the first railroad built in the West. "It is believed that the first locomotive made in the States ran over this road. It was invented by Thomas Barlow, of Lexington, as early as 1827, and was also built in Lexington."

A Lexington paper carried an advertisement of a hemp-breaking machine invented by Cyrus McCormick. He did not offer to sell the machines, but to license the building of them by local people on a royalty basis.

Ranck also says: [3] "The Phœnix Hotel has continued to exist since the year 1800. It was here that Aaron Burr lodged in 1806, and was met and welcomed by Harman Blennerhassett, the cultured but unfortunate Irishman he had so completely fascinated. It dates from Jefferson's administration. It was the scene of the sumptuous dinner to Lafayette and, later, was the

[1] Bibliography, No. 146. [2] Bibliography, No. 145, p. 28. [3] Ibid., p. 60.

stopping-place of the wily Mexican chieftain, General Santa Anna."

Suffice it to say that Lexington was a city of wealth, of commerce, and of manufacture, as well as a center of blooded stock-raising and of farming in general.

A cross-section of life as it was in Lexington among the people of the Todd business and social circles is shown by these extracts from the papers:[1]

(1817) "Byrd Smith informs those who deal with him that he has formed a connection in business with Robert S. Todd, and will trade under the firm name of Smith and Todd.

"We have now on hand 10 barrels cognac, 15 barrels Jamaica spirits, 6 casks Madeira wine, 8 casks Malaga wine, 8 casks London particular Teneriffe, 8 casks of sherry, 6 casks Holland gin, claret and port wines, Irish whisky, country brandy, a larger quantity of old whisky. Also, stock of groceries and glassware. Best chewing tobacco." On another date they offer "50,000 pounds of good hog lard."

(1818) "It becomes our painful duty to record the death of the father of our western country." (This was George Rogers Clark.)

(1820, July 13) "A public dinner for Mr. Clay."

(1821) "Smith and Todd dissolve partnership. R. S. Todd will continue in business in Lexington. All business in their establishment in Winchester and Mount Sterling will be transacted with Mr. Todd."

(1821, October 15) "Mr. Schaffer's school for instructing dancing. . . ."

(1822) Mr. Todd advertises to purchase "a quantity

[1] From files of the *Kentucky Reporter*, *Kentucky Gazette*, Lexington *Reporter and Observer*, Lexington *Public Advertiser*, *Kentucky Monitor*, *Western Monitor*, *Anti-Jackson Bulletin*, Lexington *Herald*, *Kentucky Statesman*, the *Leaders' Spirit of Washington Literary Journal*, Maysville *Eagle*.—Draper Collection, Wisconsin Historical Society.

of lard and 10 to 20 barrels of whisky of good flavor and proof."

(1822, July) "Mr. R. Wickliffe asks those who have borrowed books of him to return them."

(1822, July 4) "Celebration of Independence Day. Large party of ladies and gentlemen."

(1823, May 6) "Robert S. Todd, J.P., testifies that he attended several drawings of the second class of the Atheneum Lottery, as required by an act of the legislature, and is satisfied that the whole is conducted agreeably to the requisitions of that act."

(1823, August 7) "Charles Humphreys and other trustees ask for brick for the new theatre."

(1823, October 31) "Dr. Dan Drake will be inducted into office as Professor of Materia Medica, in the chapel of the University."

(1824, February 3) "The ladies of the Lexington Female Academy address those in attendance at seminaries of learning, asking to subscribe to a fund which will contribute to the glory, liberty, and triumph of Greece."

(1824, February) "New cotton factory. Cotton of all sizes and the best quality spun by William Oldham, sold at the new cotton factory on Main Street, a little below the First Presbyterian meeting-house, on the opposite side of the street."

(1824, July 5) "Fourth of July celebration. The military joined the country parties and passed the day with the citizens and ladies assembled."

(1824, August 27) "General Brown, by order of the President, directs that when Lafayette arrives in this country, he shall be received at all military posts with the honors due to the highest military rank in our service."

(1824, December 6) "The first assembly ball will be held December 9."

(1825, May 16) "The Harmonic Society concerts, etc."

"Gentlemen who wish to attend the Lafayette ball . . ."

"Lafayette cockades just received at the bookstore of Henry H. Hunt, Main Street."

"Cockades like those mounted by the Republicans during the Revolutionary War . . ."

"Officers of the Grand Lodge . . . R. S. Todd, of Lexington, steward of the charity fund."

(1825, May 25) "A sumptuous dinner was served Henry Clay at Maysville, at which Lafayette was toasted."

(1825, July 11) "Commencement ball at the Masonic Hall. Tickets for men may be obtained at the bar of the Phœnix Inn. Tickets for ladies on application to the managers."

(1825, July) "The Literary Festival will be celebrated in the Episcopal church on Wednesday next. . . ."

(1825, October 24) "The match race, to be run on the Lexington course . . ."

"The theatre . . ."

"The circus, lately erected in our town by Mr. Pepin . . ."

"Mr. Palen's wax figures on Short Street . . ."

"Philosophical experiments . . . Galvanic battery an excellent one."

"This evening, nitrous oxide will be administered. Ladies will be accommodated in boxes recently erected in the sun room."

(1826) "The Institute will meet . . ."

"Lexington artillery cadets will assemble for the purpose of making arrangements for the celebration of Washington's birthday."

(1826, July) "Mr. Jouett's portrait of Lafayette is now finished and can be seen at his rooms from 9 to 12 every day."

(1826, July 4) "Celebration at Sanders' Garden."

(1826, July 16) "The Institute will meet at the home of Mr. Jouett."

(1827) "The subscribers inform the public that the Rev. John Todd will commence a female seminary on April first, in Fayette County, eight miles east of Lexington, and within one mile of Walnut Hill. . . . A complete system of female education . . . The substantial branches taught in the best seminaries of the kind . . . A critical knowledge of the Latin and Greek languages."

"B. O. Peers advertises a Pestallozian school."

(1827, July) "Barbecue by citizens of Lafayette County in honor of General Jackson and the people's rights."

(1827, December 24) "Ninian Edwards offers to sell or exchange 10,000 acres of improved Kentucky land. Willing to take whisky, flour, hemp, and tobacco."

(1828) Robert S. Todd, and others, subscribe to a card defending Henry Clay against a charge of having been connected with Aaron Burr.

(1829, July 4) Dinner to Henry Clay "by citizens of Lexington and old friends."

(1829) "Lexington branch of the American Colonization Society. Object: The colonization of the west coast of Africa, with their own consent, of the free people of color. R. Wickliffe, President."

(1830, January 30) "Subscriptions opened for Lexington and Ohio Railroad."

(1831, May 11) "R. S. Todd advertises to rent his house on Short Street."

(1831, October 28) "At a literary meeting held at the Court House, sixty gentlemen signed their names for the purpose of establishing a museum for the diffusion of useful information. Lecture by Professor Caldwell, on the Moral and Incidental Influence of Railroads."

(1831, November 9) Oldham, Todd and Company purchase Fayette Cotton Factory.

(1831) "Madame Blaigue, late of Paris, opens Dancing Academy."

(1832, February 29) "Married in this city, Ninian W.

Edwards, of Illinois, to Miss Elizabeth Todd, daughter of Robert Todd, Esqr."

(1832, March) "A lecture on the use of cold water in fevers, delivered by Professor Cooke before the Lyceum."

(1833, May 2) "May Ball. Mr. Xampis' first cotillion party."

(1833) A long list of persons who had died of cholera. Mr. Xampis's name headed the list.

(1833, July 18) "The First Presbyterian Church[1] of this city has appointed next Friday as a day of Thanksgiving to Almighty God for His great mercy in removing the cholera from our city and its vicinity, and also of humiliation on account of our sins, and prayer to God for forgiveness of them."

(1833, October 22) Mr. V. Ferron opens a fencing-school.

(1833, November 7) Exhibition of paintings by Professor Cordella.

(1834, November) "Dr. Dan Drake, professor at Transylvania, endorses Stagner's Patent Truss."

(1835, January 7) "Advertisement: The railroad car leaves Lexington every morning at six o'clock. Passengers will purchase tickets. No money accepted on the car."

(1835, March 31) "Northern Bank of Kentucky, J. W. Hunt, Chairman; Robert Wickliffe and Robert S. Todd, Commissioners."

(1835, July 26) "Funeral honors for General Lafayette."

(1837, June 2) "Died in this county, on Sunday night, at an advanced age, John Parker.[2] The deceased was an old and highly respected resident of Fayette County, was amongst the earliest settlers of Kentucky and, at the time of his death, the presiding Justice of the County Court. In

[1] This was the church to which the Todd family belonged.

[2] This is one of the many references to the Parkers, kinsfolk of Mary Todd. The notices in the newspapers would indicate that in this period of Lexington life the Parkers were more prominent than the Todds.

all the relations of life he sustained an unblemished character for integrity and probity."

(1837) "Dr. B. W. Dudley did three lithotomies last Wednesday. Under his surgical care right recently there have been patients from nine different states."

(1837, August 26) "Mr. T. Vincent announces that he will teach French. Recently he has been a tutor in Mr. Thomas Jefferson Randolph's family."

(1837, October 11) "Marriage of Thomas H. Clay to Miss Mary Mentelle."

(1837, December 23) "Mr. Richardson's New Year's Ball is in preparation."

(1838, February 22) "Anniversary exercises. The day was closed with a ball at M. Giron's, prepared in his usual style of elegance and taste. After the parade the Lexington Light Infantry Company marched to the residence of Capt. R. B. Parker, to present him with a special cane as a testimonial of their regard for him as a gentleman and as an officer."

(1838, June 12) "Mr. Richardson will give a dancing party at M. Giron's. In the course of the evening the beautiful dance La Bayadere will be performed by twelve young ladies."

These quotations from Lexington and north-central Kentucky papers issued between 1817 and 1839 give a general idea of those matters that may have influenced the life of Mary Todd, directly and not-too-indirectly. Stories of fights, tragedies, and controversies, heated legal battles, and political campaigns, in which a young woman of 1830 would have had no great interest, have not been included.

In the Draper Collection,[1] there is a letter written by Mary's father, which gives more direct light on the Todd affairs. In beautiful handwriting, Robert S. Todd writes Walker Reed the following:

[1] Bibliography, No. 49, Kentucky MSS., Vol. XXXI, p. 101.

October 31, 1831

DEAR FRIEND:

From everything that I have heard, considerable opposition will no doubt be made to me in the ensuing election, particularly in that section of the country called Green River, who, as usual, have their favorites. Judging of their zeal in this case by that heretofore discovered in carrying their scheme into effect, I have no doubt Mr. Town's friends will use great exertion. I have thought it necessary to be prepared to meet them armed at all points and, for that purpose, have requested several of my friends to attend a day or such a matter earlier than usual, to counteract any scheme that may be attempted, or defeat their plans should any be attempted.

If you should find it convenient, permit me to request that you would do me the favor and drive here on Friday evening preceding the meeting of the Legislature and go down with me on Saturday. I have heard from some counties in the Green River country and my prospect of success is good, but more of this when I see you. Endeavor to get all the members to attend punctually. Write to me whether you can be here at the time I should wish, and should you not arrive at the exact time I will wait a while.

MARY TODD'S MENTALITY AND PERSONALITY IN THE LEXINGTON PERIOD

The first report of her disposition is that made by Mrs. Norris to Mrs. Helm, relating to Mary Todd in her years of adolescence — eleven to eighteen years of age. She says:[1]

"My first recollection of your sister Mary runs back to the time when your father lived on Short Street. . . . Mary Todd was then about ten years old. [This was in 1829.] She was a pupil of the celebrated Mr. Ward. He was a splendid educator; his requirements and rules were very strict; and woe to her who did not conform to the letter. Mary accepted the condition of things and never came under his censure. . . . Mary was bright, talkative, and warm-

[1] Bibliography, No. 72, p. 476.

hearted. She was far advanced over other girls of her age in education. We occupied the same room, and I can see her now as she sat on the side of a table, poring over her books, and I on the other side, with a candle between. She was very studious, with a retentive memory and a mind that enabled her to grasp and thoroughly understand the lessons she was required to learn. . . . I have nothing but the most pleasant memories of her at that time. I never heard any display of temper, or heard her reprimanded during the months I was an inmate of your father's home. Sixty-six years ago children had few privileges. We had no amusements, no parties, nor books with charming little stories to stimulate us to acts of courtesy and kindness. Our standard library was the Bible, and the shorter Catechism, which we always carried to Sunday school."

The next record [1] relates to the early part of 1832, when Mary Todd was about thirteen years old. It was written by Miss Helm and is probably an interpretation of a family legend which her mother had often heard. In this story Mary is represented as rather willful and out of control. When riding near Mr. Clay's home, she stopped, and pushed her way past obstructing servants to him. She is quoted as saying: "My father says you will be the next president of the United States. I wish I could go to Washington and live in the White House. My father is a very peculiar man, Mr. Clay. I don't think he really wants to be president. . . . If you were not already married I would wait for you."

To the account Miss Helm adds this comment: [2] "Perhaps a psychoanalyst might discover in this adventure of Mary's the seed of ambition, planted in her unconscious mind, to grow into a wish to be mistress in the White House." Perhaps so. A psychoanalyst might also connect Mary's impatience of opposition and restraint with some of her later difficulties.

[1] Bibliography, No. 73, p. 27. [2] Ibid., p. 4.

In another reference she is represented as stopping the carriage in which she was riding, to speak to an old derelict. "'Howdy, Miss Mary. You ain't never too proud to speak to me,' said old Sol. 'Too proud to speak to you!' cried Mary. 'I am proud when you speak to me.' . . . Her eyes were brimming with tears. 'You were not afraid! You are a hero!'" This last reference was to the courage which old Sol showed in the epidemic of cholera that had swept Lexington the previous summer. Miss Helm goes into this epidemic at some length, dwelling on Mary Todd's emotional reactions thereto.

Fear is generally instilled in a child very early in life. It is likely to start with the stories told by nurse-maids. It may be grounded in procedures used in training. It is very infiltrating. It penetrates a long distance from the starting-point, and as it spreads, it acquires new phases. We call these panic, worry, anxiety, or other names.

Mary Todd was as free from fear as most people get to be. Miss Helm [1] tells of one instance of the young girl's becoming panicky, but this narrative has many ear-marks of pose. Then we read that when her children were ill, her anxiety was out of the ordinary. On the other hand, her usual attitude was one of fearlessness — a fearlessness that approached the abnormal. She was not afraid to plan marriage or to undertake building up a home on slim prospects. She was not afraid to have her husband neglect his law business for politics, or to make his various political plunges. She was not afraid of crises in war, or in government; or of men, or measures. She was not afraid for the safety of her husband. Just once did fear play a major part in shaping her personality. That was the long anxiety about the debts of which we shall hear. That prolonged strain had much to do with breaking her down.

Julia Taft Bayne [2] said of Mrs. Lincoln in 1861 something that was probably equally true of her in her youth.

[1] Bibliography, No. 73, p. 120.

[2] Bibliography, No. 17.

It was: "She wanted what she wanted." She meant that Mary Lincoln was selfish and inconsiderate. This is also the opinion of a member of the family with whom I have talked. Selfishness was not a major in her make-up, however. Socialization, the educational process of late childhood and adolescence, is a process of development in the superficialities of unselfishness. Mary Todd, when she left Lexington, easily met the accepted social standards as to unselfishness.

Somewhere about seven or eight years of age socialization begins. While part of the instructors who teach this subject are the brothers and sisters, a larger part is the school and play companions. It is in this period that socialization sometimes goes wrong in such a way as to make the person a kleptomaniac or a pathologic liar. A thorough grounding in three of the Commandments, plus social training, is the preventive for these bad qualities. The training of Mary Todd was ample to protect her against them.

Children approaching adolescence usually pass through one or more "collecting" phases. This is an obsession. Were it not so regular in its development, so on-schedule, and so self-limited, there would be temptation to call it pathologic. As it is, we regard it as an experience through which the child naturally grows and out of which nearly all children come.

We have no proof that Mary Todd was ever a "collector." But when her mind began to break in later life, miserliness was one of the traits of her mental disturbance. We regard the several "money" characteristics which Mrs. Lincoln developed as a peculiarity of her mental disturbance and not as a major cause. But there is nothing to connect this with any tendency toward "collecting" in her childhood or school years. It was not an element of her personality.

Adolescence is the age of emotionalism. In this period Miss Todd was somewhat aggressive, somewhat impatient, somewhat imperious. "She wanted what she wanted when she wanted it." But we read nowhere of fits of hysteria, or great outbursts of emotionalism. For the development of these the element of strain was necessary.

Miss Helm quotes Mrs. Norris:[1] "Mary was like that — always her mood changing with every new thought. . . . Her face expressed her varying moods. . . . She had the demure shyness of a little Quakeress. . . . But presto! They now gleamed with mischief, and before you could be sure of that, her dimple was gone and her eyes were brimful of tears."

The picture is one of a person dominated by emotionalism. Some would call it temperamental, and others mercurial. We see it forming the background for the hysteria and wild emotion in which Mrs. Lincoln indulged following the deaths of her husband and three of her children.

Emotionalism became a dominant influence in shaping Mrs. Lincoln's personality. No other was more potent in changing it from the grade termed "abnormal" to that termed "pathologic," and in changing her mentality from balanced to unbalanced. And yet, when it came to the method of her madness as distinguished from its causation, emotionalism played a minor role. This is more fully discussed later.

One other quality of her emotionalism is the variation in its manifestations at different periods. In her youth her emotionalism took the form of self-assertive domineering; in her maturity, of fits of temper and hysterical mourning; after 1871 it faded from the picture almost entirely.

It must remain an unsettled question whether or not anyone could have cured Mary Todd of this fault of emotionalism. Certainly neither father nor stepmother did so, and the influence of her grandmother was worse than unavailing.

Mary Todd was reasonably attractive in society. She was a little too liable to do and say things that were rooted in

[1] Bibliography, No. 73, p. 52.

self-gratification, but her charm was much more than enough to balance. She was aggressive, determined, persistent. These qualities were a part of her constitution. There is no reason to think home, family, or society training either increased or decreased them materially.

Speaking of her social life in 1837, Mrs. Norris wrote: "Among them [the men associates of Mary Todd and herself] were many scholarly, intellectual men, but Mary never, at any time, showed the least partiality for any one of them. Indeed, at times her face indicated a decided lack of interest, and she accepted their attentions without enthusiasm. Without meaning to wound, she now and then could not restrain a witty, sarcastic speech that cut deeper than she intended, for there was no malice in her heart. She was impulsive and made no attempt to conceal her feelings."[1]

"At different times French gentlemen came to the University to study English, and when one was fortunate enough to meet Mary he was surprised and delighted to find her a fluent conversationalist in his own language."[2]

Miss Helm quotes the Louisville *Courier-Journal*:[3] "There is still living in Louisville an old lady who, for four years, was a fellow pupil of Mary Todd's at Madame Mentelle's. 'Mary Todd!' said the old lady. 'She was one of the brightest girls in Madame Mentelle's school; always had the highest marks and took the biggest prizes. She was a merry, companionable girl, with a smile for everybody. She was really the life of the school, always ready for a good time, and to contribute even more than her own share in promoting it.'"

Albert Shaw writes:[4] "Mrs. Lincoln belonged to a type of Kentucky womanhood that has not been unduly praised for grace, charm, quick wit, social adaptability, and fine loyalty in all the relations of life."

---

[1] Ibid., p. 55.
[2] Ibid., p. 53.
[3] Ibid., p. 52.
[4] Bibliography, No. 158, Vol. II, p. 238.

James Whaler, in *Green River,* speaks of

"... Kentucky
Women who adjective their love with loyal — ..." [1]

These varied opinions give an excellent résumé of Mary Todd as she was when she left her Lexington home to live in Springfield. She had trained for that forum called by some "polite society," and she was now to launch her pursuit of a husband and a home. For twenty years her inherited personality had been molded, beneficially in the main, by the association with sisters and brothers, the guardianship of parents, the teaching of schools, and the comradeship of pupils; and by the social, political, and other contacts of her Lexington life. She had had few conflicts and almost no responsibilities. Her life may be said to have been without strain. The family quarrel was the most harmful influence and, in fact, the only one of consequence to which she had been subjected.

While Miss Todd was well trained for society, it was largely what might be termed a theoretic training. She had not had beaux, nor been an active participant in balls and parties. Although she was socially alert, she was not socially minded. This was partly because of her introvert personality, and partly because of the conflicts of her home. Persons of this personality are in dire need of extrovert training, and this Mary had not had.

And this was Miss Mary Todd when she became Mrs. Abraham Lincoln.

[1] Bibliography, No. 187, p. 89.

CHAPTER FOUR

The Training of Maturity

The web of our life is of a mingled yarn, good and ill together; our virtues would be proud if our faults whipped them not; and our crimes would despair if they were not cherished by our virtues.

— SHAKSPERE

INCIDENTS AFFECTING MRS. LINCOLN

Autumn 1839 to 1851

1839 *Autumn,* Mary Todd, living with Mrs. Edwards in Springfield, met Abraham Lincoln.

1840 Abraham Lincoln in the Illinois legislature; during the year, defeated for Whig elector.
April 1, Elodie Todd (Mrs. N. H. R. Dawson) born.
Abraham Lincoln and Mary Todd engaged to marry.

1841 *January,* engagement of Mary Todd and Abraham Lincoln broken.
April 14, Stuart and Lincoln dissolved partnership; Logan and Lincoln in partnership.
September, Lincoln and Joshua Speed visited Lexington and Louisville.
October 7, Katherine Bodley Todd (Mrs. W. W. Herr) born.

1842 *November 4,* Abraham Lincoln and Mary Todd married at the Edwards home.
The Lincolns lived at the Globe Tavern.
Illinois Whigs adopted the convention system.

1843 *August 1,* Robert T. Lincoln born.
Visit from Robert S. Todd.
Lincoln defeated for Congress.
September 20, Logan and Lincoln partnership dissolved; Lincoln and Herndon partnership begun.

1844 Lincoln defeated for elector for Henry Clay.
The Lincolns lived on Monroe Street.
The Lincolns bought the "Lincoln home."

1845 Abraham Lincoln laying plans for race for Congress; practicing law actively.

1846 *March 10,* Edward Baker Lincoln born.
Lincoln elected to Congress.
1847 Lincoln attended River and Harbor Convention, Chicago; his first considerable political contact with northern Illinois.
October, the Lincolns visited Lexington *en route* to Washington.
1848 *Spring,* Mrs. Lincoln in Lexington; Lincoln in Washington.
Lincoln attended Whig National Convention, Philadelphia.
Lincoln spoke in New England and other places, as member of the Whig National Committee.
1849 *July 16,* Robert S. Todd died.
October, the Lincolns in Lexington in connection with lawsuit.
1850 *January,* Mrs. Eliza Parker, grandmother of Mrs. Lincoln, died.
February 1, Edward Baker Lincoln died.
Spring, the Lincolns in Lexington.
December 21, William Wallace Lincoln born.

CHAPTER FOUR

The Training of Maturity

WHEN MARY TODD WENT TO HER SISTER'S HOME IN Springfield in 1837, she planned to enter society, and in the back of her head was the thought that she might marry and settle in Illinois. While there, she met several important people and went to many social functions. She sustained herself well enough, but, for some unexplained reason, she decided to quit society for the time and go back to school.

When she returned to Springfield in 1839, she may have been more confident of herself; at any rate, her plans were more definite. She bade her family good-by, took the train to the river at Frankfort, and traveled by boat down the rivers to Cairo, then up the Mississippi to St. Louis, and thence by stage to Springfield. She took her sister Frances's place in Mrs. Edwards's home. Elizabeth Edwards wrote:[1] "We had a vacancy in our family—wrote to Mary to come and make our home her home; she had a stepmother with whom she did not agree."

Miss Mary Todd was now out to make a successful marriage, and she pursued her objective with intelligence, good sense, and good taste. She met Stephen A. Douglas and all the other eligible bachelors of Springfield. The Lexington record deals solely with the girls and women who were her associates and friends. The Springfield record is equally

[1] Bibliography, No. 52.

partial, but this time it is the young men who receive the attention. The young women are only secondary.

Mary Todd did not meet Abraham Lincoln when she was in Springfield in 1837. He had been living there but a few months. He was associated in the law with her cousin, Judge John T. Stuart, and he had been an important member of the legislature in bringing the capital to Springfield. For these reasons it might be expected that he would have met her. In spite of them, however, Abraham Lincoln was not good society material then. He was poor, unlearned, and just acquiring a profession; he was ugly and awkward, and his clothes did not appeal to society ladies. He had no family backing. It is easy to understand why he was not invited by Mrs. Edwards to meet her sister, and why he did not meet her elsewhere, at social functions.

By 1839 the story was different. Lincoln was now the partner of Judge Stephen T. Logan, another of Mary Todd's cousins. He was establishing himself in his profession. He had lived two years in Springfield and had participated actively in politics. He was dressing better, acquiring some social grace, meeting people, and attending parties — occasionally, at least. It would have been logical for him to meet her in 1839. Had he not, it might have been of some significance. Nevertheless, Mrs. Edwards wrote of him at that period:[1] "Lincoln could not hold a lengthy conversation with a lady; was not sufficiently educated and intelligent in the female line to do so."

Miss Todd's method of campaigning was excellent, on the whole. She attended all sorts of social affairs; she met many people. She conversed wittily and, generally, in an engaging way. She danced well. She attracted men and had ample opportunities for gauging them.

Before long, she decided that of the many young men in Springfield she preferred Lincoln, a decision that did not meet with the unanimous approval of her family and friends.

[1] Bibliography, No. 52.

In fact, on more than one occasion she was called on to defend her choice, and her customary way of doing so was to say that he was to be president of the United States. There were people who argued that when she said this, she was mentally unbalanced, and her saying it was proof.

That she made the remark, not once, but several times, can be accepted, for there are many reliable people who bear witness. Very early in their acquaintance Mrs. Lincoln told W. H. Lamon that Mr. Lincoln would be president of the United States, and " from that day to the day of the inauguration she never wavered in her faith that her hopes would be fulfilled."[1] The only question is what the significance of it was. To start with, the prediction came true. That throws the burden of proof on the opposition. If anybody has to do any explaining, it is they. Presumably they would say: " Oh, it was nothing but wishful thinking on her part, and that kind of thinking is not only poor judgment, but it often indicates a judgment which does not work true. Furthermore, that kind of thinking is destructive mentally, or at least harmful. That it came true was due to Lincoln's ability, plus the opportunity and the setting. Her thinking and saying it had nothing to do with the case, nor did it indicate vision, foresight, or exceptional judgment." So much for them and what they say. Now let us see the logic of the other side.

All her life Mary Todd had heard the story of Andrew Jackson, the plain man who had made his play for the support of the plain people. She was at an impressionable age, in 1824, when this homely "man of the people " defeated, in the popular vote, the oligarchy which had been in control of the government since its beginning. In 1828, when Mary was ten years old, Jackson won the presidency and forever ended the power of the men who had previously controlled it. He was still the dominant power in national politics when Mary went to Springfield. She did not like him, but that

[1] Bibliography, No. 100, p. 221.

made no difference. All her life she had heard of what Jackson had done, in spite of a popular conception as to the qualifications required of a president, and in the face of the most powerful opposition of aristocratic leaders in Massachusetts and Virginia.

She had known Henry Clay all her life. He, too, had won his way in spite of tradition, for he had started as the "Millboy of the Slashes." Since early childhood she had listened to talk about making Henry Clay president. Doubtless she had often said that Mr. Clay would be president. In fact, we can easily understand that talk about making somebody president was rather customary with Mary Todd.

Nor was there anything radically wrong with predicting that Lincoln would be president. He also was a plain man whose youth had been spent in poverty. As a legislator he had shown wisdom and political ability. He had been considered for speaker, and he had recently been a presidential elector. Everyone recognized that he knew how to win people. Everyone could see that he was growing mentally. His mind showed no tendency to set, to harden, and to stop. His geographic location was right. He came from Kentucky, had lived in Indiana, and was now active in politics in Illinois, a state typical of the territory that clearly was soon to become good political hunting-ground. The people in this North-west were wilderness-blazing folk, just the kind that Lincoln would appeal to.

That Mary Todd said what she did about Abraham Lincoln showed astuteness and vision, as the record proves. It showed self-confidence and indicated that she chose objectives, and then drove for them with far-sightedness and determination. We are not justified, however, in fully concluding that Miss Mary meant it when she declared that Lincoln would be president. What she said had several inspirations: it was compounded of banter, repartee, a spirit of aggressive defiance, love, faith, hope, foresight, and judgment.

After Miss Todd and Lincoln became interested in each other, courtship followed the fashion of that day. She was innocently flirtatious. She played one male acquaintance against another in a way that all women understand and most women approve. As the courtship progressed, we read less and less of Lincoln's rivals being attentive to Mary Todd.

WHY LINCOLN DID NOT MARRY IN 1841

In 1840 Abraham Lincoln and Mary Todd were in love, were engaged, and planned to marry. The belief is common that the marriage was set for a given date, in January 1841, and that Lincoln failed to appear. A part of the story is true, but the details of a projected wedding; the gathering of the company, the bride, the preacher; the awful wait for the groom, who did not appear — all that is embroidery and without foundation in fact.

There was an engagement and there were plans for a wedding. The engagement was broken and both parties suffered in many ways therefrom. But there was never a license, nor an assembly of preacher and guests. Frances Wallace wrote:[1] "No, it was as I tell you. There never was but one wedding arranged between Mary and Mr. Lincoln, and that was the time they were married."

SOME OF LINCOLN'S CHARACTERISTICS

Lincoln was of the pituitary type. His life has been studied in every detail, and he has been charged with much; but never, in the days of bitterest calumny, has Lincoln been charged with misconduct with women. William H. Herndon, who sometimes made ambiguous statements about

[1] Bibliography, No. 181.

Lincoln's fondness for the ladies, would conclude such references by saying that he was honorable, loyal, and faithful to his wife. At Springfield social gatherings he spent most of his time talking to the men. In riding the circuit he passed his spare time, including week-ends, with male companions. His mental processes were masculine in type.

He had two affairs with women that pointed toward matrimony: one with Mary Owens, and the other with Mary Todd.

He promised to marry Mary Owens, and not until August 1837 did he know whether he had been taken seriously. Nor was he certain as to how seriously he should take himself.

The following letter which he wrote to Mary Owens is a good answer to the question as to why Mary Todd and Lincoln broke their engagement in 1841; it has been printed many times, but it is needed at this point: [1]

Springfield, Aug. 16, 1837

FRIEND MARY:

You will no doubt think it strange that I should write you a letter on the same day on which we parted, and I can only account for it by supposing that seeing you lately makes me think of you more than usual; while at our last meeting we had but few expressions of thoughts. You must know that I cannot see you or think of you with entire indifference; and yet it may be that you are mistaken in regard to what my real feelings towards you are. If I knew you were not, I should not trouble you with this letter. Perhaps any other man would know enough without further information; but I consider it my peculiar right to plead ignorance, and your bounden duty to allow the plea. I want in all cases to do right, and more particularly so in all cases with women. I want at this particular time, more than anything else, to do right with you; and if I knew it would be doing right, as I rather suspect it would, to let you alone, I would do it. And for the purpose of making the matter as plain as possible, I now say you can now drop the subject, dismiss your thoughts (if you ever had any) from

[1] Bibliography, No. 9, Vol. I, p. 234. W. H. Townsend informs me that this letter is owned by Mrs. H. C. Cunningham, Weston, Missouri.

me forever, and leave this unanswered, without calling forth one accusing murmur from me. And I will go even further, and say that if it will add anything to your comfort or peace of mind to do so, it is my sincere wish that you should. Do not understand by this that I wish to cut your acquaintance. I mean no such thing. What I do wish is that our further acquaintance shall depend upon yourself. If such further acquaintance would contribute nothing to your happiness, I am sure it would not to mine. If you should feel yourself in any degree bound to me, I am now willing to release you, provided you wish it; while, on the other hand, I am willing and even anxious to bind you faster, if I can be convinced that it will, in any considerable degree, add to your happiness. This, indeed, is the whole question with me. Nothing would make me more miserable than to believe you miserable — nothing more happy than to know you were so.

In what I have now said, I think I cannot be misunderstood, and to make myself understood is the only object of this letter.

If it suits you best to not answer this, farewell. A long life and a merry one attend you. But if you conclude to write back, speak as plainly as I do. There can be neither harm nor danger in saying to me anything you think, just in the manner you think it.

My respects to your sister.

Your friend,

LINCOLN

A recital of some of the circumstances is required if Lincoln is not to be misunderstood:

Lincoln had been interested in Mary Owens. He had told her sister that if she would bring her back to New Salem, he would marry her. This he said in pleasantry, but a half-wish was father to what he said. He knew she knew what he had said, and for a while he was anxious to consider his pleasantry as a promise. Then rose up his timidity about marrying, his fear that he could not make a wife happy and that he could not care for her properly. This was his frame of mind when he wrote the letter.

Some time after the termination of the Owens affair the second sister moved into Mrs. Edwards's home, and presently Lincoln became interested in her — the witty, sprightly Mary Todd. He sought her out, but with no serious intent. Almost before he knew it, he had asked her to marry him. Scarcely had he done so when he developed the typical Lincoln reaction to prospective matrimony that is shown in the Mary Owens letter. On the one hand, he was captivated by the pretty, intelligent, cultured, and socially prominent Miss Todd, and this urged him toward marriage. But, on the other hand, he had no physical or social urge to undertake matrimony. He was poor and in debt, and with only a small earning capacity. He thought it inadvisable for him to marry, and that Mary would make a mistake in marrying him. He probably talked to her much in the vein in which he had written to Miss Owens a little more than three years before. Mary Todd reacted somewhat as Mary Owens had done. And thus ended the engagement.

Proof that this interpretation of the essentials of what happened to break the first engagement between Lincoln and Miss Todd is correct is supplied by Herndon [1] and others. Lincoln at the time called on J. F. Speed and asked him to read a letter which he had written Mary Todd. This letter was substantially the same as his letter to Mary Owens quoted above. Speed read it and told him he was a chump for writing such a letter and would be worse if he sent it. Lincoln accepted Speed's advice and destroyed the letter. But when he next called on his sweetheart, he frankly told her of his misgivings as to her happiness should she marry him: he was poor and could not provide her with the refinements she had always enjoyed; he questioned his ability to make any woman happy. Mary doubtless replied that she loved him and was willing to marry him in spite of what he had told her. She forgave him, and they cried, kissed, and made up. She did not forget, however, and the chances are that when Lincoln at a later date again talked in like manner, Miss Todd flared up and terminated the en-

[1] Bibliography, No. 75a, Vol. II, pp. 212 ff.

gagement. This is about the way it happened, in January 1841.

There is no evidence that Mary Todd was seriously disturbed by this break or that she changed her purpose, however much she changed her plans. In a letter written to a friend many months later, she shows that her interest in Lincoln continued. Their common friends the Francis family brought the young people together and provided opportunities for them to meet. In November 1842 they again became engaged, and marriage followed at once.

Mary Todd had achieved her purpose. She had prepared and trained for marriage all through her young womanhood. At its peak her plans were extended so as to include marrying Abraham Lincoln. She had accomplished her ends.

SPRINGFIELD

Sangamon County was organized in 1821, three years after Illinois entered the Union. The location of the county seat was a matter of debate, since there was no suitable village situated near the center of the county, not to mention the absence of cities and even towns. In a region within the limits of the present Springfield a village had been laid out by the surveyor, Calhoun, to which he had given his own name. Adjoining this village was a level piece of ground, known as "Kelly's field." It was located on a small tributary of the Sangamon, called Spring Creek or Branch. This field was agreed on as the location of the county seat, partly because of its level surface and natural drainage, and partly because it was in a neighborhood in which there were some homes where attendants on court could be accommodated. It did not become known as Springfield until 1828, in which year the post office was first so designated.

The court-house was a small log building, costing less than one hundred dollars. In 1832 the village of Springfield was incorporated as a town. It was just one of the small prairie villages of that pioneer period, with little organization, no improvements, and almost no school facilities.

Heinl, speaking of Springfield in these years, quotes several writers.[1] One of these, B. F. Harris, referred to the town in 1835 as follows: "Springfield is a small village of about one hundred people and twenty or thirty shanties, a hotel — a hard-looking place." However, Heinl writes: "Jacksonville and Springfield were the two most important towns in the Lincoln-and-Douglas country in 1832. In fact, no town in America north or west of St. Louis approached them in size or activity." (It was customary for those who wrote of central Illinois in that decade to couple Springfield and Jacksonville, and always to the disparagement of the former.) Another writer, Patrick Sheriff, observed, also of 1835: "Jacksonville contains about the same number of souls as Springfield but is superior in buildings, arrangements, and civilization. Many of the houses consist of brick, and the hotels are large and commodious." John Mason Peck said: "In 1834, the business and professional interests of Springfield were less than those of Jacksonville." William Cullen Bryant supplemented this by writing, with special reference to the cultural side: "Jacksonville is a better and more attractive town than Springfield."

Ninian Edwards was a judge of the Supreme Court of Kentucky and a wealthy citizen of that state before he came to Illinois. When he crossed the Ohio River, it was to serve as Territorial Governor. Later he was elected Governor of the state. His home was in the southern end.

When his son, Ninian W. Edwards, moved to Springfield, in 1833, he associated the Edwards name and prestige with the crude but ambitious prairie village, and in doing so laid some part of the foundation for its aspirations to become a center of political influence. At that time the village could not have had more than three hundred inhabitants, its

[1] Bibliography, No. 71.

buildings were primitive, and there were no public improvements.

Soon there began a contest for a new location for the state capital. A state-wide referendum vote was held on August 4, 1834, with the following result: Alton, 8,157; Vandalia, 7,730; Springfield, 7,075; Geographic Center, 790; Peoria, 424; Jacksonville, 273.

Considering that Springfield was a village of less than five hundred people, without railroad or boat transportation, and without improvements or commodious buildings, and that it was far away from the center of population, the wonder is that it got so many votes. Of the 24,750 votes cast, 28 per cent were for Springfield, 64 per cent for the two locations considerably south of Springfield and only a little more than 1 per cent for Peoria, the only city to the north.

This contest advertised the town, and it waged through several legislatures. Votes for Springfield were swapped for votes for local improvements at state expense, further advertising the ambitious town. People began to move in, that they might have ringside seats when the circus started. Among them were families with names that have since loomed large in Illinois history.

Shrewd political management was required to win the capital, in the face of the manifest wish of the people that it should be located farther to the south. After several years of preliminary agitation, and much logrolling by Abraham Lincoln and his associates, the capital came. Incidentally, its coming made the elongated legislator from New Salem a very popular man in Springfield.

In 1840 the estimated population of Springfield was 1,600. In 1850 the census gave it as 4,533; and in 1860, 9,320. (The city directory issued in 1857 gave the population in 1850 as 5,106.) In the first ten years that Mrs. Lincoln lived there, the population nearly trebled. By the end of the second ten-year period the number of inhabitants was almost six times as great as when she first arrived in town. In 1850, to Mr. and Mrs. Average Citizen the Lincolns were old settlers. The new people judged the Lincolns as they found them. Many knew little and cared less about the earlier history of either the husband or the wife.

The era was one of commercial, industrial, and transportational development. The east-and-west division of the Northern Cross Railroad started at the Illinois River in 1836 and reached Springfield in 1842. It was soon to push on to Decatur and, later, to the Indiana line. The present Chicago & Alton Railroad, then known as the Alton & Sangamon, was commenced in 1850 and opened for traffic between Springfield and Alton on September 10, 1852. It reached Bloomington not long afterwards and was in Joliet by August 1854. Then followed the Illinois Central and the Baltimore & Ohio, in the order named, but not close on the heels of the other roads. When Abraham Lincoln left for Washington and his inaugural, he had a choice of routes, between the Wabash, leading east; and the Alton, leading north to connections with the east, and also leading south to St. Louis and the eastern connections there. Transportation facilities had developed in ten years!

The building of these railroads added much to Springfield. To the west lay Jacksonville, the "Athens of Illinois," filled with professors, learned men, and cultured citizens. Some of these, like Douglas, were very much at home in Springfield. There had been many exchanges of social courtesies between these two neighbor cities, in spite of the inconveniences of stage and coach travel over prairie roads. The east-and-west railroad made it convenient for Jacksonville and Springfield to say "Howdy!" Then the railroad brought Decatur into the family. By 1854 Bloomington was reached, and it was easy for Judge David Davis to visit his Springfield friends.

When Lincoln campaigned against Cartwright for Congress, in 1846, he was able to get across two counties in the south end of his congressional district on the railroad, but in all the other counties he had to depend on stages and private conveyances. When he engaged with Douglas in their celebrated series of debates, twelve years later, they traveled by train to each of the battle-grounds.

When Lincoln, Judge Davis, and other members of the bar traveled the circuit prior to 1850, they made a few county seats by railroad, but more often they had to travel by stage or by private conveyance. Between 1850 and 1860 traveling by private conveyance was rarely necessary.

While Springfield was rapidly developing — commercially and industrially — the school of political training was also working overtime. The legislature was a testing-ground for the younger, aspiring politicians. The administrative offices caused prominent people to make their homes in Springfield for terms of years, and the courts drew the leading lawyers. The State Medical Society had been organized, and many of its meetings were being held in the capital city. The lyceum and lecture hall ranked with newspapers and ahead of books as means of adult education, and Springfield was making use of this machinery of culture. The social atmosphere of this decade was an improvement over that of the preceding one.

The Springfield to which Mary Todd came in 1839 was an incorporated town. While it had been the designated capital for two years, the seat of state government, the officials had actually been in residence only a few months and were still housed in makeshift quarters. The streets were unpaved and in winter, and after rains at all seasons, were difficult to negotiate. There was no sewage system, and no public water-supply. There were churches and schools, but not many. The Edwards family had a fine house, which stood out because there were so few in its class, or even near it. A superabundance of politics, and enough of business, Springfield had in 1840, but its supply of the something called " culture " was short.

Mrs. Lincoln stayed in Springfield during this period of more than ten years, with the exception of the time spent with her husband when he was in Congress; her two visits to Lexington (one on the way to Washington, and the other returning therefrom); and two visits to Lexington in connection with family lawsuits. Between 1840 and 1857 she bore three children: Robert, Edward, and Willie; and suffered the death of one, Edward. Bearing children, rearing them, and caring for her husband and home kept her occupied. I. N. Arnold wrote:[1] "The mother was too busily engaged with family cares and maternal duties to leave home for any considerable time."

Toward the end of the decade her father died, and his death was followed by a group of family lawsuits which caused considerable bitterness.[2] In one of these her full brother Levi O. Todd sued Lincoln, alleging breach of trust. The family frictions, which had caused some unhappiness in the Lexington days, were not quieted by the death of Mrs. Parker, Mrs. Lincoln's grandmother. Litigation over her estate helped to keep these irritations alive.

There is tradition that Mrs. Lincoln mourned extravagantly when Edward died. The shift in attendance from the Episcopal to the Presbyterian church was the result of emotionalism stirred by his death. We have no history of Mrs. Lincoln's being unduly depressed by her father's death. Nor is there any knowledge as to what was her reaction to her grandmother's death. This strong-minded old lady had taken considerable part in the conflict that arose out of the second marriage of Robert S. Todd, and Mary had been on her side. When Mrs. Lincoln visited Lexington in 1847 and 1848, she spent much of her time with her grandmother. All in all, grief consequent upon deaths was a minor factor in Mrs. Lincoln's life in this period. At least, it appears minor when contrasted with the personality

[1] Bibliography, No. 4, p. 82.
[2] Bibliography, No. 176, p. 246; and No. 186.

deterioration which followed the hysterical mourning for members of her family in later years.

POLITICS

Mrs. Lincoln may not have considered it an objective, but through these years she doubtless held close to her heart the political future of her husband. Discount as much as we choose the statements she is quoted as making about her husband's attaining the presidency, we still must know that his political advancement was a basis, if not *the* basis, of Mrs. Lincoln's hopes and plans for a successful life — successful for herself as well as for her husband.

Between 1842 and 1851 Lincoln's political career was on the rocks most of the time. In 1840 he helped to elect Harrison and Tyler, but by the time the Lincoln family bark was launched, Harrison had died, and Tyler had shifted the administration from the Whig to the Democratic fold — or that is what the Whigs said. In 1843 Lincoln was defeated for Congress. He wrote to his old friend M. M. Morris, of Menard County, saying that his being classed as an aristocrat had helped to make Sangamon County reject him, but that Menard, the part of old Sangamon in which New Salem now was, had stood by him. In 1844 he ran as a Henry Clay elector and was defeated. In 1846 he was elected to Congress, but he was limited in his political ambitions by an agreement on a rotation in this office. The agreement that got him the nomination in 1846 prevented him from being a serious candidate in 1848. In 1847 and 1848 he was in Congress, but his record did not indicate that he had a political future. That record, such as it was, hurt him in Illinois even more than it helped him.

In 1848 he made campaign speeches in New England and elsewhere. This, and the Washington contacts, laid some foundations for his future career. In March 1849 Taylor, the Whig, was inaugurated President, but he was soon succeeded by Fillmore, and the latter did not fulfill the partisan expectations of the Whigs. It was at the end of this period that Abraham Lincoln was offered the secretaryship and the governorship of Oregon Territory, of which offer it has been written [1] that it " embodied the Washington estimate of the Lincoln political stature."

Mrs. Lincoln found it no easy matter from 1842 to 1851 to maintain her faith in her husband's political future. She knew him, his wisdom and sagacity, his power to win men. She had hopes. But the record was against her. The political disappointments of this period were among those forces that injured Mrs. Lincoln's personality, though not to a great extent.

FINANCES

These were lean years financially—the leanest that Mrs. Lincoln ever knew and that Lincoln knew after the first Springfield days. John G. Nicolay says: [2] " He was so poor that he and his bride could not make the contemplated visit to Kentucky they would both have so much enjoyed."

That these were years in which the Lincolns lived sparingly, financially speaking, is amply supported by the " Springfield tradition." That there was sometimes a servant in this household of wife, husband, two children, and an occasional visiting relative is established, but that at other times there was none is also true. It is said that Lincoln took few friends home with him to meals, because his table was not very bountiful; that he milked the cows, did the necessary work around the barn and yard, and chopped the wood; that Mrs. Lincoln made much of the clothing for the two children, her husband, and herself and did most of the cooking and housework. Mrs. Wallace [3]

[1] Bibliography, No. 18, pp. 494–552.

[2] Bibliography, No. 133, p. 69.

[3] Bibliography, No. 181.

said her sister was a fine seamstress and made all the children's clothes, most of her own, and many of her husband's.

Herndon [1] tells of Abraham Lincoln and Robert eating cheese and crackers at the office because of short rations and short temper at home. The probability is that Lincoln was indulging in a habit which he had formed when he lived at New Salem. And boys of Robert's age are always ready for an extra meal!

One unfriendly critic said that Mrs. Lincoln saved on table supplies and household expense, but he poured a little sauce into the statement by saying she did this to spend on herself, particularly on her dresses. The "Springfield tradition" does not show, however, that she wore fine, showy clothes in this decade, nor do the bills at Smith's store — such as are now available — show extravagant purchases.

It is not probable that the Lincolns were ever hard pressed for money, at least after 1844. Lincoln was a thrifty man (as will appear later), and during this, the poorest decade of his married life, he was paying off some New Salem debts, helping his parents, supporting his own family, and getting ahead financially. And his wife was helping him.

But such close saving did not help her socially. Spiritually she suffered in several ways from it. It hurt her social standing, and, heavens, how that hurt her soul! It was not easy for one reared as she had been, in a roomy house with a large family and servants. Edgar Lee Masters,[2] describing one of her Springfield homes as shabby, added: "And here the daughter of the Kentucky banker abode for some time to come, with Lincoln."

To add to all this was that atmosphere of hostility or "back-fence gossip" about intimate household conditions which enters so largely into the "Springfield tradition." If so much of this has found its way into books, some must have come to Mrs. Lincoln's notice. And it was just the kind of unfriendly gossip that was most liable to encourage

[1] Bibliography, No. 75a, p. 432.

[2] Bibliography, No. 115.

her to strike back. It was tongue work, and in a battle of tongues she was equal to the occasion.

SOCIAL NEGLECT

It is not in accord with social practice for people to maintain a society status when, for financial and other reasons, they cannot keep up their end. To receive invitations, one must invite. To be entertained, one must entertain. There must be something approaching parity between scales of living on the part of those who meet on the same level. This was true in Springfield in 1845 as it is now.

When the Lincolns moved from the large Edwards house to live at the Globe Hotel; next, to a modest, rented house on Monroe Street; and, later, to the twelve-hundred-dollar home of their own — it was too much to expect the small city aristocrats to continue to have an acute interest in them. Her sisters did, and by this time Ann had married C. M. Smith and joined Elizabeth, Frances, and Mary in Springfield. So did the Edwardses, the Todds, and the Stuarts; but not the general run of the society element. Charles Arnold is quoted by B. F. Stoneberger [1] as saying: " Mrs. Edwards was the social leader of Springfield and she gave fine parties. Mrs. Lincoln was poor and she resented the way people passed her by. She was hurt and envious." If Mrs. Lincoln went to any parties or participated in any social affair or public function in Springfield in this period, there is no record of the fact. She must have done so to some extent, but I have not been able to find proof that she did.

It almost summarizes her social activities during this period to say that Mrs. Lincoln lived quietly in her home — economizing, doing without luxuries, bearing and rearing children, attending to domestic duties, paying some attention to politics, but otherwise letting the world go by.

[1] Personal communication to me.

A casting-up of the record of this decade shows that Mrs. Lincoln came through it reasonably well. Her training had been for a position in a fairly idle, rather glamorous, social world. She had had no training for motherhood except what little she had absorbed in her father's home. She had had no training in the conduct of a home where there were no slaves, rarely more than one servant, and often none — a home run on very thrifty lines and supported by a slender income. Her training for society had not equipped her for the kind of social intercourse to which she was then limited. There was a social isolation which she did not understand and which her type of mind resented. She had been compelled to live simply and to do without things, but that had not hurt her character. She had known some political disappointments, but there had been a few successes. The greatest influences of her life just then were wifehood and motherhood — home.

CHAPTER FIVE

Rounding Out

Life is a quaint puzzle. Bits the most incongruous join with each other and the scheme thus becomes symmetrical and clear.

— Bulwer-Lytton

INCIDENTS AFFECTING MRS. LINCOLN

January 1851 to March 1861

1851 *January 17,* Thomas Lincoln (Abraham's father) died.
Lincoln practicing law.

1852 Henry Clay and Daniel Webster died.
Pierce elected President.
Lincoln, candidate for Whig elector, defeated.
Lincoln practicing law.

1853 *April 4,* Thomas Lincoln (Tad) born.
Lincoln practicing law.
December, Emilie Todd visited in Springfield.

1854 Abraham Lincoln candidate for Senate; beaten by Lyman Trumbull.
Todd estate settled.
February 10, the suit of Oldham, Todd, and Company vs. A. Lincoln dismissed.
Whig party dying.
October 4, speech on Nebraska question.

1855 Abraham Lincoln in Cincinnati on McCormick Reaper case.
Republican party organizing.

1856 *February,* the Lincolns gave a large party.
May 29, "Lost" speech delivered at Bloomington.
Lincoln joined the Republican party.
Lincoln defeated for nomination for vice-president.
Lincoln began to have faint hopes of being a presidential possibility.
November, Buchanan elected; Frémont defeated.
November 23, Lincoln went to Chicago for three weeks.

1857 *Summer,* Mrs. Lincoln traveled to Niagara Falls and New York.

Mrs. Lincoln laughingly told Mr. Lincoln that her next husband would be a rich man. "I sigh when I think poverty is my portion," she wrote.
September 8, Abraham Lincoln in Chicago on Rock Island Bridge case.
September 5–30, second story added to Lincoln house.
B. H. Helm visited Springfield.
Lincoln began to take politics more seriously and to dress better.

1858 Lincoln candidate for Senate; beaten by Douglas.
June 16, "House Divided" speech.
August to October, Lincoln-Douglas debates.

1859 Lincoln wrote autobiographical sketch for Jesse Fell. Fell wrote the first Lincoln biography.

1860 *February 27,* Cooper Union speech.
May 18, Lincoln nominated for president.
November 7, elected President.
November 21, Lincoln went to Chicago to consult Hannibal Hamlin, I. N. Arnold, and Ebenezer Peck, about cabinet positions; Mrs. Lincoln accompanied him.
December 20, South Carolina seceded.

1861 *January 10,* Mrs. Lincoln in New York shopping.
January 24, Mrs. Lincoln back in Springfield.
February 11, Lincoln and his family left Springfield for Washington.
February 18, Jefferson Davis inaugurated as President of the Confederate States of America.
February 23, Lincoln arrived in Washington.
Mrs. Lincoln in New York, Metropolitan Hotel.
March 2, Mrs. Lincoln arrived in Washington.

CHAPTER FIVE

Rounding Out

THIS DECADE BEGINS WITH MR. AND MRS. LINCOLN living quietly with their two children in their own home. At the start of it, she was a little over thirty-two years old; at the close she was more than forty-two. Lincoln was nine years and ten months her senior. In 1851 Robert was over seven years old and was going to school (a private academy in Springfield), and Willie was a baby in arms. It was a period in which one more son was added to the family. There was no death of any close relative of Mrs. Lincoln's; in that respect the decade was a serene one. When they moved to the White House, Robert was past seventeen and in college; Willie was in his eleventh year; and Tad lacked one month of being eight years old. Willie had been attending school in Springfield and was regarded as a good student, well up in his studies and abreast of the best of his class. On the other hand, there is no record that Tad had been in school up to this time.

Mrs. Lincoln bore four boys. This alone as her contribution to society entitles her to commendation. In that era four children to the family was the requirement for continuance of the family stock, since the death-rate was high. She and her husband brought the requisite number of children into the world, and at intervals that prevented the home from being overcrowded, thus affording the parents opportunity to give attention to each. Had it not been for the death of Edward at four years, the children would have been close enough in age to have made effective the educational and social value of fraternal contacts and influences, without being so close as to overtax the mother's time and energy. As it was, Robert was too old to exercise much influence on the lives of Willie and Tad, nor did they help him much. In the grouping of the children in their activities, we find Willie and Tad in close and constant association, while Robert stood apart. Those men with whom I have talked of their Lincoln associations have referred to themselves as playmates of Robert or playmates of Willie and Tad, but never as playmates of Robert *and* the younger boys. Had Edward lived, he would have bridged this gap.

Bearing these children was a wholesome influence on Mrs. Lincoln's character. In the childbearing of itself she was lucky or efficient; she had no mishaps, and her children were good physical specimens. Her own mother died in childbirth, as did her half-sister Mrs. Herr, and Lincoln's sister Mrs. Grigsby. The maternal death-rate in that day was high. There were many widowers, and stepmothers were not scarce.

As the mother of babies Mrs. Lincoln was a success. She carried all four of her children through the vicissitudes of babyhood, and that was then no mean accomplishment. Her mother and her stepmother were not so lucky or so capable, since each lost one baby. Her own sisters and sisters-in-law were likewise less successful than she. It is a pretty good guess that in Springfield about 1850 at least one fourth of the babies failed to survive babyhood, and on Mrs. Lincoln's level probably the expectation was a survival rate of, say, less than five sixths. Mrs. Lincoln landed all of hers safely in the two-to-six-year period. She and her husband both are to be credited with sparing these babies inheritable and congenital diseases and with carrying them safely through babyhood. It is not of record that Lincoln was fond of feeding and milking the family cow, but this was a part of his contribution to the health of the babies. Mrs. Lincoln scores high as a mother care-taker of babies. This experience was also a wholesome influence on her personality.

In the last half of the Springfield score of years Mrs. Lincoln as the mother of older children had many problems to meet. Much has been said of her mother relationship in these years, and much of that written about the next five years applies to the Springfield experiences as well as to those of Washington. Her record as the mother and trainer of children two to twelve years of age is not so good as for the earlier period. In the home phases of child education, as distinguished from those of the school, the "Springfield tradition" is that the Lincoln boys were not well trained. At times the mother punished them, even whipped them; at other times she permitted them unrestrained liberty; and at still other times her method lay between these extremes. She did not maintain uniformity in either her attitude or her method. The Springfield and the Washington "traditions," and even some part of the record, show that Lincoln's parental attitude was one of license rather than of liberty. He was "a kid with the kids." Julia Taft Bayne's recital of what she and her brothers saw and even participated in establishes that, and there is ample corroborative evidence. This as a parental attitude has very serious shortcomings, but it has the virtue of consistency. Mrs. Lincoln's was neither consistent nor uniform. It is probable that in the training of her children she was guided by her remembrance of her father's household—partly when her mother directed five, partly when her grandmother and aunt managed the household, and principally when her stepmother was doing what she could for her own large brood and the half-dozen stepchildren.

She was not able to keep contagion out of her home. Lincoln's correspondence with the Kellogg family in Cincinnati, in which scarlet fever is mentioned, refers to the same disease in the Springfield Todd families. Edward

Lincoln died of diphtheria. Years later Tad died of a pleurisy that was possibly tubercular. Willie is said to have died from an acute malarial infection. Katherine Helm quotes [1] from a Washington paper as follows: "The White House levee on Tuesday will be omitted on account of the illness of the second son of the President, an interesting lad of about 8 years of age, who has been lying dangerously ill of bilious fever for the last three days. Mrs. Lincoln has not left his bedside since Wednesday night, and fears are entertained for her health." This account was wrong by nearly four years as to Willie's age, but it was probably right in other particulars. Acute "bilious fever" is malaria, and acute bilious fever fatal in one week is pernicious malaria. Willie died in February, and malaria in Washington in that month is due to relapses, which are often pernicious. Mrs. Lincoln's letters contain references to attacks of malaria, and Elizabeth Keckley's statement that Willie rather suddenly took a turn for the worse and died, fits malaria fairly well. Pernicious malaria is recognized as a preventable disease. If Willie did not have pernicious malaria, he had some other form of preventable disease — at least, as we now know preventable disease.

It is somewhat apropos to say that Lincoln had smallpox. This occurred while he was in the White House. In fact, when he wrote and when he delivered the Gettysburg address, he was in that three-day febrile period of smallpox which precedes the eruption. The speech was written, as Dr. William E. Barton [2] has shown, in greatest part within twenty-four hours of its delivery. Soon after the exercises the President went to a room in his host's house to rest. On the way back to Washington he complained of headache and lay down much of the time. Before the next cabinet meeting he was broken out, and the diagnosis was made. We find Lincoln saying of the office-seekers: "Let them come. I now have something I can give them." The Stoddard account of Lin-

[1] Bibliography, No. 73, p. 197.

[2] Bibliography, No. 10, p. 97.

coln's attack of smallpox goes into much detail, both from the clinical standpoint and as to the measures of control which were undertaken. All contacts, including the family, were vaccinated. Mrs. Lincoln deserves credit for the fact that, though her husband had smallpox and while ill was cared for in the home, she and Tad escaped the disease.

These incidents are cited to add to the showing that the Lincoln household was at least unfortunate with respect to preventable diseases. Present-day careful mothers prevent their families from having diphtheria, scarlet fever, smallpox, tuberculosis, pleurisy, and bilious fever.[1]

Barton[2] has this to say of Mrs. Lincoln as the mother of children older than babies: "She was not a model mother. She was too nervous, too impetuous; her chidings and her caresses depended too much upon her own moods. In times of sickness she was too anxious and too excitable to be a good nurse. But she loved her children passionately."

SOCIAL INFLUENCES

In the second decade of the Springfield life Mrs. Lincoln's social position was better than in the first. We find the Lincolns entertaining their friends and political associates more frequently, and they are known to have attended some dinners and more formal affairs.

Mrs. Lincoln's sister Elizabeth Edwards was ambitious for her very capable, though not very aggressive, husband. She hoped to see him in the "seat of the mighty" once occupied and adorned by his father, Governor Ninian Edwards. When the legislature was in session, Mrs. Edwards was accustomed to entertain some of the politically powerful.

[1] While it has no direct bearing, it is of some interest that Mrs. Lincoln's father died of cholera, and Lincoln's mother of milk-sickness. Mrs. Lincoln did not keep contagion out of her home, it is true; at the same time she was not less successful than were other mothers of the period. Measured by present-day standards, her record in this particular would be called a poor one; but using the standards of her day, it was good enough.

[2] Bibliography, No. 9, Vol. I, p. 326.

At times she gave large and elaborate receptions. Mr. and Mrs. Lincoln were usually present. Incidentally, there eventually grew up some rivalry in husband-promotion between these ambitious sisters.

On one occasion the Lincolns gave a reception to which they invited five hundred people. Most of them came, though a conflicting reception held in Jacksonville caused some of the invited guests to absent themselves.

The society people of Springfield had more time for Mrs. Lincoln in this second decade. It is also certain that the Lincolns were spending more money on entertaining. It follows that the social neglect from which Mrs. Lincoln suffered, and which did much to strain her personality, was less in evidence.

The following letter[1] written by Mrs. Lincoln to her half-sister Emilie Todd Helm, February 16, 1856, shows that there were many parties in Springfield, which the Lincolns were attending and of which, at least on one occasion, they were hosts:

"Within the last three weeks there has been a party almost every night, and some two or three grand fêtes are coming off this week. I may surprise you when I mention that I am recovering from the slight fatigue of a very large, and I really believe a very handsome, entertainment — at least, our friends flatter us by saying so. About five hundred were invited, yet owing to an unlucky rain three hundred only favored us by their presence. And the same evening in Jacksonville Col. Warren gave a bridal party to his son who married Miss Birchall of this place, which occasion robbed us of some of our friends. You will think we have enlarged our borders since you were here. Three evenings since, Governor Bissell gave a very large party. I thought of you frequently when I saw so many of your acquaintances beautifully dressed and dancing very happily. . . . The first part of the winter was so quiet."

[1] Bibliography, No. 73, p. 121.

In November 1856 Mrs. Lincoln wrote to Mrs. Helm of the improvements in Springfield:[1] "You can scarcely imagine a place improving more rapidly than ours. Almost palaces of homes have been reared since you were here. Hundreds of houses have been going up this season, and some of them very elegant. Governor Matteson's house is just completed. The whole place has cost him, he says, $100,000, but he is now worth a million."

Between 1851 and 1861 Mrs. Lincoln stayed very closely in Springfield, as behooved the mother of three boys, one an infant. The cottage on Eighth Street was their home during the entire period. In fact, the Lincolns called this house home for about seventeen years of the somewhat more than eighteen years of their joint Springfield life. The house was a one-story-and-attic frame cottage during thirteen of the years that the Lincoln family occupied it. Nevertheless, it was ample for the mother, father, and three boys. Besides the main house there was an ell, together providing a bedroom for the parents, a children's room, parlor, dining-room, kitchen, and some space besides — a great luxury of room and accommodation according to the standards of Lincoln's youth, and with less crowding than even his wife had been accustomed to when she was of her children's age. The second story was not added to the house until September 1857. On the authority of a statement by Bunn to Conkling, and a letter by Gurley, A. J. Beveridge says:[2] "While Lincoln was in Chicago on the Rock Island Bridge case (September 8–26, 1857), Mrs. Lincoln had the half story of their house made into a full second story, the whole house painted, and the rooms papered."

There was a stable, a large yard, and room for a garden, though relatives say that the family did not make use of the space for either flowers or vegetables. Help was scarce and hard to keep, and Lincoln was now a busy lawyer and an active politician, while Mrs. Lincoln was occupied with

[1] Ibid., p. 123.

[2] Bibliography, No. 18, p. 605.

nursing and caring for the baby born in 1853, besides looking after two older boys, as to both home care and preparation of lessons for school.

I. N. Arnold is authority for the statement that there were some dinner parties, for which the food was outstandingly good. Doubtless Mrs. Lincoln exchanged visits with her three sisters and her many Springfield cousins. She was visited by Emilie Todd, later Mrs. Helm, who probably divided her Springfield stay between the homes of her three Springfield half-sisters. No other member of the Lexington family ever came to visit Mrs. Lincoln.[1] If Levi's daughter got there before Mrs. Lincoln went to Washington, she stayed with Mrs. Smith. It is not known that Mrs. Lincoln left Springfield in this period except to go to Niagara Falls and the East in 1857. How could she? There was no one to care for the baby, not to mention the older boys. She went to Alton for a day to attend one of the Lincoln-Douglas debates, but there is no record of her hearing any other of these epoch-marking discussions. She was in Chicago at least once, in November 1860. There must have been a few other trips that we do not know about. St. Louis is within one hundred miles of Springfield, yet we have no proof that she was there. Perhaps the bitterness of factional strife, and the blind, irrational distrust and hatred of Lincoln that was so manifest in the South after 1856, kept her from visiting some of the Kentucky friends of her youth. Whatever the reason may have been, no one accused Mrs. Lincoln of being a gadabout while she lived in Springfield. On the contrary, during these years she was a "home body." Her life may have been very humdrum and everyday and exceptionally free from all external causes of emotional reaction.

[1] Robert S. Todd visited Mrs. Lincoln and the other Springfield daughters when Robert Todd Lincoln was a few weeks old.

POLITICS

Between 1851 and 1861 Lincoln ran for the Senate twice and was defeated both times.

The first of these defeats, that by Lyman Trumbull, he and Mrs. Lincoln are said to have been very bitter about. Beveridge says:[1] "Mrs. Lincoln was determined her husband should win, and when she saw the triumph of Trumbull her anger was so fierce, unreasoning, and permanent that she refused then and ever afterward to speak to the wife of the victor, Julia Jayne, the intimate of her young womanhood and until now her closest friend." There is confirmation of the fact that Lincoln's failure in this contest was a source of disappointment and caused him to lose faith in some of his friends; it is also true that Mrs. Lincoln was even more disappointed, but I am assured by descendants of Senator Trumbull that, according to the family tradition, the statement exaggerates the facts. The night of the Trumbull nomination the Lincolns attended something of a reception given by Mrs. Edwards at her home, and there met the Trumbulls. The meeting was a friendly one, and no bitterness or unpleasantness is intimated by any of the several biographers who tell of this event. Miss Julia Jayne was one of the few who were in attendance when Mrs. Lincoln was married, and if there were bridesmaids, Miss Jayne was one of them. It is true that in later life, as Mrs. Trumbull, and especially in the Washington years, she and Mrs. Lincoln did not see much of each other. The Trumbull success in the senatorial campaign may have been in part responsible, but it is probable that political differences between Lincoln and Senator Trumbull were the principal reason for any coolness there may have been. Senator Trumbull and Lincoln were usually in opposing political parties, or in opposing factions of the same party. The

[1] Bibliography, No. 18, p. 286.

statement that Mrs. Lincoln and Mrs. Trumbull never spoke afterwards is not true. It has some bearing on this question that, when President Johnson adopted and advocated the Lincoln reunion policy—making it the Johnson reconstruction policy, which was the real reason for his impeachment by the opposition — Trumbull committed political suicide by voting against Johnson's removal. Trumbull went down to his political death in support of the policies of Abraham Lincoln. It is even more to the point that when Mrs. Lincoln's pension bill was before the Senate, and she was being abused openly and covertly, Senator Trumbull was her staunch defender.

The second contest for senator was likewise lost, but, in spite of that fact, strategically this was the greatest political success in Lincoln's life, the presidency alone excepted. The Lincoln-Douglas debates did three things of supreme tactical advantage for Lincoln. First, they tied him closely to, and coupled him in the public mind with, the new party to which he had given his allegiance two years before. Lincoln had to win a right of leadership in this new party—the party that was soon to choose him as its presidential candidate; that was to carry the political burden of winning a civil war; and that was to remain dominant in American politics for many years. Second, they made Lincoln nationally known. When a Congressman, he had stumped for Taylor in New England. He had made a few other speeches outside of his own state. But until the reports of the Lincoln-Douglas debates were read, the country at large had heard very little of Abraham Lincoln of Illinois. Barton[1] attributes the great rush to write campaign biographies in Illinois in 1860, and Fell's urge to write the sketch for a Pennsylvania paper in 1859, to the abysmal ignorance of the general public about the party candidate. In 1856, after the Republican convention had nominated Frémont for president, a certain number of delegates voted for Abraham Lincoln as nominee for vice-

[1] Bibliography, No. 12.

president. When he was given this information as news, Lincoln said these delegates must have been voting for the then better-known Abraham Lincoln of Massachusetts. The third advantageous result of the Lincoln-Douglas debates was the setting up of questions which were certain to eliminate Douglas from Illinois, and national, politics. In 1860, Douglas was one of the four candidates for president, but the position which Lincoln had forced him into on the slavery question, in these debates, made it impossible for the Democratic party to unite on him as its candidate. In the election the Democrats split their vote between the Douglas ticket and that headed by Breckinridge. The vote for these two tickets, when added, surpassed the vote for the Lincoln ticket, but under the electoral law Lincoln was elected President. Had there been no division in the Democratic party in 1860, it would have won. That the Democrats split their vote and failed was a result of the Lincoln strategy in 1858.

Barton[1] says that Abraham Lincoln kept rather well out of politics from 1849 to 1854. General Winfield Scott was his party candidate in 1852, and Lincoln was a candidate for elector from Illinois. Both were defeated. In the latter part of 1854 the Republican party in Illinois was launched, but Lincoln did not join at that time. Not until 1856 did he take the plunge from the dying, or dead, Whig party to the new one. Lincoln participated in the campaign of 1856, but not in a conspicuous way.

In 1860 Lincoln was the nominee of the state Republican convention for president. He received the nomination in Chicago a few weeks later, and his electors triumphed at the general election in November. In March 1861 he was inaugurated as President.

Thus in this decade he was defeated as a candidate for elector, and twice as a candidate for senator; and he witnessed the death of the political party to which he belonged.

[1] Bibliography, No. 9, Vol. I, p. 287.

He held no office and received no salary from any division of the government.

The effect of these several failures on Mrs. Lincoln could not have been other than bad. Of this there is some confirmatory evidence as to the first of the senatorial contests. Mrs. Lincoln was buoyed through many a disappointment, however, by the faith she had in her husband's political acumen and personal popularity. Those who think Mrs. Lincoln was shrewder and a better politician than her husband—and there are many who are on record to that effect—cite as one bit of proof the fact that in this decade she prevented her husband from re-entering the Illinois legislature. He had been a candidate for United States senator and as such had achieved an enviable reputation, in spite of defeat. Nevertheless, he was anxious to accept election to the legislature. She recognized that this would not be good politics and finally so convinced him, causing him to forgo his yearnings and decline the position.

There was little in the record of the first half or three fourths of their married life to sustain her faith in her husband's political future. But in 1858 came the Lincoln-Douglas debates, and with them a recognition of her husband's political possibilities. In November 1860 the country decided that she had been right when she said Abraham Lincoln would be president. On March 4, 1861 her second great objective was achieved. In this decade the combined influence of political events, of Lincoln's political successes and failures, on Mrs. Lincoln's personality was good, or, at least, more wholesome than not.

FINANCES

Financial worries for the Lincolns were less acute in the fifties than in the forties. This is of importance, because when Mrs. Lincoln later became unbalanced, money was the thread which ran through the fabric of her aberrations. The

Freudian school says that when such is the character of a disturbed mentality, the source may be found in a scarcity of money in the earlier years of life, or in an unsatisfied yearning for money at some time. Many would say that the Todds must have had a money mania, and that Mary inherited a money-madness streak. They might add: Was not her father a banker?

In the second decade of the Springfield life Lincoln's income was rising. He was an attorney for the Illinois Central Railroad, and that corporation was his best client from the financial standpoint. In this period he was engaged in the McCormick reaper litigation and in the Rock Island Bridge case. William H. Herndon, referring to Lincoln in this second decade, wrote: "And now he began to make up for time lost in politics, by studying law in earnest." Milton Hay and Herndon both wrote of Lincoln's waste of time from his studies in telling stories and in making contacts, so necessary for a good trial lawyer; but they also show that there were periods, especially after Lincoln returned from Congress, when he was a rather studious lawyer, attending closely to the business of the law and collecting moderately well.

"Many lawyers and judges in Illinois became rich men during the period before the Civil War; but their wealth was not acquired by practicing law or administering justice. It was obtained through wise and far-seeing investments, for professional earnings were moderate." [1]

Thus Beveridge opens the second of two chapters which deal more closely than others of his biography with the personal characteristics and affairs of the future President. He drew on such reliable witnesses as Whitney, Swett, Herndon, Davis, and Arnold, for evidence that Lincoln in this period was never without cases and clients. In lower courts he excelled as a pleader before juries. But, in spite of his reputation as a jury pleader, Beveridge acclaims him

[1] Bibliography, No. 18, p. 552.

as best before the state Supreme Court. Commenting on the aspects of Lincoln's character suggested by the opening paragraph quoted above, Beveridge says that Lincoln was not an investor, but that he collected his fees and held on to them. This writer then describes at length several of Lincoln's more important cases, some of which brought in good fees. In one — the Illinois Central case — he charged a fee so high that the railroad would not pay it without suit. It was compelled to pay, and, paying, retained Lincoln as one of its lawyers up to the time he became President. He plunged into the Rock Island Bridge case and earned back some of the money spent as he traveled round in his senatorial campaigns. In August 1859 Lincoln wrote to Governor J. W. Grimes of Iowa:[1] "I lost nearly all the working part of last year giving my time to the canvass, and I am altogether too poor to lose two years together."

In this decade Mrs. Lincoln was a beneficiary of two wills. Robert Parker had left his estate to his wife for her use during her lifetime, but it was entailed for the benefit of the grandchildren, of whom Mrs. Lincoln was one. The settlement of this estate resulted in a lawsuit which took Abraham Lincoln, with his wife, to Lexington for his fifth, and what proved to be his last, visit. The estate was considerable, but the division was into many parts.[2] Mrs. Lincoln was also a beneficiary by reason of the death of her father, Robert S. Todd. His estate, too, was a considerable one, but again there were many heirs, and Mrs. Lincoln's share was not large. However, the sums received from these estates in the first half of the decade contributed somewhat to the financial ease of the Lincolns.

The truth is that in the second decade of the Springfield experience the Lincolns were not spending much money, but they were living tolerably well and were not having to worry about means to meet expenses. In Arnold's narrative of their life in Springfield there is evidence of progressive

[1] Letter dated August 1859.

[2] Bibliography, No. 176, pp. 242 ff.

improvement in financial status as the years passed. He says:[1] "Lincoln lived simply, comfortably, and respectably, with neither expensive tastes nor habits. His wants were few and simple. He occupied a small, modest, comfortable, wooden cottage such as is found everywhere in the villages of our country. In the later Springfield years this cottage had been enlarged and made more pretentious. . . . He was in the habit of entertaining in a very simple way. Mrs. Lincoln often entertained small numbers of friends at dinner, and somewhat larger groups at evening parties."

There is no reason for thinking the Lincolns had financial worries in this decade. They were living on a scale that suited Mrs. Lincoln reasonably well. The financial experience of this period did not contribute to her breakdown.

MRS. LINCOLN'S PERSONALITY IN THIS PERIOD

Mrs. Helm visited her half-sister in Springfield in the first half of this range of years. She based the following statement[2] partly on what she then saw and partly on her observations during her stay in the White House:

"It has also been said that Mr. and Mrs. Lincoln were not happy. Mrs. Wallace denies this emphatically, and the present writer's knowledge bears out Mrs. Wallace's assertion. They understood each other thoroughly, and Mr. Lincoln looked beyond the impulsive word and manner, and knew that his wife was devoted to him and to his interests. They lived in a quiet, unostentatious manner. She was very fond of reading, and interested herself greatly in her husband's political views and aspirations. She was fond of home and made nearly all her children's clothes. She was a cheerful woman, a delightful conversationalist, and well-informed on all the subjects of the day. The present writer saw Mr. and Mrs. Lincoln together for some part of every day for

[1] Bibliography, No. 4, p. 82. [2] Bibliography, No. 72, and No. 73, p. 116.

six months at one time, but saw nothing of the unhappiness which is so often referred to. Many of Mr. Lincoln's ways, such as going to answer his own doorbell, annoyed her, and upon one occasion a member of her family said: 'Mary, if I had a husband with a mind such as yours has I wouldn't care what he did.' This pleased her very much and she replied: 'It is very foolish — it is a small thing to complain of.' "

Frances Wallace's statement to which Mrs. Helm refers was as follows:[1] " They did not lead an unhappy life at all. She was devoted to him and her children, and he was certainly all to her that any husband could have been. . . . And they say that Mrs. Lincoln was an ambitious woman. But she was not an ambitious woman at all. She was devoted to her home."

One of the men who knew the Lincolns in this period was Arnold. He was the friend of Mrs. Lincoln then, and he stood by her loyally in her Gethsemane. He wrote:[2] "I must not omit to mention the old-fashioned, generous hospitality of Springfield, proverbial to this day throughout the state. Among others I recall the dinner parties given by Mrs. Lincoln in her modest and simple home. There was always, on the part of both host and hostess, a cordial and hearty western welcome which put every guest perfectly at home. Mrs. Lincoln's table was famed for the excellence of many Kentucky dishes. . . . Yet it was her genial manners and ever kindly welcome, and Mr. Lincoln's wit, humor, anecdote, and unrivaled conversation, which formed the chief attraction."

Henry B. Rankin first met Abraham Lincoln in the forties, but it was not until the fifties that he moved to Springfield and entered the Lincoln-Herndon office in a minor capacity. I have discussed Mr. and Mrs. Lincoln with Rankin, and what he told of them is in accord with what he said in the two books he has written. In the In-

[1] Bibliography, No. 181.

[2] Bibliography, No. 4, p. 82.

troduction to the second of these books[1] Ida M. Tarbell wrote: "They are a precious contribution."

Rankin writes: "I was a verdant youth of nineteen when I was calling on her at her home sixteen years after she became Mrs. Lincoln, and I had the temerity to ask her how and when she made her first acquaintance with Mr. Lincoln." Mr. Rankin, when a boy in the law office, took a copy of the *Southern Literary Messenger* to the Lincoln home, and there met Mrs. Lincoln. He was charmed by her grace and good manners, and her kindness to a country boy newly come to town. Her evidence of culture and education won his admiration. He has written the kindliest description of her of which I know. From it the following quotations are made:[2]

"She thought quickly, spoke rapidly. Without intending to wound, she sometimes hurt in sarcastic or witty remarks. . . . It was remarked to me by one who had known Mrs. Lincoln long and very intimately that her frank and spirited manner, her candor of speech and independence of thought, often gave offense where none was meant. . . . She was never ungracious toward strangers, nor did she ever intentionally wound a friend. . . . Always and everywhere she showed her refinement and dignity of character. . . . I shall not in this writing seek for, or endeavor to set forth, all the sources or motives, nor follow the trail, of either the personality or the criticism of Mrs. Lincoln's foes — much less try to account for their animosity. . . . The writers who have exhausted the resources of both gossip and fiction to write Mr. Lincoln's early life down in a way calculated to cheapen and coarsen those years with as much vulgarity as possible are the same writers from whom have come the attacks on Mrs. Lincoln in even worse caricatures. . . . I ask you to hear something about her life as I know it. . . . In none of these situations [the text recites a great many] did I ever detect in Mrs. Lincoln aught but the most wifely

[1] Bibliography, No. 148, p. 13. [2] Bibliography, No. 149, Chapter ix.

and matronly proprieties and respect toward her husband and her friends. She adapted herself cheerfully to all those exacting functions required of Lincoln in his public life. . . . I beg pardon of any reader for trailing my pen through such trivial scandals. I have done it in the briefest possible way. It is done to show the injustice and cruelty of much of the false insinuations against Mrs. Lincoln that have found their way into history. . . . The few I have mentioned show how distorted many simple acts and incidents may be made to appear when taken apart from their relation to other facts with which they were connected."

What we find in the Lincoln biographies that follow Herndon about Mrs. Lincoln's personality from 1842 to 1851 is not favorable to her. Beveridge's opinion is summed up in the title which he uses for the chapter dealing with this period. It is: "Years of Discipline." The title bears evidence of having been chosen from the following paragraph, in which he indicates his opinion of the effect on Lincoln of his wife's behavior:[1]

"Thus began his continuous and lifelong tutelage in humility, his instruction in patience, and the practice of that supreme virtue which was to continue without ceasing, year after year, decade after decade, as long as he lived. . . . For his wife soon unchained that temper which grew more savage through the years, and was exhibited in the sight and hearing of many. She speedily became a 'she-wolf,' as Herndon long afterward described her to Weik without knowing that John Hay, as secretary to the President, had used a similar but stronger and even more picturesque phrase about Mrs. Lincoln."

That part of the Browning diary available is creditable to Mrs. Lincoln, though little is said, and one hears much, about what is in the suppressed part. Until that is known we cannot weigh this diary.[2]

[1] Bibliography, No. 18, p. 356.

[2] A foot-note in the chapter on Mrs. Lincoln in Barton's *Life of Abraham Lincoln*, Vol. II, p. 416, reads as follows: "If any future biographer of Lincoln shall present

Lloyd Lewis wrote of the "Springfield tradition":[1] "Springfield knew Mrs. Lincoln of old; her erratic nerves, her wild, sudden rages of temper."

B. F. Stoneberger, whose father rented the Lincoln house and whose family lived there for several years, has told me of conversations with Lincoln neighbors.[2] Charles Arnold, who lived across the street, gave him the following estimates of Mrs. Lincoln: "She was an educated woman, and very ambitious for her husband. She was a very set woman. She kept Mr. Lincoln from making several mistakes that would have been fatal politically. She kept nagging her husband on. Mr. Lincoln called her 'Puss,' and so did we. We didn't think Puss Lincoln got a square deal."

Herndon wrote:[3] "In her domestic troubles I always sympathized with Mrs. Lincoln. The world does not know what she bore or how ill adapted she was to bear it."

STRIKING A BALANCE

Miss Mary Todd beginning her Springfield career was a brilliant society girl with a boundless ambition and great determination. Mrs. Mary Lincoln ending her Springfield life, in 1860, was a sedate woman, but still with a boundless ambition and great determination. Her twenty years of Springfield life had added much without spoiling much. She had failed to achieve several of her wishes, and these disappointments had sharpened her temper and made her irritable. As to her irascible disposition within the family circle, the evidence is reasonably conclusive, even though it bears the

other evidence, taken from an important document whose use is now forbidden for any purpose derogatory to the character of Mrs. Lincoln, I suppose myself to be familiar with that document; and while observing, as I am bound in honor to do so, the conditions under which it is permitted to be read, I have taken its content fully into account in my estimate of Mary Lincoln." This evidence follows a discussion by Barton in which he reviews such of the charges as can be quoted.

[1] Bibliography, No. 101, p. 133.

[2] Personal communication.

[3] Bibliography, No. 75a, p. 230.

marks of exaggeration. When it comes to personality deterioration manifested beyond this range, the evidence is not convincing. She went through twenty years of experiences for which she had been poorly trained except in two or three fields. Many of these experiences were trying, especially to an ambitious, aggressive woman with small capacity for accepting disappointments. Her trials had not overreached her power of resistance, however; her fiber was tough enough to withstand what came to her. Her personality had changed somewhat in its non-essentials, but it had built up in some directions while it was being torn down in others. Balancing the account, I think Mary Lincoln of 1860 was, in many respects, an improvement over Mary Todd of 1840. However, she was approaching the limits of her capacity to withstand. It will be shown shortly that before she reached the White House, she gave one manifestation that she was in trouble, or was nearing it.

THE SPRINGFIELD LIFE IN 1860 AND 1861

After Mr. Lincoln was endorsed for president by the Illinois state convention, he remained at home almost continuously until he started for Washington, in February 1861. Perhaps at no time before in his adult life did he remain so long in one city as he did between his trip to New York for the Cooper Union speech and his departure for the inauguration in Washington. Perhaps never before or after did he make so few speeches. He did not practice law. None of this, nor all of it, meant that time hung heavy on his hands, or that he was without occupation. His family did not see a great deal of him that year, in spite of his being tied to Springfield.

The business of getting nominated was arduous, and that of being elected was still more so. In receiving the numerous delegations, Mrs. Lincoln had an opportunity to meet a great many national characters, and usually she did the right thing, although once she came near showing her newness to like situations by proposing to serve refreshments when to do so was not proper socially and would have been hazardous politically. The husband candidate threaded the maze of political expediency with skill, and the wife met the bands of visitors and pilgrims adroitly, saying the appropriate thing always.

In this campaign the political attacks were uncommonly harsh and raw. The question of slavery excited bitterness. The cartoons were vile, and the charges made in newspaper columns and political speeches were exceptionally rapacious. The Lincolns had been through several campaigns since their marriage, and there is no evidence that the shafts directed against her husband hurt Mrs. Lincoln particularly. There were no attacks on her. Things were "coming her way," and in such times her personality was not likely to suffer; it was restraint and disappointment that tended to curdle the milk of her composition.

It was not difficult to foresee that Springfield and Sangamon County were not to support Lincoln. On election night he stayed up receiving returns until he learned that he had carried his own ward. Knowing that his city and county had gone against him, he soothed his soul with the local returns — the vote of his nearest neighbors — and went to bed and to sleep. The loss of the home town must have hurt Mrs. Lincoln somewhat, but the returns showed that her husband was to be president, and that recompensed for the loss of Springfield. She could foresee that Lincoln would lose Lexington. She knew that her own family was not supporting him. Many old friends everywhere were deserting, and that also hurt. But again success was more than an offset.

Following the election the press of the South was very bitter toward Lincoln. In December the threats of secession were made a reality by the action of South Carolina. In the first months of the next year other states followed suit. Then the Confederate government was organized. Civil War was begun. This sequence of events was very disturbing to Lincoln as he awaited his opportunity. He was constantly busy writing letters, reading papers, advising and being advised, listening, thinking, planning, and perhaps worrying. All of this must have registered on his wife, but her personality seems to have been equal to the strain.

In January 1861 there occurred the first act of Mrs. Lincoln indicating that she might not be mentally " right " —the first suspiciously false note. This developed in connection with a trip she took to New York to make purchases, some of which, according to the papers, were for the White House. The details as well as the significance of this visit will be set forth more fully in the following chapter.

Robert S. Todd.
From a portrait owned by Mrs. Emilie Helm.

GENEALOGICAL CHART OF MARY TODD LINCOLN

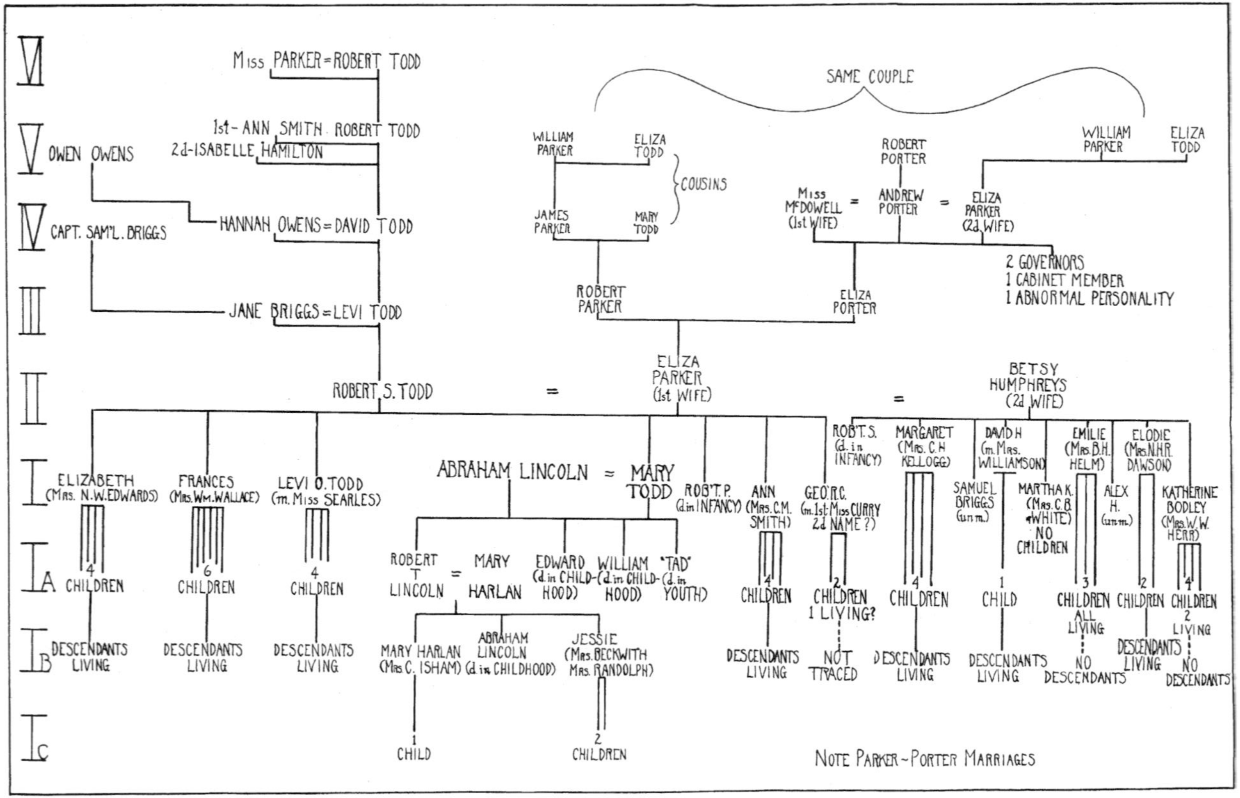

By permission of Mr. Meserve

"Tad" Lincoln.

From a photograph in the Frederick H. Meserve collection.

By permission of Mr. Meserve

Robert Todd Lincoln.

From a photograph in the Frederick H. Meserve collection.

By permission of Mr. Meserve

William Wallace Lincoln.

From a photograph in the Frederick H. Meserve collection.

The Main Street house of Robert S. Todd, Lexington, as it appears today; the second of Mrs. Lincoln's Lexington homes.

One of the buildings occupied by Transylvania University when Mary Todd lived in Lexington.

Morrison Hall, Transylvania College.

One of the first daguerreotype cameras
brought to America, imported by
Transylvania University;
now in Sayre Institute, Lexington.

Planetarium in Transylvania College, made and mounted by Thomas Harris Barlow, of Lexington, while Mary Todd lived there.

The Ninian W. Edwards residence, Springfield.

Parlor of the Ninian W. Edwards residence, Springfield.

The Globe Tavern, Springfield, where the Lincolns went to live when they were married. Robert was born here.

The Monroe Street cottage, Springfield, where the Lincolns lived when Robert was a baby.

From a drawing from memory.

The Lincoln residence, Springfield.

The youthful Lincoln.
From a photograph taken in Princeton, Illinois, July 4, 1856.

The youthful Mrs. Lincoln.
From a photograph owned by Oliver R. Barrett.

The Anderson Building, United States Soldiers' Home, Washington, D. C., where the Lincolns lived during the summer, 1861 to 1864.

By permission of Mr. Cameron

Abraham Lincoln while President.

From a photograph owned by S. R. Cameron, Chicago.

By permission of Mr. Meserve

The White House during Lincoln's administration.
From a photograph in the Frederick H. Meserve collection.

The Clifton House, Chicago.
From a picture owned by The Chicago Historical Society.

XX

The house, on Washington Street (now Boulevard), Chicago, *owned by Mrs. Lincoln, in which she lived in 1866 and 1867 (indicated by the crosses).*

Bellevue Place Sanatorium, Batavia, Illinois. A window of Mrs. Lincoln's room is seen directly above the swing.

By permission of Mr. Sweet

Ear-rings owned by Mrs. Lincoln;

now in the possession of Homer Sweet, Battle Creek, Michigan.

Mary Todd when about twenty years old.

From a portrait painted from a daguerreotype, by Katherine Helm. The portrait is now owned by William H. Townsend.

By permission of Mr. Cameron

Mrs. Lincoln.

From a photograph owned by S. R. Cameron, Chicago.

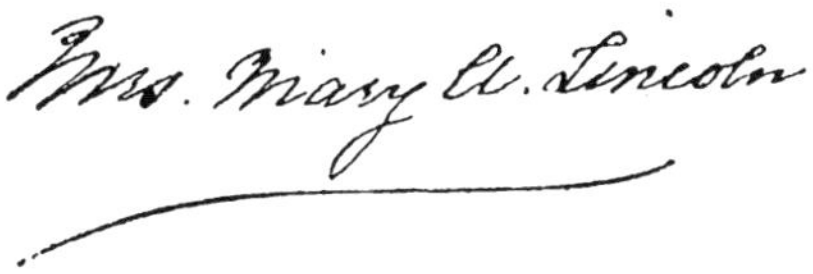

No. 1

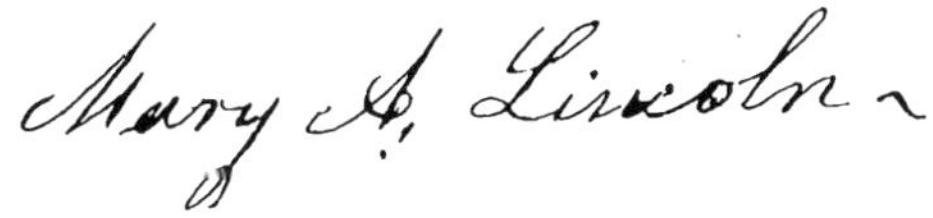

No. 2

No. 3

No. 1. Signature from a copy of a book on character written by Miss Chandler, *owned by Oliver R. Barrett.*

By permission of Mr. Barrett

No. 2. Signature from the back of a photograph of Mrs. Lincoln, *owned by Oliver R. Barrett. The writing is probably that of Mrs. Lincoln.*

By permission of Mr. Barrett

No. 3. Mrs. Lincoln's signature, *from one of her letters in the possession of the John Hay Library, Brown University.*

By permission of the John Hay Library

Mrs. Lincoln,
from a photograph owned by Oliver R. Barrett.

Mrs. Lincoln.
The puffiness of the face indicates a possible myxœdema.

CHAPTER SIX

The Peak and a Decline

Men in great place are thrice servants.

— Francis Bacon

INCIDENTS AFFECTING MRS. LINCOLN

March 4, 1861 to April 14, 1865

1861 *March 4,* Abraham Lincoln inaugurated as President of the United States.

April 15, President Lincoln called for 75,000 volunteers.

May 10, President Lincoln proclaimed martial law; Civil War on.

May 23, Colonel E. E. Ellsworth killed; his body lay in state in the White House.

June 3, Stephen A. Douglas died.

Spring, it was becoming evident that there was to be a friction between the White House and Washington " high society."

Summer, Mrs. Lincoln visited Saratoga, New York, and Long Branch, New Jersey.

September 1, Mrs. Lincoln visited Niagara Falls.

October 30, Willie Lincoln wrote a poem eulogizing Colonel Edward Baker.

November, Mrs. Lincoln had returned to the White House from her several trips.

1862 *February 20,* William W. (Willie) Lincoln died.

March 9, Battle of the Monitor and the Merrimac.

April 6–7, Battle of Shiloh. Samuel B. Todd killed.

June, Pekin, Illinois, a Council of the Union League organized.

Summer, President and Mrs. Lincoln spent most of the season in the Anderson cottage, Soldiers' Home, Washington.

September 16–17, Battle of Antietam.

September 22, Emancipation Proclamation issued.

September, Mrs. Lincoln visited New York City, at the Metropolitan Hotel.

November, in the Illinois congressional elections, the vote indicated that the people were not behind the administration.

November 29, Mrs. Lincoln returned from a visit to New England.

December 21, Mrs. Lincoln in Philadelphia, Continental Hotel.

1863 *January 1,* slaves declared free.

January 12, Richardson, Democrat, elected Senator from Illinois.

April, President and Mrs. Lincoln and Tad visited the Army of the Potomac.

June, Yates prorogued the Illinois legislature.

July 1–3, Battle of Gettysburg.

July 4, surrender of Vicksburg. David H. Todd seriously wounded at Vicksburg.

July, Mrs. Lincoln thrown from carriage, and her head badly hurt.

August, Alexander H. Todd killed at Baton Rouge.

September, Mrs. Lincoln at Fifth Avenue Hotel, New York City.

September 20, General B. H. Helm killed at Chickamauga.

October, Mrs. Helm visited Mrs. Lincoln in the White House for one week.

November 19, Gettysburg address.

November, creditors of Mrs. Lincoln threatened to sue her.

December 3–7, Mrs. Lincoln in New York City, Fifth Avenue Hotel.

1864 *February 22,* General Grant appointed Commander-in-Chief.

Spring, bitter feeling shown by General Frémont.

April 28, Mrs. Lincoln in New York City, Metropolitan Hotel.

June 7, Lincoln nominated for president the second time by Union, or Republican, party.
June 24, Mrs. Lincoln in Boston.
August 29, McClellan nominated for president by the Democrats.
August 31, Mrs. Lincoln in Manchester, Vermont.
August, Battle of Mobile Bay.
September 3, Atlanta fell.
November, President Lincoln re-elected.
December, Robert T. Lincoln in the army on the staff of General Grant.

1865 *January 5,* Yates elected Senator from Illinois.
January 17, Levi O. Todd died.
March 4, Abraham Lincoln inaugurated as President for the second term.
March 22, President and Mrs. Lincoln visited City Point.
April 3, Richmond fell.
April 4, President and Mrs. Lincoln visited Richmond.
April 9, General Lee surrendered.
April 14, President Lincoln assassinated.

CHAPTER SIX

The Peak and a Decline

WHEN MRS. LINCOLN LEFT SPRINGFIELD FOR WASHington she had gained everything in life that she had set out to accomplish. Matrimony had been the goal of her young womanhood, as was meet and proper; it was the goal of every girl she grew up with. She and they accepted that as true, gloried in it, and talked about it no small part of their time. Well, she had married; and, more than that, she had outmarried any of them. Her husband was the President elect. She had outmarried her three sisters. Lincoln had proved a better catch than Edwards, the promising son of a rich father — the grand chief of Illinois public life for years. Ninian W. Edwards was a prominent man in Springfield and in Illinois, but his success did not compare with that of Abraham Lincoln. Dr. William Wallace was an important man and well-to-do, a physician in Springfield; but Frances's husband could not match position with Mary's. And, however successful C. M. Smith was as a business man, as a matrimonial catch Ann's husband was rated below that of her sister. No other Springfield girl had done so well as Mary. Julia Jayne's husband was Senator Lyman Trumbull, but a president outranks a senator. None of the Lexington girls had made a match which compared with Mary's, seen by the light of 1861. She had boasted that Lincoln would be president; helping to make him so had been one of her aims. Well, he had been elected!

Motherhood had been one of her plans, also — as was both customary and proper. She had borne four sons. Three of them were going with her to the White House. She and her husband had wanted economic security. That, too, they had. They owed no one; they had a home and several other pieces of real estate; there were a fair number of good loans and some ready money to their credit. It is easy to understand that Mrs. Lincoln went away from Springfield feeling that her life had been a success, and she had very good reasons for being both satisfied and happy.

Now a new vista was opening. What were to be her aims for the future? She was of a nature that did not wait for Fortune to lay things in her lap. When Opportunity came her way, intent upon knocking at her door, it was in her make-up to be at the gate waiting. If, perchance, she got a late start, she would at least be ready to open the door while the knocking was still going on.

Undoubtedly her first endeavor would be to make her husband's administration a success, in so far as she could. To effect this, the social life of the administration must be successful. Diplomats must be impressed; the wives of senators and congressmen must be kept friendly; the Washington resident society must be so pleased that they would help to establish a background for her husband's efforts. Perhaps she could help to make friends for the administration among foreign governments. She could talk about their literature with their representatives, and with those from France in their own language. A war was on, and the friendship of foreign representatives was unusually important. She was ambitious, and few deny it. She had social ambitions, and in Washington social ambitions may become political.

To discharge the duties of a wife and mother continued to be a major objective. It is customary for the outgoing Mistress of the White House to invite the incoming Lady to visit her. On the occasion of this visit, the one explains to the other just how the domestic affairs are conducted and introduces her to what may be called "the management." The incoming Lady accepts the invitation and absorbs as much information as she can. All of this is by way of training for the job in hand. Actually, none of the details of the housekeeping are attended to by the President's wife. Mrs. Lincoln, however, interfered with household management rather more than others had done before her, thus showing her lack of training in organization and administration. Had she left more of this routine to others, she would have escaped some of the censure that was poured on her head.

The duties of his office are so strenuous that the President has little time for his family, and the First Lady has few opportunities to minister to her husband's comforts. There is authority for the statement that Mrs. Lincoln improved such opportunities as she had. She was criticized for leaving the President too much alone while she shopped in New York, but these criticisms even from her enemies died down. Contradicting the charges that she neglected her husband is the evidence that she laughed with him and even joked at rare intervals, bossed him, made him take rest and indulge in diversion, and dispelled his gloom when he was in the depression sector of his cyclic personality. Doubtless she did some things that added to his worries — all mates do. But she also helped her husband over some rough places. Lincoln stole away to play with the children when he could. Julia Taft Bayne [1] tells of his doing so in 1861, and many others have confirmed it. More than one man was shocked and some were outraged — and they told the world so — over the play of the President with his boys.

Mrs. Lincoln's mother care continued. Willie was in his eleventh and twelfth years. Great is the need of wisdom in the mother of a child of that age. Tad was eight years old

[1] Bibliography, No. 17, p. 109.

when he went to Washington, and twelve when he left. He, too, greatly needed a mother's care. In the White House period Robert was in college and did not come in for much of his mother's attention.

For the discharge of her duties in this epoch, Mrs. Lincoln's training rated from good to superior. She and her husband had been married eighteen years, and therefore she had been trained for her duties as his wife. She had had seventeen years of training as a mother. For the social, political, and diplomatic duties she had also had an unusual training. Very few First Ladies have had such thorough preparation.

If she analyzed the situation in 1861 — as she probably did — she must have felt that she would be equal to her new responsibilities. She had met problems before and had found solutions for them. Her training for life had proved good enough, and what she had not learned in her youth she had been able to acquire. Her training for the new field had been exceptionally good; she was prepared for most that she could foresee. Whatever new problems arose, she would find a way to meet them.

Dr. William E. Barton says of her that she was naturally timid, and her courage was that of will-power; she drove herself to be courageous, in spite of her timidity. I disagree with Barton as to this characteristic of Mrs. Lincoln; I think that she was fearless — almost needlessly, blindly, so. She entered life in Washington in high spirits, with no signs of trepidation or fear. She was confident, happy, and hopeful.

She little knew that an unkind fate was just round every bend in the road — lying in wait for her, ready to strike when and where the blow would hurt worst.

In 1861 Mrs. Lincoln traveled a good deal. She went to New York City and to the seashore. There was a moderate number of formal parties and dinners. By the summer of

1861 the attitude of society toward the Lincolns became noticeably hostile — perhaps no more than in March, but more openly so. The progress of the war was a source of uneasiness and unhappiness. Ellsworth, the dashing young leader of the Zouaves, was killed, and the Lincolns had his body carried to the White House. The Battle of Bull Run had a profound effect on Washington psychology.

Early in 1862 Willie died, and there followed a prolonged period of grief. (While Judge David Davis deplored the death of Willie, he thought it might serve to prevent Mrs. Lincoln from doing things for which she was being criticized and which were reflecting on her husband.) Thereafter the social atmosphere of the White House was of another kind. Mrs. Lincoln wore mourning clothes and mourning jewelry and she wrote on mourning stationery. There were no more public receptions or balls, and very few dinners. The Lady of the White House devoted her energies to visiting hospitals, convalescent stations, and camps.

The purely social efforts of Mrs. Lincoln and the administration were not soon renewed after the death of Willie. The social historians generally give two years as the length of the social eclipse attributed to the period of mourning. When there was some suggestion of awakening, in 1864, the color was more military and political than social.

In 1863 the horrors of war and the perplexities that arose out of it were many, but the spirits of the presidential family were on the mend. In the latter part of the year it was plain that the war was being won. The statesmanship and major war strategy of the President were gaining for him the confidence of thinking people, and this hopeful condition was being reflected in the family circle.

In 1864 there was a political battle, and political excitement always stimulated Mrs. Lincoln. To her this election meant as much as did that of 1860. It offered the only solution she could see for her financial problem. It meant indorsement of the Lincoln policies, and four more years of power and position.

The Lincolns were greatly encouraged in November 1864. The President's own state had voted for him. Those new friends in the north end had proved staunch; some of the old central Illinois supporters who had wandered off politically were now friendly. The victory of arms was in sight; the critics had been silenced. The Lincoln sagacity and wisdom were recognized.

In the spring of 1865 Mrs. Lincoln's spirits were again buoyant. She emerged from the introvert state of insularity, separateness, and resentment in which she had been most of the time since Willie's death. She regained some of that ambition and drive — termed by some aggressiveness, and by others audacity — which characterized her personality and which was so much in evidence in 1861. The war was drawing to a close, and Lincoln was laying his plans for the aftermath. There was work to be done, and he was giving his wife a chance to help.

Came the second inaugural.

And then April the fourteenth!

FINANCIAL WORRIES

There should have been no financial worries for the Lincoln family during their years in the White House. For Lincoln there were none. He went there owning a moderate amount of real estate and having a fair accumulation of liquid assets. He received a salary of twenty-five thousand dollars yearly, which was much beyond his simple needs, considering that the government bore most of the expense of the presidential household. He was not only a man of plain tastes and few wants, but thrifty and careful and a good enough business man. He had told William H. Herndon to keep the old law sign up. When he was through in Washington, he expected to take up his old work and his old partnership, and he never doubted his ability to make the best living he had ever made. For Mrs. Lincoln, however, the White House years were a financial nightmare.

In the latter part of January 1861 she and a party, of which her merchant brother-in-law, C. M. Smith, was one, went to New York City to do some shopping. Mrs. Lincoln had sewed to some extent for herself and family, and she had employed the best dressmakers in Springfield; but she was now about to enter Washington social life and wanted a wardrobe befitting the occasion. A. T. Stewart and the other great New York merchants extended credit and courtesy to her as the President's wife. At this point is recorded her first evidence of poor judgment in money matters; the peculiar direction and bent of this error were later to become a quality of her insanity. She bought dress-goods, particularly silks, and ornaments, and jewelry for her neck and ears, and used this newly acquired credit to the breaking-point. Her purchase of lace curtains for the White House is not easily understood.

During four years Mrs. Lincoln continued to use her credit. Her husband had no knowledge of all this. The best information we have of the harrowing experience comes from Mrs. Keckley.[1] Mrs. Lincoln began negotiations for dresses with Elizabeth Keckley on March 5. The dressmaker used the material bought in New York in making fifteen or sixteen dresses in the spring and early summer of 1861. Dressmaking was somewhat halted by the death of Willie, in 1862. Thereafter Mrs. Lincoln wore mourning, but in time her black garments became of an expensive kind, and mourning jewelry was costly.

Mrs. Keckley says: " In endeavoring to make a display becoming her exalted position, she had to incur many expenses. Mr. Lincoln's salary was inadequate to meet them, and she was forced to run in debt. She bought the most expensive goods on credit, and, in 1864, enormous unpaid

[1] Bibliography, No. 85, pp. 15–28.

bills stared her in the face." Mrs. Lincoln is quoted as saying:[1] " I have contracted large debts of which he knows nothing and which he will be unable to pay if he is defeated." Mrs. Lincoln was strong in her counsel to Lincoln to run for a second term, and one of her reasons was that she hoped to be able in the second term to save enough to pay these bills. Mrs. Keckley wrote: " The debts consisted chiefly of store bills. . . . Altogether the amount was $27,000. The principal part of this was owed to Stewart. . . . She owed at the time of the President's death $70,000." The debts had gradually piled up year by year, but if the high figure given by Mrs. Keckley is correct, it was not so until 1865. Mrs. Morrow wrote:[2] "When Mrs. Lincoln entered the White House she plunged into an orgy of spending that lasted four years. In 1863, Mrs. Lincoln owed $27,000, and New York creditors threatened to sue her." At times threats were made to ask Mr. Lincoln to pay the bills, and at other times suggestions were made of the unpleasantness of publicity. Mrs. Keckley wrote that sometimes Mrs. Lincoln was hysterical over financial worries and fears.[3]

Ben Perley Poore[4] grouped the several forces responsible for the undoing of Mrs. Lincoln as her social-political-personal enemies. His grouping is comprehensive, but it leaves out two factors for which Mrs. Lincoln, rather than her enemies, was responsible, and both are too important to be overlooked: one was her emotional mourning; the other, her anxiety due to the debt.

---

1 Bibliography, No. 85, pp. 149, 204.

2 Bibliography, No. 121, p. 145.

3 I have seen a bill for more than $3,000, rendered by Galt and Company in 1865. This bill represented jewelry, silverware, and ornaments purchased by Mrs. Lincoln during two months prior to April 14, 1865.

4 Bibliography, No. 141, p. 115.

POLITICS

To be a successful politician one must have a certain mental and emotional make-up, either inherited or acquired by experience. One must know practical psychology: how the individual thinks and, what is more important, how the mob thinks — or, is it not better to say, feels. One must be a strategist in human emotions and conduct, or an opportunist. One must have a certain quality of detachment, known by some as being " hard-boiled."

The politics of the Lincoln period were the most difficult that any president has ever known. To the ordinary difficulties were added those peculiar features which war develops — and this was a civil war. The political intricacies were again doubled. Lincoln's war politics were based upon a concept of the Constitution, under which he proposed to reconstruct the Union. Many who gave him full support in his war policies were bitterly opposed to his foundations for reconstruction. This added to the difficulties of his war politics. Ranking well up in the list of difficulties were those which pertain to the first national success of a political party. In this instance the new party was an admixture of old-line Abolitionists and their new political affiliates, and between the two groups was an unbridgeable chasm. Abraham Lincoln was a master politician and handled the situations that arose as no other man could have done. Nevertheless, all well-informed persons know of the bitterness with which Lincoln was attacked by his antagonists in the North, and even in his own state, during the war period.

Mrs. Lincoln was also a politician of no mean ability and with much desire to indulge. Indulge she did. Her activities were bitterly resented for two reasons, for only one of which was she responsible. Her mind was so constituted that she could not play politics with detachment. She thought of politics in terms of offices to be filled. Her letters show that she was often engaged in seeking jobs for relatives or personal friends. The many letters she wrote in which she was not advocating relatives or friends for office generally showed a tendency to punish or reward for old political scores. She was alert in her efforts to protect her husband from those who, she thought, intended to use him. She threw her influence, by correspondence and otherwise, against those who had injured him or had tried to do so. Could she have had her way, the President's Cabinet would have been limited to men who met one standard, and that: Had they been fair to Mr. Lincoln? Would they be loyal to him? Politicians resented the very personal way in which she played politics.

In this period Mrs. Lincoln began to show conspicuously a quality which grew out of a personality trait of an earlier period. In her young womanhood she was gossipy, interested in talking and writing about people and events, and somewhat indifferent as to the consequences. In the Washington period she began to make, or she showed an increased habit of making, direct, sharp, personal references to politicians and others whom she did not like or distrusted. This quality was much more in evidence after 1865; in fact, it was a characteristic of her deteriorated personality in the later period.[1]

The other group of antagonisms above referred to, and for which she was not responsible, was her Southern antecedents and affiliations.

For the light they shed on the Washington popular mind in the spring of 1861, let us read some comments by Albert Shaw:[2]

"Prejudice and slander now [1860–1] found fresh opportunity. Some vestiges of these prevailing misunderstandings lingered in the popular mind for more than half a century. . . . When Abraham Lincoln came to the center

[1] See letter to James Gordon Bennett, October 4, 1862, in the Brown University Lincoln Collection, and many others.

[2] Bibliography, No. 158, Vol. II, p. 232.

of the stage he was encompassed by invisible walls of prejudice and animosity. . . . Few people could overcome the feeling that Lincoln was merely the glorified rail-splitter. . . . There were unfounded rumors that Lincoln was part Negro. . . ."

This is a mild statement of the bitter antagonism to Lincoln and the resultant vilification of him which was the order of the day in 1860 and '61 and continued in part until 1865. Following his assassination, the country at large tried to make amends, and Washington kept step. All has been done that could have been to correct the false statements that were made about him.

Some of the charges against Mrs. Lincoln, quoted by Shaw, were as follows:

"The extreme antislavery elements, and these became increasingly large, grew deeply suspicious because Mrs. Lincoln had come from Kentucky. It was enough for the censorious fanatics that her own brothers and other relatives were living in the South and were serving in the Confederate Army. Some people have believed until this day that Mrs. Lincoln was a Southern spy in the White House. The extreme elements in the South, on the other hand, hated Mrs. Lincoln because, in point of fact, she was intensely loyal to her husband and to the Union cause, although of Southern origin. People in the back districts of all the Southern states were told that Mrs. Lincoln had Negro blood in her veins and was profligate in her personal life. . . . Mary Todd, Lincoln's wife, had been more unpleasantly criticized from various standpoints private and public than any other woman in the long succession of Mistresses of the White House. . . . Far more intense and more penetrating, however, was the sectional prejudice due to the cleavage between North and South. The nation's capital city — always a hotbed of malicious gossip — was dominated in the social sense by Southern sympathizers. The District of Columbia, wedged in between Virginia and

Maryland, was sullenly hostile to the idea of having the Lincoln family in the White House."

Mrs. Lincoln's case differs from that of Mr. Lincoln. There has been no great effort to refute the lies that were told of her, and, as Shaw says, " Some vestiges of these . . . misunderstandings lingered in the popular mind for more than half a century." So great were the walls of prejudice and animosity against her, and so few were the defenders, that Shaw's designation, " vestiges of misunderstandings," is not strong or broad enough.

Laura C. Holloway, one of the most widely read of the historians who have dealt with the social side of official Washington, expresses the following estimates and opinions of Mrs. Lincoln: [1]

" Mrs. Lincoln did not rightly estimate the importance of conciliatory address with friend and foe alike, and seemed not conscious of the immense assistance which as the wife of a public man she had it in her power to give her husband. . . . She was very ambitious. . . . Mrs. Lincoln was a fortunate woman, in that she secured the measure of her ambition, but it was the impartial judgment of her friends that she was not a happy person. . . . She was fond of society and pleased with excitement. She would have made the White House socially what it was under other administrations, but that was impossible. She found herself surrounded on every side by people who were ready to exaggerate her shortcomings, find fault with her deportment on all occasions, and criticize her performance of all her official duties. . . . Mrs. Lincoln was a lone woman during much of the time she spent in the White House. . . . The New Year's reception of 1865 was the most brilliant entertainment given by the administration."

Edna M. Colman assayed her as follows: [2]

" She was willful, impulsive, and quick-tempered. . . . In her the social graces were highly developed. . . . High-

[1] Bibliography, No. 80, pp. 528–44.
[2] Bibliography, No. 44, pp. 287–318.

spirited, independent, and with a frankness that was often offensive and a wit that could be caustic, she failed to win the hearts of the people. . . . From the very beginning, criticism and prejudice made her path a difficult one. She was accused of disloyalty and, in later days, of actually supplying information to the South."

On one occasion Mrs. Lincoln talked to Mrs. Keckley about a charge that she was a Southern sympathizer which appeared in the Chicago *Tribune,* telling her: "The *Tribune,* instead of saying three of my brothers are in the Southern army, might have said, my half-brothers." And she added: "I have not seen them since they were infants. . . . My early home was truly a boarding-school."

Instead of multiplying citations, let us see what are the facts about Mrs. Lincoln's relatives in the armies.

She had several relatives in the Confederate Army; three were killed in battle, and two died subsequent to the war from wounds. Her full brother George R. C. Todd was a surgeon in that army. Doctor Todd had been estranged from the family, however, long before 1861. Two of those killed in battle were her half-brothers, and a third half-brother was severely wounded. General B. H. Helm, the husband of a half-sister, was a Confederate officer and was killed. General Helm had married into the family fifteen years after Mrs. Lincoln left home. Another brother-in-law to be, W. W. Herr, was a Confederate soldier, but the war was over when he married her half-sister; Mrs. Lincoln never saw him.

But she was not without relatives in the Union Army. Mrs. Wallace's son-in-law was in that army. Two cousins, Porter by name, had the title of general in McClellan's army. Several of the Todd relatives and connections in Illinois fought under the Stars and Stripes. Her full brother Levi O. was Union in his sentiments, but his age and the condition of his health prevented his taking part in hostilities; he died in 1865. In all probability Mrs. Lincoln had more relatives in the Northern army than in the Southern. And, finally, the Kentucky Todds were a branch of the Pennsylvania stem.

SOCIETY

Washington society was well organized in 1860. The first aristocracy had been carried down with the fall of John Quincy Adams in 1828; Jackson had sacked the town socially in his day; but gradually the social nobility had come back into their own, and they had had almost thirty years in which to "dig in." It was a Democratic régime, with a big D, but when it came to setting up the word with a lower-case letter, the thing did not go. There was an interruption with the Whigs and Harrison in 1840. That was not much of a change because Harrison was cut from the same pattern as they; but, more important, he was shortly replaced by Tyler. There was a slight interim with Taylor and Fillmore, but on the whole the social flow from Jackson to Buchanan was wonderfully even, as politics go in a capital city.

Genevieve Forbes Herrick,[1] writing of the present-day organization of society in Washington, illustrates her story schematically. Her illustration zones society, and the zones and their occupants, from within outwards, are these:

In the center are the "cave-dwellers." Next in social influence are the "money-bags." Third in rank are the "residential highbrows," including the "Georgetown highbrows." Then come fourth, the "diplomatic corps"; fifth, the "army-and-navy circle"; and, last, the "political group."

She assigns the Civil War as the birth period of present-day Washington society with its system of zoning. It is true that the present personnel inherited the organization

[1] Bibliography, No. 77.

from a crew which began operating in Civil War time, but beyond that her statement misleads.

Society is not creative. It does not originate; it merely co-ordinates existing forces, organizes them, and lays down rules for them. It is a machine, and not a genetic force. The Civil War organization took over an older order. There were "cave-dwellers" in Washington when the Lincolns arrived, and they were intrenched. Mr. Poore, Mrs. Ellett, Mrs. Clemmer, Miss Colman and Miss Holloway tell who they were and what were their credentials. We read such names as Mrs. Alexander Slidell, Mrs. Rose Greenhow, Mrs. Givin, Mrs. Jeffry, Mrs. Sallie Ward Hunt, Mrs. Charles Eames, Mrs. Woodbury, Mrs. Pickens, Mrs. Parker, Mrs. Hoover, the Misses Green, and the Tayloes. Mrs. Ellett records at least a score more of ladies each of whom belonged to what are now known as the "cave-dwellers," the "army-and-navy circle," or the "money-bags." Most of them were Southern Democrats, with fortunes dependent on slavery. Many of them were from New England and the industrial East, with fortunes founded on industry and commerce. The combination of the business East and the slave-holding South was on a satisfactory basis in the drawing-room. For thirty years these "cave-dwellers" had reigned with but little to disturb their serenity.

Then came the rise of a new party without antecedents. That was horrible to contemplate! There were zealots and Abolitionists among its adherents. But the big "X" quantity was those who were coming from beyond the mountains, from the lands whence Indians had been expelled but recently. They were the "great unwashed." The "cave-dwellers" viewed them with alarm, just as their social forbears had viewed Andrew Jackson when he burst in at the head of his ruffians in March 1829. (At least, that is the way Washington society regarded it.) Was there to be another Polly Eaton? The Abolitionists were "poison," but most of them had education and culture. These Westerners were likely to scalp one!

Of the Lincolns they knew almost nothing. Mr. Lincoln was very ugly and awkward; he could not possibly have good manners. Some of them may have remembered him when he was in the House, but probably not; he had been just one more congressman living in a second-rate boarding-house. A few could report on Mrs. Lincoln. Mrs. Sallie Ward Hunt had known the Todds in Lexington, but that was many years ago; so had the Breckinridges, and the Clays of the second generation, and Benjamin Gratz and his family. Mrs. Jacob Thompson may have remembered her from the old congressional boarding-house, but she did not know much about her and she probably had left Washington before the inauguration.

The "cave-dwellers" are a very shrewd lot; they have considerable power of adaptability. They decided to attend the first reception. Mrs. Ellett wrote:[1] "At Mrs. Lincoln's first drawing-room reception the élite of the metropolis was in attendance. . . . Not only was the élite of Washington society represented, but the wealthy and fashionable circles of nearly every state from Maine to Louisiana, and from the Atlantic to the Pacific." She commented on the success of Mrs. Lincoln at this reception: "Mrs. Lincoln seemed to have impressed foreigners most favorably. . . . Her spirit was equal to any emergency." Of Mrs. Lincoln at the inaugural ball she said: "All eyes were turned on Mrs. Lincoln, whose exquisite toilet and admirable ease and grace won compliments from thousands."

But presently there came a change. Mrs. Lincoln was not treated as she had expected to be — for one reason by one, for another by another. She resented this. She unleashed her vitriolic tongue. What she said was carried to the "cave-dwellers." They did not talk back, for that is not their way; they turned "thumbs down," and the technique

[1] Bibliography, No. 53, pp. 521–60.

consisted in ignoring the President's wife. They felt that they were strong enough to do that. And they were, so far as the present was concerned. Poore, writing of the presidential New Year's reception in 1862, said:[1] "The crowd, indeed, as looked upon by old residents, appeared to present new faces almost entirely." Poore said of another function: "Washington society refused to be comforted. Those within its charmed circle would not visit the White House nor have any intercourse with the members of the administration."

Mrs. Herrick in her sprightly story states:[2] "The things that are written and the things that are said—above all, the things that are whispered." The gossip about Mrs. Lincoln began with whisperings, but ended otherwise—when it ended at all; it found its way into the newspapers and thus to the eyes of the person most concerned.

Here are some of the charges, culled from books in most instances, and special newspaper stories in others:

From Mary Ames Clemmer:[3]

"It was the misfortune of Mrs. Lincoln to be the only woman personally assailed who ever presided in the White House. . . . Yet in reviewing the character of the Presidents' wives we shall see that there was never one who entered the White House with such a feeling of self-satisfaction, which amounted to personal exaltation, as did Mary Lincoln. To her it was the fulfillment of a lifelong ambition. . . .

"Mrs. Lincoln, presuming to abolish the time-honored but costly state dinners of the White House, increased her personal unpopularity to an intense degree. . . .

"The newspapers teemed with gossip concerning the new Lady of the White House. While her sister-women sewed, scraped lint, made bandages, and gave their all to country and to death, the wife of its President spent her time in

---

[1] Bibliography, No. 141, p. 115.

[2] Bibliography, No. 77.

[3] Bibliography, No. 41.

rolling to and fro between Washington and New York, intent on extravagant purchases for herself and the White House. Mrs. Lincoln seemed to have nothing to do but to shop, and the reports of her lavish bargains in the newspapers were vulgar and sensational in the extreme.

"Letters of rebuke, of expostulation, of anathema even, addressed to her personally, came in from every direction. Not a day did not bring her many such communications denouncing her mode of life, her conduct; calling upon her to fulfill the obligations and meet the opportunities of her high station. . . .

"Thus, while disgracing the state by her own example, she still sought to meddle in its affairs. . . . Prodigal in her personal expenditures, she brought shame upon the President's House by petty economies which had never disgraced it before. . . . From the moment Mrs. Lincoln began to receive recriminating letters, she considered herself an injured individual, the honored object of every jealousy and spite, and a martyr to her high position. . . .

"It was not strange that Mrs. Lincoln was not able to leave the White House for five weeks after her husband's death. . . . It was her misfortune that she had so armed public sympathy against her, by years of indifference to the sorrows of others, that when her own hour of supreme anguish came there were few to comfort and many to assail . . . led to the accusation which so aroused public sympathy against her: that she was robbing the nation's House, and carrying the national property with her into retirement. This accusation, which clings to her to this day, was probably unjust.

"The public also did Mrs. Lincoln injustice in considering her an illiterate, ignorant woman. She was well born, gently reared, and her education above the average given to girls in her youth. She had quick perceptions and an almost unrivaled power of mimicry. . . . Can write a more graceful letter than one educated woman in fifty. . . .

"The career of Mrs. Lincoln had chilled the people to expect little from the feminine administrator of the White House, but from Martha Patterson they received much. . . . From the nation's Home which they had redeemed and honored, the Johnsons went back. . . ."

Poore wrote of the ball given in February 1862:[1] "Most of the Senate was present, but not many from the House. . . . There was no dancing, nor was it generally known that Mrs. Lincoln had been up the two nights previous watching at the bedside of her two sick children. Both the President and Mrs. Lincoln left the gay throng several times to go up to see their darling Willie. . . . The Abolitionists throughout the country were merciless in their criticism of the President and Mrs. Lincoln for giving this reception when the soldiers were in cheerless bivouacs or comfortless hospitals, and a Philadelphia poet wrote a scandalous ode on the occasion, entitled, *The Queen Must Dance*."

Mrs. Keckley wrote:[2] "I do not forget, before the public journals vilified Mrs. Lincoln, that ladies who moved in the Washington circle freely canvassed her character among themselves. They gloated over many a tale of scandal that grew out of gossip in their own circle."

W. O. Stoddard, writing out of his experiences while resident in the White House, said:[3]

"People in great need of something spry to write about or talk about are picking up all sorts of stray gossip related to assorted occurrences under this roof, and they are making strange work of it. It is a work they will not cease from.

"The fact that she [Mrs. Lincoln] has so many enemies strikes you as one of the curiosities of this venomous time, for she never in any way has harmed one of the men or women who are so recklessly assailing her. She says she is willing to do her duty and to sit through the evening while

[1] Bibliography, No. 141, p. 121.
[2] Bibliography, No. 85, Preface, p. 15.
[3] Bibliography, No. 168, p. 52.

her guests are pulling her to pieces. . . . Every woman who has yet arrived has come as a critic, and not one of them will be capable of doing her kindly justice. They will show no mercy. . . .

"She was well educated, of good family, and was noted for her keenness of wit. She was well prepared for her duties in Washington. But that she should make a success here, under such circumstances, under the focalized bitterness of all possible adverse criticisms, was simply out of the question. . . . She has done vastly better than ill-natured critics are willing to admit. They are a jury impaneled to convict on every count of every indictment which any slanderous tongue may bring against her, and they have already succeeded in so poisoning the popular mind that it will never be able to judge her fairly. . . .

"She is accused of being a traitor. . . .[1]

"Mr. Lincoln's vilest foes are writing direct to Mrs. Lincoln. They are willing to vent their infernal malice upon his unoffending wife. . . .[2]

"Society women call socially in pretended exchange of social courtesies, but really in order to gather ammunition with which to attack her. . . .[3]

"She has no lack of visitors, but the old-time society of the city of Washington has been shattered to its foundations and the social structure of the new takes form slowly."

Stoddard depicted the charm of this old-time society — which he calls antediluvian — its grace and its beauty; but he states that it was an aristocracy founded on slavery; it sensed that its day was at an end, and it used all its powers to checkmate the forces that were destroying its position. Such is human nature and always has been, and on all social levels.

Charles Francis Adams tells of a visit to Mrs. Eames's salon, saying: "If the President caught it at Sumner's dinner, his wife caught it at Mrs. Eames's reception. All man-

[1] Bibliography, No. 168, p. 35. [2] Ibid., p. 36. [3] Ibid., p. 176.

ner of stories about her were flying around. She wanted to do the right thing but, not knowing how, was too weak and proud to ask. Servants are leaving because they must live with gentlefolks."

W. H. Russell wrote in the London *Times:*[1] "I was agreeably disappointed in Mrs. Lincoln, as the 'secesh' ladies in Washington had been amusing themselves by anecdotes which could scarcely have been founded on facts." He went to a reception at the White House, March 30, 1861, and wrote: "Only two or three ladies were in the drawing-room. The Washington ladies have not yet made up their minds that Mrs. Lincoln is the fashion."

Barton[2] gives some of the abusive things that were said of Mrs. Lincoln, among them: that she did not love her husband and was planning to elope with a Russian count; that she was a Confederate spy in touch with the Confederate Army through her relatives, some of whom visited at the White House—in ribald songs around campfires her name was joined with that of Jefferson Davis; that she was heartless and vain, giving balls and dinners when the nation was in distress, and war was levying its toll; that she discontinued state balls and dinners to save her money; that she neglected her husband to travel. These stories Barton pronounced "as false as they were foul." He says of her that she was loyal to the country and to her husband.

Among other charges against Mrs. Lincoln, found cited in Honoré Willsie Morrow's book and in other places, were these:[3]

A cabinet member accused her of falsifying the White House accounts in 1862.—Lincoln beat his wife while drunk.—Lincoln forbade Sumner the house because of indiscretions with Mrs. Lincoln.—"There are spies in the White House."—"Mrs. Lincoln is a spy."

So far as her Washington social aims were concerned,

[1] Bibliography, No. 121.
[2] Bibliography, No. 9; No. 11; No. 15, p. 334.
[3] Bibliography, No. 121, No. 122, and No. 11.

Mrs. Lincoln was a failure. For this undertaking she had considered herself highly qualified. She had embarrassed herself financially in securing an equipment of clothes and jewelry. She had taken the job seriously and had set about it with her accustomed energy and aggressiveness. The opposition had been too strong for her. The hostility of the social atmosphere in March 1861 she had failed to change. She heard many of the charges against her. They hurt her; they seared!

MOURNING

Within these four years Mrs. Lincoln suffered two of the three major tragedies of her life. Her emotional reactions to these two deaths left her a wreck. Her recovery from the first was incomplete when the second blow fell. Her financial worries after June 1865 were so great that she appeared to recover from the second loss with a rapidity that was not expected. She sought support for her pension bill rather than listeners for the story of her sorrows. The recuperation was superficial, however — the marks were on her soul to the end of her journey.

THE DEATH OF WILLIE

In February 1862 the Lincolns lost Willie, their third son. Elizabeth Grimsley wrote of Mrs. Lincoln:[1] ". . . and with it [Willie's death] had gone part of the doting mother's heart also, which was never more to find peace and comfort, mourning and refusing to be comforted, as only such impassioned natures yield to grief."

Mrs. Lincoln did not attend the funeral of this son. Nor did she ever attend the funeral of any of her immediate family.

Mrs. Keckley, writing of March 1862, said[2] that so

[1] Bibliography, No. 67.

[2] Bibliography, No. 85.

prolonged and profound was her depression that Mr. Lincoln once put his arm around her and, pointing toward a hospital for the insane which lay within view, made the remark: "Mary, if you do not control yourself we will have to put you over there."

Emilie Todd Helm is the authority for the statement that, subsequent to the death of Willie, Mrs. Lincoln had hallucinations. An entry in her diary, made while she was a guest in the White House in October 1863, reads:[1] "After I had said good-night and gone to my room last night, there was a gentle knock at the door and Sister Mary's voice said, 'Emilie, may I come in?'"

Mrs. Lincoln then attempted to console Mrs. Helm on the recent death of her husband by telling her the dead still lived and could visit their loved ones. Quoting Mrs. Lincoln from the diary: "'. . . When my noble little Willie was first taken from me there was not a ray of light. . . . If Willie did not come to comfort me I would still be drowned in tears, and while I long inexpressibly to touch him, to hold him in my arms, and still grieve that he has no future in this world that I might watch with a mother's heart — he lives, Emilie. He comes to me every night and stands at the foot of my bed with the same sweet, adorable smile he has always had; he does not always come alone; little Eddie is sometimes with him, and twice he has come with our brother, Alex.'"

And Mrs. Helm continues: ". . . It is unnatural and abnormal, it frightens me. It does not seem like Sister Mary to be so wrought up. She is on a terrible strain and her smiles seem forced."

THE DEATH OF LINCOLN

The death of the President came to Mrs. Lincoln without preparation. In August 1866 she said to William H.

[1] Bibliography, No. 73, p. 226 ff.

Herndon:[1] " I often told Mr. Lincoln that God would not let any harm come to him. He had passed through four long years — terrible and bloody years — unscathed." In his account of Lincoln's death W. J. Ferguson says:[2] " Mrs. Lincoln was the first person to realize what had happened. She sprang to the front of the box and called for someone to stop the escaping murderer. Then she sank back in a chair, apparently in a daze. The account which pictures Mrs. Lincoln's dress as covered with blood is incorrect, since no blood flowed from the wound until the bearers started with the wounded man to the house across the street." The general contemporary reports picture Mrs. Lincoln as following crying loudly, almost yelling, in her grief. Poore wrote: " Mrs. Lincoln in a frantic condition was assisted in crossing the street, uttering heart-rending shrieks." The descriptions of her mourning subsequent to the night of his death use such terms as " convulsions," " spasms of grief," " convulsive sobbing," as was the case when Willie died. She remained in bed for several weeks, her violent emotional outbreaks painful to hear and very distressing to all. She did not attend her husband's funeral, but she did insist that Willie's body be carried home with that of his father.

For several weeks President Johnson was not able to function from the White House, because Mrs. Lincoln's sorrow had so undermined her health that she could not assume the task of moving.

These two violent emotional disturbances, occurring within about three years of each other, were important causes of Mrs. Lincoln's personality disintegration. After the death of Willie her conduct was very plainly toward the introvert type, and so it ran for two years. The reaction of 1864, followed by the greater normalcy of 1865, was of great assistance; but before she was well established in it, the calamity of 1865 befell her.

[1] Bibliography, No. 75a, p. 514. [2] Bibliography, No. 58.

CHAPTER SEVEN

Taking Toll

Pompey bade Sulla recollect that more worshiped the rising than the setting sun.

—Life of Pompey

INCIDENTS AFFECTING MRS. LINCOLN

May 1865 to May 20, 1875

1865 *May 4,* President Lincoln buried in Springfield, Illinois.

May 22, Mrs. Lincoln and family left Washington for Chicago; they arrived May 24 and went to the Tremont House.

May 31, Mrs. Lincoln moved to a Hyde Park boarding-house.

June 11, Mrs. Lincoln wrote to Governor R. J. Oglesby, laying down conditions as to the Lincoln tomb.

December 22, Mrs. Lincoln and Robert in Springfield; Mr. Lincoln's body transferred to tomb.

1866 Mrs. Lincoln in Chicago.

Robert T. Lincoln, in Chicago, was studying law in the office of Scammon, McCagg, and Fuller (afterwards Chief Justice Fuller).[1]

May 22, Mrs. Lincoln bought and occupied the house on West Washington Street.

September 6, Mrs. Lincoln interviewed by Herndon, St. Nicholas Hotel, Springfield.

November, Herndon delivered his lecture on Ann Rutledge and Mrs. Lincoln; Robert bitter against Herndon for the Ann Rutledge myth and other statements.

1867 Mrs. Lincoln in Chicago.

February 26, Robert Lincoln admitted to the bar.

Robert Lincoln in the firm, Scammon and Lincoln; lived with his mother at 375 West Washington Street (old number).[2]

---

[1] Edwards's Chicago Directory.

[2] Bailey's Chicago Directory.

March, Mrs. Lincoln first wrote Mrs. Keckley about selling her jewelry.

March, Mrs. Lincoln expressed bitterness against Herndon for the Ann Rutledge lecture.

April 14, President Andrew Johnson in Chicago; Mrs. Lincoln in Springfield to visit the Lincoln tomb.

May 1 (about), Mrs. Lincoln rented her West Washington Street house and moved to the Clifton House.

July, Mrs. Lincoln in Racine, Wisconsin.

September 19, Mrs. Lincoln in New York. The proposed auction episode.

October 13, Mrs. Lincoln was boarding with D. Cole, at 460 West Washington Street, Chicago (old number).

November, Mrs. Lincoln's brother-in-law, Dr. William Wallace, died.

1868 Mrs. Lincoln traveled in New England, Pennsylvania, and elsewhere. In Chicago much of the time, at the Clifton House.

Robert Lincoln was practicing law alone; living at the Tremont House.[1]

May 16, Senate failed by one vote to depose President Johnson on impeachment.

June, Mrs. Lincoln in Chicago.

July to September, Mrs. Lincoln in Cresson, Pennsylvania.

September 1, Mrs. Lincoln expected to sail for Europe, but did not.

September 24, Robert T. Lincoln married Mary Harlan.

Later in the autumn, Mrs. Lincoln with Tad went to Europe.

November, U. S. Grant elected President.

1869 *January 25,* Mrs. Lincoln's letter written from

[1] Edwards's Chicago Directory.

Frankfurt am Main, Germany, was read to the Senate.
February, Mrs. Lincoln and Tad in Frankfurt am Main.
October 12, Robert's daughter, Mary, born.
December 3, Mrs. Lincoln and Tad in London.
December 29, Mrs. Lincoln and Tad in Frankfurt am Main; Tad in school.

1870 *February 12,* Mrs. Lincoln in Florence, Italy.
March 22, Mrs. Lincoln and Tad in Frankfurt am Main; Tad in school.
May to August, Mrs. Lincoln and Tad in Germany; Tad in school.
May 2, Mrs. Lincoln's pension bill passed the House.
May 19, Mrs. Lincoln visited Tad in school at Ober Ursel, near Frankfurt.
June 29, Mrs. Lincoln in Frankfurt am Main.
July 14, The pension bill passed the Senate.
August 17, Mrs. Lincoln in Frankfurt am Main.
September 1 to December, Mrs. Lincoln and Tad in England.

1871 *January and February,* Mrs. Lincoln and Tad in London; Tad in school.
March, Mrs. Lincoln and Tad sailed for home; Tad ill.
May, Mrs. Lincoln and Tad were staying with Robert Lincoln and family on Wabash Avenue in Chicago; Tad's illness continued.
June, Mrs. Lincoln and Tad at the Clifton House; Tad seriously ill.
July 15, Tad died at the Clifton House; funeral from Robert's home on Wabash Avenue; burial in Springfield.

1872 and 1873 Mrs. Lincoln's name not in Chicago or Springfield directories.[1]

---

[1] I have found nothing which tells definitely where Mrs. Lincoln was between the autumn of 1871 and the spring of 1874. There is no record on the subject, and

1874 Mrs. Lincoln's name reappeared in the Lakeside Directory of Chicago; address, Grand Central Hotel.
April 6, Mrs. Lincoln sold the Washington Street house.
Summer, Mrs. Lincoln in Waukesha, Wisconsin, drinking the waters for her health.
Winter, Mrs. Lincoln in Florida.
1875 *Until March 12,* Mrs. Lincoln in Florida.
April, Mrs. Lincoln at the Grand Pacific Hotel, Chicago.
May 19, Mrs. Lincoln tried for sanity.

---

no letters written by her during this period have come to light. She was in Chicago at times, for Dr. Willis Danforth testified that he treated her after Tad died and prior to 1875; she was living in Hyde Park when he treated her. She probably was in Chicago in April 1874, when she sold her house. Mrs. Fitzgerald, who was her companion nurse, says that Mrs. Lincoln was often in Springfield and traveled considerably. These are about the only known facts for these years.

CHAPTER SEVEN

Taking Toll

AFTER A PERIOD OF EMOTIONAL ILLNESS WHICH CONfined her to bed, and the length of which irked many people, Mrs. Lincoln left the White House, May 22, 1865, and went with her family to Chicago. There she lived rather obscurely, simply, and inexpensively for several years. She spent most of the time in boarding-houses, though she lived at the Clifton House for a while, and for another period in the house she purchased on West Washington Street.

She devoted her attention to Tad. She dabbled somewhat in spiritualism, and she visited her husband's tomb from time to time. She traveled a good deal, sometimes to the mountains and other resorts because this was the period in which she gave most evidence of ill health. Other trips were for the purpose of attempting to sell her wardrobe and of promoting her pension bill. There was one long European trip, the ostensible purpose of which was to educate Tad. The underlying purpose unquestionably, however, was to escape the bitter debate when the pension bill should come up in Congress. By that time the auction episode had taught her what politicians and newspapers could do in this line, and doubtless Senator Sumner had warned her what to expect. Possibly another reason for this trip was her poor health; this she gave when discussing her proposed journey. She had planned to go to Europe earlier than she did, and had even engaged passage. She assigned her poor health and her poverty as reasons for waiting. Probably the marriage of her son Robert was also a factor.

Within one week of Mrs. Lincoln's arrival in Chicago from Washington (May 24, 1865), she was in a quarrel with Governor Oglesby and the Lincoln Monument Commission, but this disagreement was not serious. In it she was opposed editorially by the Springfield *Journal;* but she was supported by the Chicago *Tribune*. She won most of her contentions, and, having been victorious, she appeared to be satisfied. When Lincoln's body was moved to its permanent resting-place, on December 22, 1865, Mrs. Lincoln and Robert went to Springfield to witness the transfer. Tad, being in Racine at school, did not go. Elizabeth Keckley mistakenly writes [1] that Mrs. Lincoln did not visit her husband's grave until April 14, 1866.

Robert knew that his mother was mentally unbalanced, for he had written his fiancée to that effect as early as 1867.[2] When Mrs. Lincoln was in Europe in 1870, she wrote her daughter-in-law affectionate letters in which there is no suggestion of bitterness against Robert; but after 1871 and until 1875 there are no letters to be found, to Mrs. Robert Lincoln or to anyone else — at least, none that I have been able to locate. Mrs. Fitzgerald was with her as an attendant, and from Eddie Foy (the actor), her son,[3] we learn that in this period the family thought it advisable to have Mrs. Lincoln guarded. That she was in Chicago part of the time is shown by the testimony of Dr. Willis Danforth. Undoubtedly she traveled a great deal — Eddie Foy's statement indicates that. Significance lies in her restlessness, and also in the fact that she avoided her family and friends.

The re-election of Lincoln in 1864 had meant a great deal to Mrs. Lincoln. It was gratifying to know that his policy had won, his wisdom been vindicated. And, then, the

---

[1] Bibliography, No. 85, p. 226.
[2] Bibliography, No. 73, p. 267.
[3] Bibliography, No. 60.

war was drawing to a close. Success in battle had helped to win the election, and winning the election had speeded the end of the war. Beyond all this the early spring of 1865 was a harbinger of hope for her. She saw a possibility of paying the bills owed the New York City and the Washington merchants — a possibility that she could not have seen if the election had gone against her husband. It is likely that Mrs. Lincoln intended to renew her struggle for social recognition. She was now in a strategic position, and the old group that had opposed her so effectively in 1861 had lost slaves, property, and caste, and were no longer able to turn "thumbs down." That she and her husband hoped to see their son Robert married to Mary Harlan, the daughter of their close friends, Senator and Mrs. James Harlan, is undoubtedly true. They hoped to see him finish his formal education and launch himself in his chosen profession. They hoped for a family of grandchildren. They would see Tad, also, finish his education and take a place in the world.

Certain it is that she had political aims. President Lincoln was contriving to present his idea of reconstruction to the country, and his wife was being given certain tasks. We can readily understand that Mrs. Lincoln in March 1865 was well out of her "Slough of Despond" and again felt herself headed for success.

When she left the White House at the end of May 1865, the picture was different. She had lost her husband, her position as First Lady of the Land, her ambitions, her hopes, and her opportunities. All was ashes. Nothing for which she had planned and striven remained to her. She had her two boys, and that was all.

After she had begun to emerge from her hysterical emotionalism, she did as it was her nature to do: she set a new goal — financial independence. The explanation of this as her objective is easily understood. Her debts were unpaid — Mrs. Keckley said they totaled $70,000 when Lincoln died. Since he left no will, his estate was to be distributed by law. The inventory showed that it amounted to over $100,000 in good securities, not counting the value of the real estate. Under the Illinois law, Mrs. Lincoln would eventually receive one third of the personal property, amounting to something less than $40,000. She needed nearly twice that amount to pay her debts. If she paid them, she would be penniless. Her creditors were not patient and could be expected to become more insistent. Even if she escaped the debts, the earnings of her widow's portion would be inadequate to meet her needs. She must get additional revenue. This became her great purpose and about her only one, beyond that of mothering her sons.

For the first time in her adult life she found herself untrained for the pursuit of her major objective. She had helped her husband to make money by saving in the Springfield days, but that experience was not adequate for the need which now confronted her. How was she to get the debts paid and to find money for her living? The story of her plans and schemes, some of them far-seeing and wise, and some foolish, will be next discussed. We cannot understand Mrs. Lincoln unless we keep in mind the mess she had got herself into, her desperate need, the objective for which she was striving, and her eventual achievement of that aim.

Before the end of June 1865 the necessity of paying the old debts became a source of trouble. In that month and for the remainder of the year Mr. Williamson and B. F. Davis were writing letters on this subject. It was proposed in Boston, New York, Philadelphia, and perhaps other cities that funds be raised by public subscription to pay the financial obligations of the widow of the martyred President. Several newspapers took up the suggestion. Mr. Williamson had a scheme for collecting money to pay them, and this met with some enthusiasm from Mrs. Lincoln at first. There are several letters to him in which she was very cordial and from which one can readily infer that she thought he was her friend and would be able to raise a substantial sum to apply on her obligations to her creditors. Later in the year the tone of the correspondence indicated that Mrs. Lincoln thought him more interested in A. T. Stewart, Lord and Taylor, and Galt and Company, than he was in the President's widow. That Williamson was quite active is shown by a letter from Secretary of the Interior James Harlan, later Robert Lincoln's father-in-law, saying that Williamson was pressing for payment of Mrs. Lincoln's debt. That he spoke from the standpoint of the creditors was evident. Mrs. Lincoln closed his relation to the matter by the following letter:[1]

Chicago, Nov. 10th, 1867.

MR. WILLIAMSON

MY DEAR SIR:

Your note is received and you will allow me to say, that I have not the least intention of going to Europe. If I should ever do so, with my present means, it would be with the hope, that I might live more comfortably there on my small income, than here. You men have the advantage of us women, in being able to go out in the world and earning a living. There need be no more correspondence on the subject of sending your daughter one of my dresses. When they are returned to me I shall do so. — I am having chills, every other day, therefore I am unable to keep up a correspondence with any one — therefore my silence, with this explanation, and with your good sense and feeling, will not be attributed to any want of friendship. I am greatly indisposed and my physician orders quiet — as little writing and reading as possible. This climate is very trying to me in the winter season. When my dresses are returned to me, I will remember my promise, I cannot do so before. My health is too poor, for me to be disturbed by idle rumors. I would gladly keep up a correspondence with yourself and other friends, if I could do so without injury to myself. At the proper time, my promise, regarding your daughter, will be kept — so there will be no more writing on the subject — I have given up housekeeping and am boarding in the plainest

[1] Original Letter in the Lincoln Collection, Brown University, Providence, Rhode Island.

manner, so I can appreciate your expression, about high prices — I wish we, all, could be unmindful of our daily necessities, by having sufficient to live upon. There is no more expensive place than Chicago. I am writing, with a fever on me after a chill — and against a positive promise given my physician. So, in the future, my silence by all friends, I hope, will be understood.

I remain, truly your friend

MRS. L.

From the summer of 1865 and until 1870 the urge to get money was an obsession with her. I have read many of her letters written between 1865 and 1871, and in most of them she complains of poverty, of the poor way in which she, Robert, and Tad are compelled to live; and always coupled with this theme is the subject of money-getting. She wrote often of people to whom Lincoln had loaned money before he went to Washington, and of measures for making them pay the estate. In one collection of her letters, there are ten written in 1866 dealing with her poverty and the humiliation and discomfort it occasioned her, and with efforts to get more money; there are eleven written in 1867 and one in 1868, dealing with these two themes.

In the later months of 1867 Mrs. Lincoln shifted her efforts to get money from the plan for a national subscription to the proposed auction.

THE WARDROBE AUCTION EPISODE

Mrs. Keckley says that Mrs. Lincoln discussed selling some of her clothing and jewelry, in order to raise money to pay her debts, as early as 1863. In 1864 she again mentioned the subject. In 1865 she told Mrs. Keckley: "We will leave the White House poorer than when we came. . . . Lizzie, I may see the day when I shall be obliged to sell a part of my wardrobe."

When she went to Chicago in May 1865, she remained there for a year or two. She and Tad boarded in the

Tremont House, the Hyde Park Hotel, the Clifton House, and in one or more boarding-houses and lived for one year in the Washington Street house. Together they had a yearly income, from Abraham Lincoln's estate, of about $3,400.

In March 1867 Mrs. Lincoln wrote Mrs. Keckley for the first time about selling her wardrobe, saying: "I cannot live on $1,700 a year." She would have to give up her house, and board. In August she wrote Mrs. Keckley to meet her in New York to arrange for the sale of her clothes. After one or two postponements they met there, September 17, 1867.

A New York firm had been in negotiation with Mrs. Lincoln for the sale of her wardrobe and jewelry and had convinced her that enough would be realized to pay off the debts and to add something to her store of bonds. The scheme was visionary and reflected discredit on the judgment of those who proposed it; it was in poor taste; it was bad political policy. Further discussion of its shortcomings is not necessary. In so far as Mrs. Lincoln was responsible for her participation, she was censurable.

But the storm which broke when the scheme was published was far beyond the limits of justice. The papers boiled with condemnation. Mrs. Keckley says: "The newspaper denunciations which particularly hurt her were those in the New York *Evening Express,* and New York *World,* and Chicago *Times*. . . . But above all, she complained of Thurlow Weed and the Albany *Evening Journal*." On January 13, 1868 Mrs. Lincoln wrote to Mrs. Orne:[1] "I understand the New York *World* is visiting its spleen and spite against the government by attacking poor me. Broken down as I am with my agonizing sorrow it might at least have spared me this cruelty."

The Albany *Journal* said editorially: "Mrs. Lincoln has dishonored herself, her country, and the memory of her lamented husband." Thurlow Weed wrote further in his

[1] Letter in the Lincoln Collection, Brown University, Providence, Rhode Island.

paper: "The Republicans, through Congress, would have made proper arrangements for the maintenance of Mrs. Lincoln had she so deported herself as to inspire respect. No president's wife ever before accumulated such valuable effects. Those accumulations are suggestive of fat contracts and corrupt disposal of patronage."

The Pittsburgh *Commercial* said: "Mrs. Lincoln, whose judgment and taste have never been rated high . . ." The Cleveland *Herald* commented: "It has been believed that charity and oblivion were the cloaks that should cover Mrs. Lincoln's career as Mistress of the White House. It took $100,000 to make good the spoliation at the White House, and let it be proved who had the benefit of such plundering." The Philadelphia *Evening Telegraph* asked how had Mrs. Lincoln managed to squander $25,000 in less than two years. The Norwich (Connecticut) *Advertiser* said: "There is a nasty history connected with this Lincoln woman's occupancy of the White House that will come out some day." The Hartford *Evening Press* wrote: "The exhibition she has recently made of herself surprises no one."

Some of the papers, and particularly the Springfield (Illinois) *Journal,* took a kindlier view, alleging that she was insane and that this proposed wardrobe sale was another proof of the fact. On October 9 the New York *Tribune* printed a letter, signed B, which said: "No doubt Mrs. Lincoln is deranged — has been for years past, and will end her life in a lunatic asylum."

The *Ohio Statesman* wrote in a different vein. It was Democratic and found here an opportunity to discredit its opponents. It said: "The bitterness and ferocity of the Republican press in their attack on Mrs. Lincoln is without a parallel in the history of newspaper warfare. Blackguards and slanderers join in the effort to traduce the wife of a man whom they profess to be without a peer. Such things are disgraceful."

Mrs. Lincoln read these abusive articles and was dumbfounded. She complained of Weed, ascribed his bitterness to an old quarrel; complained of the New York *World* and of the Chicago *Republican,* a paper owned by Bunn and other Springfield men who had fattened on patronage given them by her husband. She gained nothing by striking back; she only made matters worse.

After shifting the plan several times — Mrs. Lincoln displaying great indecision, unsound judgment, and bad taste at every turn — the matter was dropped, with some financial loss and more loss of prestige. The fight had continued for about three months when she returned to Chicago in utter rout. On January 28, 1868 she wrote to Mrs. Keckley: "I am so miserable I feel like taking my own life"; and: "The probability is I shall need few more clothes. My rest is near at hand."

In the course of time the debts were cleared up. It is said that the merchants scaled their bills somewhat. Some of the congressional appropriation of the President's salary to Mrs. Lincoln was used to pay a part; Mrs. Lincoln is said to have paid a part; and the Republican campaign committee, still another. With this the incident closed.

Soon after the passing of this auction episode, in the autumn of 1867, Mrs. Lincoln sold her household furniture to John Alston, in whose house in Hyde Park, Chicago, she was then living. She received $2,094.50, paid in two notes "given by John Alston to Mary Lincoln."

It is worth noting that this transaction, unlike the wardrobe episode, did not lead to newspaper notice or to abuse. The papers made no comment on this sale, and the politicians raised no row. Probably no one heard of it until the story appeared in the Chicago *Tribune* many years later.[1]

The household goods thus sold were doubtless some she had used when she lived on Washington Street — though

[1] March 20, 1927.

not all, for in March 1870 she wrote her daughter-in-law about things in that house:[1] ". . . Anything and everything is yours. . . . My mind was so distracted with my grief in that house, 375 [West Washington Street], I cannot remember where anything was put. It will be such a relief to me to know that articles can be used and enjoyed by you. . . ."

The knowledge of this sale to Mr. Alston is of some service in disclosing one source of Mrs. Lincoln's money. She continued to make sales of furniture, clothing, books, jewelry, and miscellaneous articles whenever that was possible. All of this is of importance, in that it shows the fixedness of her purpose to convert her personal property, such as clothes and furniture, into cash and bonds — to get all the money she could.

THE PENSION FIGHT

A much better illustration of Mrs. Lincoln's money obsession is shown by her persistent, pushing effort to get a pension. This effort was finally successful, and the victory solved her economic problem, thus offsetting some of the harm done her peace of mind as well as her personality by the rancor of the fight.

In 1868 and until 1870 she concentrated her plans and expended her energy in this cause, but ever and anon her mind would hark back to the possibilities of a national subscription. In a letter, undated, but written probably some time in the autumn of 1869, Mrs. Lincoln compared the gratitude of the country to Mrs. Rawlins with its ingratitude toward her, saying:[2]

"We have so recently seen an exhibition of the extent of the influence in the case of Mrs. Rawlins — in whose case almost a hundred thousand dollars was raised — whilst I, the beloved wife of the great and good man whose life was

---

[1] Bibliography, No. 73, p. 281.

[2] Letter in the Lincoln Collection, Brown University, Providence, Rhode Island.

sacrificed in his country's cause, have often to endure privations which I would not venture to whisper to anyone. I mention all this by way of showing you what General Grant can do if he so desires. With my knowledge of Mr. Sumner's great and noble nature, rely upon it he will highly appreciate your communication to him — and depend upon it he will be heard from regarding it. One word from General Grant could do everything — he cannot possibly withhold it. But there is one thing, my dear Mrs. Orne, I earnestly request — it is this — that whatever views your friends write you regarding the probable result of the action in Congress — do not withhold them from me even if they are not flattering to the cause. I would prefer not to deceive myself with vain hopes — and yet when I think of failure I tremble much. My situation mortifies me very much now — without a recognition either in shape of a pension or a generous allowance I can only see still greater future discomfort."

(The purpose of this letter was to secure the aid of Mrs. Orne in obtaining the pension. She especially wanted Mrs. Orne to use her influence directly and indirectly on President Grant.)

In 1927 the Springfield (Massachusetts) *News* carried the following news items: [1]

"Washington, Sept. 16 — Letters of Mrs. Mary Todd Lincoln, widow of the Great Emancipator, indicate very bitter days after her husband's decease. The country was not so grateful as it should have been. It had other heroes whom it was rewarding on a more generous scale. The letters are more than 50 years old and were recently disposed of at auction sale here.

"They were written when Mrs. Lincoln, broken in courage and health by financial and other worries that came upon her after the assassination of her husband, wrote appeals to friends in power asking them to use their

[1] September 16, 1927. Copies of these quotations were sent me by George F. Hambrecht, Madison, Wisconsin.

influence to have Congress pass an appropriation for her assistance. . . .

"Mrs. Lincoln . . . wrote to Mrs. Orne, wife of Representative Orne of Chicago, saying: 'Gen. Grant, whose services to his country were certainly "not superior" to my husband's, within the last 18 months has had three elegant mansions presented to him, a salary of $13,000 which he now enjoys. On New Year's day he is to be presented with $100,000, an elegant library in Boston, and the prospect of his being made president with his salary increased to $25,000 a year. Life is certainly "couleur de rose" for him, if it is all darkness and gloom to the unhappy family of the fallen chief.'

"The following letter was written from Marienbad, where Mrs. Lincoln had been ordered to go by her physician: 'How strangely surprising are the events that are hourly occurring in our lives! I went into F. — only 20 minutes away by rail — to get Taddie some school books — see my physician about a new medicine he had given me — and see the papers. An English paper said that Senator Conn had decided against me on the ground that I had property to the amount of $65,000. A fearful and wicked invention of the enemy, which infamous falsehood will consign me to a most painful state of existence all my days — Will your country with all its noble hearted men allow this? Neither you or I believe it — I became very sick — I was assisted into a cab — went to the house of this good friend — My physician was sent for and after seeing me he declared another attack of sickness such as I had in the winter would follow if I were hurried away — and he said that I must not leave this place.'

"There were 12 letters in all and in one on January 13, 1870 . . . she said: '. . . But do you tell me that already this Congress has given an appropriation to Grant to refurnish the White House? Whilst the wife of the great chieftain whose life was sacrificed for his country — living in an uncarpeted apartment — ill in bed without a menial to hand her a cup of cold water. It appears strange that God in His mysterious providence permits such terrible changes and contrasts. My only prayer now is that my life will soon be passed. My health has completely broken down by privation I have been called upon to pass through. . . .'

" It is surprising to learn that the nation at the time was so cold to lend any aid to the widow of the martyred President. But it is regarded as apparent that in those days the country had an eye only for the living heroes of the time and was very generous to Grant. Lincoln, it is recalled, has become great only in recent times. They used to say bad things of him in his lifetime. Now he is apotheosized to the skies and most deservedly so. If the nation did not provide the widow with a decent home to live in and a decent income, it has erected in Washington a Greek temple to the memory of Lincoln, costing more than $3,000,000. . . .

" The country has since been more generous to the widows of the Presidents and has been disposed to appropriate $5,000 a year for them. . . ."

The pension bill was drawn by Senator Sumner, or at his instigation, though he did not introduce it. It went into the Senate of the Fortieth Congress on January 17, 1869. On January 25 the Honorable Benjamin Wade of Ohio, president of the Senate, had the following letter read in the Senate chamber: [1]

To the Honorable Vice-President and Members of the Senate:

I herewith most respectfully present to the Honorable Senate of the United States an application for a pension. I am a widow of a President of the United States, whose life was sacrificed in his country's service. That sad calamity has greatly impaired my health, and by advice of my physicians I have come over to Germany to try the mineral water, and during the winter to go to Italy. But my financial means do

[1] Bibliography, No. 38, January 26, 1869.

not permit me to take advantage of the urgent advice given me, nor can I live in a style becoming the widow of the chief magistrate of a great nation, although I live as economically as I can. In consideration of the great services which my deeply lamented husband has rendered to the United States, and of the fearful loss I have sustained by his untimely death — his martyrdom, I may say — I respectfully submit to your honorable body this petition, hoping that a yearly pension may be granted me that I may have less pecuniary cares.

I remain

Most respectfully,

MRS. ABRAHAM LINCOLN

The letter was written from Frankfurt am Main, Germany, but as reproduced in the *Globe* (*Record*) bears no date and no postmark. It was referred to the Committee on Pensions, where the bill had already gone. This bill did not pass the Fortieth Congress. When General Grant was inaugurated as President, March 4, 1869, an extra session of the Forty-first Congress was called. The pension bill was reintroduced in the Senate,[1] becoming Senate Bill No. 19, and in the House, becoming House Bill No. 1950. In the Senate it was referred to the Committee on Pensions, consisting of Senators Edmunds of Vermont, Tipton of Nebraska, Spencer, Pratt, Brownlow, Schurz, and McCreery. The Senate bill never got beyond this committee, though when House Bill No. 1950 had passed the House and came into the Senate, the Senate committee report was read into the record. It was charged by Senator Sumner that the committee tried to smother the bill, and there are indications that the charge was true. For instance, one of the obstructing measures that was voted down was a motion to postpone indefinitely.

After the bill had been in the Senate for much more than a year, it was finally forced onto the floor for general debate. Many parliamentary devices were tried to defeat it without a direct vote and without open debate. There were several

[1] Bibliography, No. 45, Senate Proceedings, Forty-first Congress.

other motions that appear to have been made with intent to kill it without having a record made. Finally the issue was joined. It began with the reading of the adverse Senate committee report, which was said to have been unanimously indorsed by the committee. Senator Edmunds did not participate in the debate after his opening statement (it was said he had been ill for some time), and the burden of the opposition was carried by the second on the committee, Senator Tipton. This gentleman and several others insisted that the Senate accept the committee report as a conclusion based on deep study, and that the Senate vote be in accordance with it.

The report was drawn on legal and parliamentary lines, in the main. It opposed the bill because (1) President Lincoln was not a military officer; (2) there was no precedent for such a pension; (3) the proposal was not in line with the policy of the government; (4) Mrs. Lincoln was not destitute.

Congress had voted her $22,000 of Mr. Lincoln's salary, and the report of her husband's estate showed that it had inventoried $110,000 in bonds and stocks, of which Mrs. Lincoln's portion was $36,765.60 — a total of $58,765.60, not including her part of the real estate.[1]

So far the report was worthy of careful consideration, at least. But it proceeded to insinuate that Mrs. Lincoln had appropriated public property for her own use in "no inconsiderable amount"; that she had been the beneficiary of public subscriptions; that approximately $60,000 was enough for any American widow, though it might not be for royalty; and it closed as follows: "Other facts bearing on this subject which it is probably not needful to refer to, but which are generally known, and evidence in respect to which is in the possession of the committee," etc.

The debate was long and at times bitter. The earlier speeches in opposition, delivered by Senators Edmunds,

[1] Mrs. Lincoln did not share in the real estate.

Morrill, and Howell, were confined to the legal and precedent parts of the report. Senator McCreery said Lincoln was a frugal man and had left his wife provided for. He began the personal trend of the later discussion by criticizing Mrs. Lincoln for traveling in Europe. Senator Thurman was opposed to the bill for legal reasons; so was Senator Saulsbury. Then Senator Yates of Illinois broke into the discussion with a bitter speech, from which the following is taken: "There are recollections and memories, sad and silent and deep, that I will not recall publicly, which induce me to vote against this bill. . . . A woman should be true to her husband. . . . I will not go into details. . . . My tongue is sealed. . . . I believe that, could Mr. Lincoln speak from the abodes of heaven, he would say as I do. . . . This is not a case to which we should extend charity. . . . I happen to know that she and her family all through the war sympathized with the Rebellion."

This bitter personal tirade against Mrs. Lincoln helped to pass the bill. Senator Howell rose to say: "I utterly refuse to take cognizance of slanders against the lady." Senator Saulsbury said: "I protest here against any imputations against the character of Mrs. Lincoln." Senator Trumbull said: "She is a lady known to the country, and of her personally I need not speak. . . . The widow of Abraham Lincoln, she was his companion in the most trying period of this country's history. . . . She shall not suffer." Senator Corbett explained that Mrs. Lincoln was in Europe to educate her son. This evoked a storm of protests against education of boys in Europe and of criticisms of royalty and those who aped it. Senator Fenton said: "Mrs. Lincoln may be indiscreet, she may have forfeited a measure of the respect naturally given to one in her position; yet she is the widow of Abraham Lincoln."

Then Senator Tipton attempted to bring the discussion back to a personal basis. He referred to the wardrobe-selling episode and the consequent condemnation of Mrs. Lincoln.

Senator Cameron told of his association with Lincoln in his Cabinet: " He often talked with me about his finances. He once told me he was worth ten thousand dollars. . . . He may have saved a little while President. . . . He was a frugal man. . . . A great deal of the opposition to this bill is due to prejudice — political prejudice and social prejudice — got up in this city. . . . When Mr. Lincoln and his family came here, the society of Washington was very adverse to him or to any other Republican family that might come here, and they were in a great measure ostracized. The ladies and even the gentlemen — the gossips of the town — did all they could to make a bad reputation for Mrs. Lincoln, and they tried to do so for the President. They failed as to the President, but they did carry their venom so far as to destroy the social position of his wife." Senator Morrill said: " She has abundant stores. Anyone who knows her character knows that she does not spend her money for nothing. If she ever had it, she has it now. She should come home and educate her boy here. She should not be encouraged to go abroad."

This is what was said on the floor in open session. It found its way into the newspapers and was read by Mrs. Lincoln. What was said in open meeting was tame compared with what was said in other surroundings. Said the Committee Report: " Other facts . . . not needful to refer to, but which are generally known . . ."; those other facts which Senator Yates " will not recall publicly. . . . My tongue is sealed."

On July 14, 1870 the bill passed the Senate by a vote of 28 to 24. Twenty senators did not vote, among them Senator Harlan. Of the seven members who, Senator Tipton said, voted against the bill in committee, Senator Schurz voted for it on the floor; Senators Tipton, Pratt, and McCreery voted against it on the floor; Senator Edmunds was paired against it; and Senators Spencer and Brownlow were absent without tie.

The bill had passed the House on May 2, 1870 with the following vote: "yeas, 85, nays, 77; not voting, 77."

THE FIRST TRIP TO EUROPE

The first European trip, that of 1868 to 1871, did not meet with the full approval of Judge David Davis, Tad's guardian, but, on the other hand, he offered no great objection. The record shows that the trip caused him trouble in keeping the estate accounts straight, and he said more on that score than he did in opposition to the trip itself.

The reason Mrs. Lincoln usually gave for the trip was to secure the best educational advantages for Tad. On July 18, 1868, however, she wrote Mrs. White from Cresson, Pennsylvania, that she expected to sail from Baltimore on August 1, that her address until October 1 would be Edinburgh, and that she was going because of her own health, saying:[1] "In my very feeble health I am endeavoring to catch every mountain breeze in hopes that strength may be given me for the sea voyage before me. In my hours of great bodily suffering which now occur quite frequently . . . I am suffering so much. I am scarcely able to sit up. . . . I have brooded so much over my great loss that, with others, I now feel assured the change that I am now about making is the only thing left me to prolong my life."

Mrs. Lincoln delayed starting for Europe several months. After she got there, she wandered very little, living inconspicuously and quietly. General Adam Badeau wrote:[2] "While I was Consul-General in London, I learned of her living in an obscure quarter, greatly neglected. I went to see her and invited her to my house. She declined in fine style, her note of thanks betraying how rare such courtesies had become to her." He added: "She went abroad doing

[1] Original Letter owned by Oliver R. Barrett, Chicago, Illinois.

[2] Bibliography, No. 73, p. 272. General Badeau wrote in the New York *World;* his letter was quoted and commented on by P. L. Shipman, Louisville *Courier-Journal.*

strange things and carrying the honored name of Abraham Lincoln into strange and sometimes unfit company, for she was greatly neglected and felt the neglect." This statement is true, provided the term "unfit company" is interpreted as meaning company entirely proper, but not on Mrs. Lincoln's former social level; otherwise, it is not.

Her letters indicate that she was interested above all else in promoting the passage of her pension bill. She was resentful and bitter when she learned of supposed friends who had failed her and enemies who had abused her. Her money urge dominated her letters from Europe, but they were gracious and kindly toward the correspondents and their families. They are the letters of an intelligent and a courteous, but not a well-poised, woman. Incidentally, I do not recall a letter written by Mrs. Lincoln in this period that does not contain some reference to her poor health. Such allusions are more numerous in this period than in any other.

Almost immediately upon their arrival in Germany, Tad went into a boarding-school, and his mother located herself where she could see him frequently. This two years was a very profitable season for emotional and backward Tad. He progressed satisfactorily in his studies, for one thing. German discipline supplied just his need. There is no wonder that his brother, Robert, was well pleased with him when they met again in March 1871. He traveled with his mother somewhat, but not enough to interfere with his studies. The latter part of his foreign schooling was in England.

In the winter of 1870–1 his mother had a severe cough, and her physician advised her to go to Italy. In March, Tad and his mother started home. He may have been ill when they left Europe, for he was ill when they landed. Mother and son went on to Chicago. There Tad was ill during the entire spring, and until death took him.

THE DEATH OF TAD

The Chicago *Tribune* published the following:[1]

"At 7.30 on yesterday [Saturday] morning Tad Lincoln died at the Clifton House on Wabash Avenue, where he had been staying since his return from Europe. The cause of his death was dropsy of the chest. The first symptoms showed themselves while he was abroad, but it was not until his return, the middle of May, that his condition became alarming. The disease made its appearance in the left chest, afterwards attacking the right chest, and soon after it caused death by compression of the heart. He was convalescent at one time, but he got up one night slightly clad and swooned. This was followed by a relapse, after which he grew steadily worse. He was attended by Dr. Charles Gilman Smith."

The administrator's report to the Sangamon County Court shows that Drs. H. A. Johnson and N. S. Davis were called in consultation.

The Chicago *Tribune*[2] said that Tad's body was removed from the Clifton House to the home of his brother, Robert, on Wabash Avenue, Chicago, where there were brief funeral exercises and a sermon by a Baptist minister, after which the body was taken to the Edwards home in Springfield. The funeral services were held in the First Presbyterian Church, Springfield. The *Tribune* story also states that "Mrs. Lincoln was not able to accompany the body of her son to Springfield, owing to her complete prostration caused by her intense grief and her continued watching at the bedside."

A fatal pleurisy developing in an eighteen-year-old boy and lasting six months was probably tubercular in origin. It may have been due to infection with some microbe other than the tubercle bacillus, but the chances are against that.

About one week after Tad's death Robert wrote Judge Davis that his mother was doing as well as could be ex-

[1] July 16, 1871. [2] July 18, 1871.

pected. In writing this he measured what was to be expected by his recollection of her hysterical outbreaks on the occasion of other deaths in their immediate family. The meager information we have from other sources is that Mrs. Lincoln mourned in 1871 as she had done in 1862 and in 1865, after the deaths of her son and her husband.

Mrs. Lincoln was now a woman fifty-three years old. The physiology of a woman of that age may be such that the maintenance of emotional calm is not easy. She was passing out of the stage of life in which headaches may be prominent. After the beginning of 1865 we find but two references to her having violent headaches: one, May 22, 1865, as she left the White House; and the other, November 23, 1867, during the auction episode. She was now approaching the age when migraine and most other forms of sick headache are not a source of much trouble, but she was not quite in this zone of equanimity at the time of Tad's death.

Between 1871 and 1875 Mrs. Lincoln must have been in a very abnormal frame of mind. There is almost no record. She wrote no letters which have remained behind, talked with no people who later grew reminiscent, and created no scenes that found place in the newspapers. What we know of her life in these years is limited to what Dr. Willis Danforth testified as to her health; the reports of what her companion nurse (Eddie Foy's mother) observed; the gossip about her presence in Waukesha, Wisconsin, drinking the waters; and a stay in the mild winter climate of Florida. Mrs. Lincoln's wanderings in Europe took her several times to resorts having reputations as "cures," and more than once she reported that her physicians had advised her to go to Italy, where the breezes were balmy, or to some other place where her physical well-being would be promoted.

THE FIRST TRIAL

Mrs. Lincoln was in Florida in the winter of 1874–5. Robert, a man of prominence, married and the father of three children, was living with his family in Chicago. On March 12, 1875 Mrs. Lincoln telegraphed Dr. R. N. Isham that her son was very ill; to go to see him and to take care of him until she could get there. Doctor Isham, greatly surprised, called on Robert and found him well and at work in his office. They telegraphed Mrs. Lincoln that there was no cause for worry, and that she should remain in Florida. Persisting in her delusion, however, she started for Chicago. When she reached Chicago, Robert met her at the train and took her to the Grand Pacific Hotel, where she remained until May 20.

Her conduct was so abnormal that Robert Lincoln advised with his friends and those of his father and mother as to what should be done. Confinement in an institution seemed to be unavoidable. That could be brought about only by having an insanity investigation and trial, legal procedures which required the filing of charges. These charges, signed by Robert T. Lincoln, were duly filed.

The case was heard, May 19, 1875, by Judge M. R. M. Wallace.[1] The jury chosen to hear the evidence was: Dr. S. C. Blake, Charles B. Farwell, J. McGregor Adams, S. B. Parkhurst, Lyman J. Gage, C. M. Henderson, James A. Mason, D. R. Cameron, William Stewart, S. M. Moore, H. C. Durand, and Thomas Cogswell. Dr. S. C. Blake was city physician, and the others were the leading wholesale merchants and bankers in Chicago. The lawyers were, B. F. Ayer, Leonard Swett, and I. N. Arnold — the ablest in the city, and old friends of Mrs. Lincoln and her husband. Mrs. Lincoln was present.

[1] Bibliography, No. 46, May 19, 1875, p. 596.

The testimony against the defendant falls under three heads:

A number of people who had had opportunity to observe her behavior in the Grand Pacific Hotel during the month or more she had lived there preceding the trial related what they had seen her do and heard her say; actions that differed from ordinary, normal behavior.

A second array of witnesses, representatives of retail business houses at which Mrs. Lincoln traded, told of the reckless way in which she purchased goods — particularly dress-goods, toilet articles, jewelry, and household goods. She would buy cloth by the bolt; would purchase a store's entire stock of something. Her detailed bill at Gossage's, the principal retail dry-goods house of the time, was put in evidence.

Five physicians, Drs. Willis Danforth, R. N. Isham, N. S. Davis, H. A. Johnson, and C. G. Smith, testified. The last four gave opinion evidence. In substance, it was that Mrs. Lincoln was of unsound mind and not in mental condition to manage her property.

Dr. Danforth testified more in detail, to the effect that she was of unsound mind and incapable of managing her property:

"In 1873 I treated Mrs. Lincoln several weeks for fever and nervous derangement of the head, and observed at that time indications of mental disturbance. She had strange imaginings; thought that someone was at work on her head, and that an Indian was removing the bones from her face and pulling wires out of her eyes. I visited her again in 1874 when she was suffering from debility of the nervous system. She complained that someone was taking steel springs from her head and would not let her rest; that she was going to die within a few days, and that she had been admonished to that effect by her husband. She imagined that she heard raps on a table conveying the time of her death, and would sit and ask questions and repeat the supposed answer the table would give. . . ."

He continued: "Her derangement is not dependent on the condition of her body, or arising from physical disease. I called upon her a week ago . . . when she spoke of her stay in Florida, of the pleasant time she had there, of the scenery, and of the manners and customs of the Southern people. She appeared . . . to be in excellent health, and her former hallucinations appeared to have passed away. She said her reason for returning from Florida was that she was not well. She startled me somewhat by saying that an attempt had been made to poison her on her journey back. She had been very thirsty, and at a wayside station not far from Jacksonville she took a cup of coffee in which she discovered poison. . . . I . . . am of opinion that she is insane. On general topics her conversation was rational."

Robert Lincoln's testimony, in part, was as follows:

"I do not know why mother thought I was sick. . . . I have not been sick in ten years. . . . I met her in the car upon her arrival from the South, and upon meeting me she was startled. She had the appearance of good health, and did not seem fatigued by the trip. I asked her to come to my house, but she declined, and went to the hotel. . . . She told me that at the first breakfast she took after leaving Jacksonville an attempt was made to poison her. I occupied a room adjoining hers that night [the night after her arrival in Chicago]. She slept well that night, but subsequently was restless, and would come to my door in her night-dress and rap. Twice in one night she aroused me, and asked to sleep in my room. I admitted her, gave her my bed, and slept on the lounge. . . . About April 1 she ceased tapping at my door, as I had told her that if she persisted I would leave the hotel.

"I went to her room April 1 and found her but slightly dressed. She left the room in that condition under some pretext, and the next I knew of her she was going down in the elevator to the office. I had the elevator stopped, and tried to induce her to return to her room. She regarded my interference as impertinent, and declined to leave the elevator, but I put my arms about her and gently forced her. She screamed, 'You are going to murder me.' After a while she said that the man who took her pocketbook had promised to return it at a certain hour. She said the man was a wandering Jew she had met in Florida. She then took a seat next the wall, and professed to be repeating what the man was saying to her through the wall. . . .

"I called on her the first week in April, and she told me that all Chicago was going to be destroyed by fire, and that she was going to send her valuables to some country town. She said Milwaukee was too near Oshkosh, where there had been a terrible fire the night before. She told me that my house would be the only one saved, and I suggested to her to leave her trunks with me. The following Sunday she showed me securities for $57,000 which she carried in her pocket. She has spent large sums of money recently. She has bought $600 worth of lace curtains; three watches, costing $450; $700 worth of other jewelry; $200 worth of soaps and perfumes; and a whole piece of silk.

"I have had a conference with her cousin and Mayor Stuart, of Springfield, and Judge Davis, of the Supreme Court, all of whom advised me in the course I have taken. I do not regard it safe to allow her to remain longer unrestrained. She has long been a source of great anxiety. . . . She has no home, and does not visit my house because of a misunderstanding with my wife. She has always been kind to me. She has been of unsound mind since the death of her husband, and has been irresponsible for the last ten years. I regard her as eccentric and unmanageable. There was no cause for her recent purchases, as her trunks are filled with dresses she never wears. She never wears jewelry."

The jury brought in a verdict "that the said Mary Lincoln is insane, and is a fit person to be sent to the State Hospital for the Insane; that she is a resident . . . ; that her age is 56 years; that her disease is of unknown duration;

that the cause is unknown; that the disease is not with her hereditary; that she is not subject to epilepsy; that she does not manifest homicidal or suicidal tendencies; and that she is not a pauper." This verdict was signed by each of the jurors above mentioned.

"Whereupon, upon the verdict aforesaid, it is considered and adjudged by the Court that the said Mary Lincoln is an insane person. And it is ordered . . . that a summons be issued to the said Mary Lincoln commanding her to appear before this Court and show cause, if any she has or can show, why a conservator should not be appointed to manage and control her estate."

In accordance with the findings, Mrs. Lincoln was committed to a private sanatorium, and her son, Robert T. Lincoln, was appointed conservator.

The trial was quietly conducted, and the crowd which filled the court-room was awed and kindly. The newspapers handled the story in a very sympathetic way, both in their news columns and editorially.

In this part of Mrs. Lincoln's life there were few influences that made for the good of her personality, and many that worked against it. Among those that were most harmful were: the death of Tad and her emotional breakdown thereafter; the quarrels with the politicians and the press about the debts, including the notoriety over the auction episode; the battle in Congress over her pension; and the minor disagreement over the location of President Lincoln's tomb. She was hurt by the Herndon lectures, and this added slightly to the aggregation of woes that broke her down.

CHAPTER EIGHT

Mending Her Fences

How many women are born too highly organized in sense and soul for the highway they must walk with feet unshod.

— O. W. Holmes

MRS. LINCOLN—HER LAST YEARS

May 20, 1875 to July 16, 1882

1875 *May 20–September 10,* in Bellevue Place Sanatorium, Batavia, Illinois; thereafter with Mrs. N. W. Edwards, Springfield.

1876 In Springfield with Mrs. Edwards.
June 15, in Chicago for her second trial.
October 1 (about), left Springfield for Pau, France.
December 1, ". . . had been in Pau six weeks."

1877 *April 12,* in Pau.
Went to Marseilles and Naples.
April 22, in Sorrento.

1878 *July 4,* in Pau.

1879 *December,* in Europe, mostly in Pau.
Injured by fall.

1880 *October,* reached America.

1881 In Springfield.
Autumn, went to New York to be treated by Dr. Lewis A. Sayre.

1882 *January 16,* pension increased to $5,000 a year by Congress, which also voted her $15,000 in addition.
March, returned to Springfield.
Summer, suffered from boils; refused to go to the seashore.
July 16, died in Springfield.
Buried in the Lincoln tomb.

CHAPTER EIGHT

Mending Her Fences

THE NATURE OF MRS. LINCOLN'S IMMEDIATE REACTION to the tragic episode of her trial, the testimony she heard, and the verdict of the jury is indicated by the following extracts from the Chicago *Tribune:*[1]

"During the absence of the jury, Robert T. Lincoln approached his mother and extended his hand. She grasped it fondly, remarking with a degree of emphasis, 'Robert, I did not think you would do this.' . . . The verdict was received by Mrs. Lincoln without any visible emotions. She was stolid and unmoved. . . . Subsequently she was . . . taken to the Grand Pacific Hotel to remain over night under proper guards. . . . About 11.30 o'clock last night it was found necessary to send for an officer to watch over Mrs. Lincoln, whose lunatic symptoms became quite violent. . . ."

ATTEMPT AT SUICIDE

When the jury at Mrs. Lincoln's first trial returned their verdict, they used a form, the blanks of which they filled in. Some findings not suggested by the form were written in. One of these written-in statements was that Mrs. Lincoln ". . . had no homicidal or suicidal tendencies." The first

[1] May 20, 1875.

needs no comment, but certain events and some things Mrs. Lincoln said about suicide call for notice.

Elizabeth Keckley[1] wrote that Mrs. Lincoln once discussed suicide with her, about 1863. In January 1867 she wrote Mrs. Keckley that she was tempted to commit suicide. The danger that Mrs. Lincoln would take her own life was one possibility that was talked of at the meeting of physicians and friends held on the Saturday before May 19, 1875.

On May 21 the Chicago dailies carried a story relating an attempt at suicide made by Mrs. Lincoln the previous day. In some way she had eluded her attendants, left the hotel, gone to a drug-store in the Grand Pacific Hotel, and asked for some laudanum and camphor for neuralgia of her arm. Knowing her mental condition, the druggist told her to call again in half an hour, at which time it would be ready. When she left, he trailed her to Rogers and Smith's drug-store, Adams and Clark streets, where he heard her order the same drugs. Slipping into the prescription department, he told the clerk the circumstances, whereupon the clerk declined to sell laudanum to Mrs. Lincoln. She then went to Dale's drug-store and repeated the order, and again the sleuthing druggist was able to prevent the sale. After this she returned to the Grand Pacific drug-store and was given a bottle of colored camphor water, labeled "Laudanum and Camphor." She left the drug-store and, while under observation, drank the mixture. In ten minutes she returned for more of the same medicine. She was given a bottle of the same placebo, and this she swallowed.[2] Meanwhile her son, who had been summoned, arrived and took his mother in charge.

There is no reason to disbelieve this story because of the jury verdict, or for any other reason. Many people have momentary urges to self-destruction — many thoroughly sane people. If such people yield, it is done promptly and under impulse. There is no evidence that these urges with

[1] Bibliography, No. 85, p. 364.

[2] Bibliography, No. 38, May 21, 1875.

Mrs. Lincoln were more than momentary, or that she ever had any trouble in resisting them. The nature of her mental malady was such that efforts at suicide were not to be expected.

Prior to 1875 she never had long periods of deep melancholia, if she ever had at any time. In 1879 and 1880 she was alone in Europe. If she had wanted to commit suicide, she had ample opportunity then, not to mention the chances she had while in Springfield and New York. Experience proved this part of the verdict right.

NEW OBJECTIVES

As Mrs. Lincoln rode to the sanatorium in the private car of a railroad president, she was under the charge of the court and in the immediate care of physicians. If her eye images could have registered on her brain, she would have seen the beautiful Fox River valley in its spring robes of flowers, trees in new life, and pastures of green grass where dairy cows were grazing. It was a beautiful panorama, but it could not register. The highways into Mrs. Lincoln's brain were closed. Could her ears have registered, she would have known that birds were singing. But her mind lay covered by the ashes of her hopes, and nothing could penetrate from the outside world. Her husband and three of her children were dead; her ambitions were blasted; she had no future; her friends had deserted her; her son had more than failed her—his had been the blow that started her to Batavia; a court had decreed her insane; her property had been taken from her.

She did not long remain hopeless. Within a few days she had decided on a policy. Her first desire was to get away from the sanatorium. She set to work on this with some of her old-time energy. Again she took up her pen, not used to any great extent since her battle for a pension. When this objective was reached and she was in her sister's home, she began a drive to have the court declare her sane. Following this, she resolved to disprove the statements made by Dr. R. J. Patterson in his letter, and by witnesses at the first trial. In the summer of 1875 she had read Dr. Patterson's letter saying that she could not restrain herself; if released, she would wander continually and widely, and no one could stay her. She knew that much of the testimony at her trial related to her inability to manage her property and to her uncontrollable urge to spend money lavishly.

She made a great resolve, which dominated her conduct up to the moment of her death. She would show the world that she could restrain herself; that she could master her urge to buy like a spendthrift; that, far from being a slave to "wanderlust," she could live quietly in one place.

MRS. LINCOLN IN THE SANATORIUM

Mrs. Lincoln reached Batavia after nightfall on May 20. She remained there until the following September 10. During these several months she wrote many letters in her effort to be released; this desire was the theme of the Bradwell correspondence. She complained of the attendant's being with her constantly, of the windows' being barred, and of the loss of her property. She was considerably disturbed about nine trunks of dress-goods and curtains which had been removed to Milwaukee and were held in storage there. The agitation led the newspapers to send reporters to investigate. They found that the institution was an attractive building, in which one could recognize a little resemblance to the White House. Mrs. Lincoln had a very pleasant room. An attendant was with her. There were bars on the window. The patient was allowed much liberty, however; she and her attendant drove frequently in a carriage; she was allowed to shop in Aurora. She did not appear to be unhappy in her surroundings.

The reporters said she talked as though the sanatorium was the White House, and Mr. Lincoln was within. During much of the time when in her room, she kept the curtains drawn, and lighted the room with candles. She had great quantities of dress-goods and lace curtains, mostly in closets in unopened packages. A great deal of such merchandise had been returned to the stores that sold it to her. Some merchants made a practice of accepting her orders, delivering the goods, and then sending for them within a day or two.

The continued "battering," public and private, through newspapers and other channels, finally caused Dr. Patterson to write a letter to the press. In this he said that Mrs. Lincoln could not restrain herself, and that no one else, outside of an institution, could. If she were released, she would wander over the country, dissipating her estate. If he ever became convinced to the contrary, he would gladly recommend that she be released.

Accepting this as an honest statement, Mrs. Lincoln began a campaign, direct and indirect, to have her sister Mrs. Edwards ask that she be sent to the Edwards home in Springfield. Finally Dr. Patterson and, presumably, Robert Lincoln and Judge Wallace gave consent. On September 10, 1875 N. W. Edwards escorted Mrs. Lincoln from Batavia to his home. She remained there quietly enough until about October 1, 1876.

In June 1876 Mrs. Lincoln and Mr. Edwards asked Judge Wallace to reopen the case. The request was granted. The jury impaneled for this hearing consisted of Dr. R. M. Paddock, D. J. Weatherhead, S. F. Knowles, Cyrus Gleason, W. J. Drew, D. Kimball, R. F. Wild, W. G. Lyon, C. A. Chapin, H. Dahl, W. S. Dunham, and William Roberts. The attorney was Leonard Swett. Robert Lincoln did not appear, but he was represented as offering no opposition and waiving all technicalities. Dr. Patterson did not appear. The only witness was N. W. Edwards. He is quoted as swearing: "They say she is of sound mind. . . .

Her friends all say she is capable of managing her property. . . ." And, finally: "We think she is sane and capable of managing her property." [1]

This jury found that Mary Lincoln was sane. The conservator was ordered to make a report to the court, to restore Mrs. Lincoln's property to her, and then to be discharged.

The Chicago *Tribune* of June 16, 1876 said: "Mrs. Lincoln was adjudged sane and her property was restored to her control. The proceedings were of an amicable nature. . . . The whole proceedings occupied but a few minutes. . . ."

The action was based on a petition of Mary Lincoln in which she averred that: "She is a proper person to have the care and management of her estate." Every point in the petition relates to property. The newspaper report reads that the jury verdict was: "Mary Lincoln is restored to reason, and is capable to manage her estate."

The proceedings and the outcome of this trial indicate that there had been an agreement to declare Mrs. Lincoln sane without giving much attention to the facts. The only testimony given the jury was opinion evidence, and that, hearsay. It is a reasonable conclusion that Robert Lincoln, Mr. and Mrs. N. W. Edwards, Mrs. William Wallace, Judge John T. Stuart, and other members of the family, Mr. I. N. Arnold and other friends had agreed to let Mrs. Lincoln have her way, and believed that in doing so she would not harm herself or her estate. Events justified this agreement. After 1876 Mrs. Lincoln's mind undoubtedly was just as much disorganized as it had been in 1875, and in 1882 it was more so. But in spite of that, she so conducted herself as to justify the course her friends had taken. She carried out her resolution in spite of her personality deterioration.

[1] Proceedings, June term, County Court, 1876, Hon. M. R. M. Wallace, Judge.

THE SECOND TRIP TO EUROPE

Mrs. Lincoln remained in Mrs. Edwards's home until October 1, 1876—not much more than three and a half months after this verdict, and thirteen months after her return there from Batavia. On December 1, 1876 she was in Pau, France. A letter shows that she was there on April 12, 1877, and she probably remained until the spring of 1878, when she went to Italy.

A letter from Robert Lincoln, written to Rev. Henry Darling of New York, dated November 17, 1877, said:[1] "My mother is now somewhere in Europe but she has, for unfortunate reasons, ceased to communicate with me, and I do not know her present address although, of course, I can by writing to some of her friends obtain it in case of need."

By July 1878 she was back in Pau and suffering great pain from boils. By August her weight was down to a hundred and ten pounds. So far as we can discover, Mrs. Lincoln stayed closely in Pau, going nowhere except for one short trip, first to Marseilles and then to Italy. She seems to have taken an apartment and to have lived quietly and very much alone. She wrote few letters; in fact, I do not know of one. She was now sixty years old and considered herself in feeble health.

In December 1879 she was on a step-ladder fixing the curtains in her simple home, in which she appears to have done her own work, when she fell and hurt her back—seriously, she thought. This was in Pau. When she was able to travel, she returned to America, arriving in October 1880.

She went to Springfield, to stay in Mrs. Edwards's home. After about a year there, still troubled by the effects of her fall, she went to New York City, to be under the care of Dr. Lewis A. Sayre, the leading orthopedic surgeon of

[1] Letter in the Chicago Historical Society, Chicago, Illinois.

America in his day. (Mrs. Lincoln may have chosen him because relatives of his were prominent in the life of Lexington. They were the founders of Sayre Institute, one of the several colleges in Lexington during her residence there.)

She spent much of the winter of 1881–2 in New York City, living in a quiet, inexpensive boarding-house. In interviews, given after her death, Dr. Sayre said he did not have a very vivid mental picture of Mrs. Lincoln; she seemed to be very poor, and complained frequently of her inadequate means.

While she was under Dr. Sayre's care, Congress increased her pension to five thousand dollars a year. President Garfield had been assassinated recently, and the bill to increase this pension accompanied one for Mrs. Garfield's relief. Congress also voted her another sum of money. On this occasion Senator John A. Logan's pension and bonus bill stirred no controversy, and it went through without interference.

In March 1882 Mrs. Lincoln returned to Mrs. Edwards's home, and there remained until July 16, 1882. In the early summer she was again afflicted with boils, and was very ill and uncomfortable. Her family tried to persuade her to go to the seashore, but she would not.

Between the date when Mrs. Lincoln left Chicago for Batavia and July 1882, seven years and two months elapsed. Nearly four of these years were spent in Europe, and more than three in Mrs. Edwards's home, the remainder being divided between the sanatorium at Batavia and Dr. Sayre's in New York.

The record of Mrs. Lincoln's life at Pau is most incomplete. But she must have deported herself in a seemly fashion. She was alone, but she got into no difficulties. She is entitled to credit for self-restraint.

Laura C. Holloway writes:[1] "In the autumn of 1880 she [Mrs. Lincoln] returned to the United States. She was no better from her long journeyings. Her mind was as unsettled as it was in 1875. . . . She was, from the time of Mr. Lincoln's death, a mental and physical wreck; and it was patent to her family that she would never recover from the catastrophe which had overwhelmed her."

As to her conduct in Springfield, we have some testimony from her two sisters Elizabeth Edwards and Frances Wallace and from Dr. T. W. Dresser; that of various of her relatives given in personal communications, and of several friends, likewise given. This is substantially what they all agree on:

She lived very quietly in her sister's home. Her room was on the second floor, where she remained nearly all the time. Frequently during the day she would have the curtains drawn and candles lighted, as she had done in the sanatorium. She would see no one in her room except relatives and close friends. There were times when she refused to see even her sisters.

Her rooms were cluttered with silks and other dress-goods and lace curtain material. One relative said there were sixty trunks and boxes. There was an excess of jewelry.

At intervals her conversation showed that her mind was quite disordered, but most of the time she talked very sensibly. She did not have storms or tantrums; was not demonstrably emotional; had no " spells "; spoke much about her dead; had many spiritualistic trends; cherished some animosities; liked to discuss people and to gossip. Most of her gossip was about people she once knew well and events of the past.

Callers on Mrs. Edwards sometimes saw her pass through the halls. She did not speak, as a rule. She was likely to be dressed in black, and sometimes overdressed. Occasionally she would chat of the old days with some visiting friend

[1] Bibliography, No. 80, p. 544.

thus encountered. The children of the town, going to school, would pass the Edwards home in some awe because of stories they had heard.

When Mrs. Edwards drove out, she was sometimes accompanied by Mrs. Lincoln. On these occasions Mrs. Lincoln sat in a rear corner of a closed carriage. Stopping in front of the stores, Mrs. Edwards would go inside to shop while Mrs. Lincoln remained in the vehicle. At times old friends would go to the conveyance to hand in bundles or to assist Mrs. Edwards, and Mrs. Lincoln would speak to them quietly.

B. F. Stoneberger[1] describes her in this period as a frail, small woman who would go into a dry-goods store, purchase some dress-goods by the yard, throw her purchases across her arm, and go away. Those who saw her making purchases would repeat stories of her trunks of unused dress-goods.

Summing it up, her behavior in Springfield, before going to Europe and afterwards, was that of a calm, quiet woman, sixty years old, indulging in memories, nursing her dislikes, occasionally rebelling against her immediate family and friends, but usually quiet and inoffensive; hoarding her possessions, but with no interest in them.

She had a mild, emotional insanity which caused her to act as does a case of schizophrenia[2]—living alone, apart, and letting the world take care of itself.

[1] Personal narrative.

[2] "Bleuler's term for dementia precox, representing split personality." Bibliography, No. 48.

CHAPTER NINE

Financial Security and Insecurity

The horse doth with the horseman run away.

— Abraham Cowley

CHAPTER NINE

Financial Security and Insecurity

As THE RESULT OF THE 1875 TRIAL OF MRS. LINCOLN, the jury wrote into the verdict the following:[1] ". . . to show cause, if any she has or can show, why a conservator should not be appointed to manage and control her estate." Her son, Robert T. Lincoln, was appointed conservator, and shortly thereafter the estate was turned over to him. Much of the testimony in this first trial had been to the effect that Mrs. Lincoln was not mentally in condition to manage her business affairs.

The result of the 1876 trial was a verdict[2] which read in part: "Mary Lincoln is restored to reason and is capable to manage her estate." This decision was responsive to testimony the jurors had heard from Ninian W. Edwards, the only witness who testified. In accordance with it Robert T. Lincoln filed his report, which was approved, and the conservator was discharged.

That these sanity trials should have revolved round matters of money was natural, since aberrations on this subject were an outstanding quality of Mrs. Lincoln's thinking at the time of her court appearances and for many years prior thereto. Worry about finances was not the fundamental cause of her mental disturbance, but financial worries largely contributed to the process of change through which her mind and personality went. Many of her great difficulties

[1] Bibliography, No. 46, 1875.

[2] Ibid., 1876.

arose out of controversies over money and property. When her intellectual processes had become disordered, money and property dominated her talk, her letters, and her acts. Though they did not originate her trouble, they contributed to it and finally characterized it.

Levi, her grandfather, and Robert S. Todd, her father, appear to have had property acquisitive qualities of mind of no small order, but these functioned easily and always within the limits of normalcy. Levi, having returned from war, acquired fine farming properties in the Blue-Grass region of Kentucky and owned a good home property adjoining that of Henry Clay, in the close vicinity of Lexington. Robert S. Todd was a banker, a merchant, a manufacturer, a farmer, and a politician. He was a good illustration of the " business man in politics." He frequently held offices of profit, and there was never a charge that he did not know and did not always respect the laws of *" meum et tuum "* in his business relations. He wanted what was coming to him, but he respected the rights of others.

Mrs. Lincoln's grandfather on her mother's side willed his considerable property to his widow, but entailed it to his descendants. The widow handled the property well. At her death the heirs fell into dispute, and litigation over the estate followed. And about this time the Robert S. Todd heirs — some of them also Parker heirs — were quarreling and litigating over their father's estate. This somewhat different behavior or mental quality, as well as the financial happenings themselves, is significant in a study of the personality and mentality of Mrs. Lincoln.

We know nothing positive about Mary Todd's finances when she lived in Lexington, and such consideration as is given them must be based on inference. Robert S. Todd, her father, was a business man of standing, who lived in a good house and moved in the best circles. He certainly earned enough to keep his family well and to accumulate property.

The children of the first wife spent some of their time in the very fine home of their mother's mother, the " Widow " Parker. Her grandmother was fond of Mary and doubtless gave her much. However, the Todd family was a large one; there were fourteen children who were reared, supported, educated, and established by their father. The scale of living in Lexington, in the social group in which the Todds moved, was high for that time, though it would not be now; society was not then on a basis of competitive expenditure.

We can infer that Mary Todd the child and Mary Todd the young woman never suffered for the comforts of life; always had plenty of food and good clothing, and the privilege of buying what she needed. She should never have had any of those money longings that corrode the characters of some people, both rich and poor. It is also a reasonable inference that Mary Todd was never able to be lavish in the expenditure of money or to be extravagant, had she cared to be. Probably she did not care to be. The best conclusion is that the money hunger which Mrs. Lincoln later showed was not present when she was in Lexington.

There is no information as to how Elizabeth Edwards's sisters were financed when they lived with her. Her statements show that she wrote to Frances and Mary in Lexington, offering them a home with her. This may have meant that when they lived in her home, they were at no expense for board, lodging, and laundry; but it does not mean that the hostess sister paid for their clothes, their travel, or their incidental expenses. We may infer that Mr. Todd must have given his daughters money to pay the expense of travel and incidentals when they left home. They went away with clothing, and no doubt he sent money to them from time to time afterwards, though not a great deal. The home ties were strained; not many letters were exchanged; Frances and Mary both married in Springfield with none of the family from Lexington in attendance. It is not likely that there was a monthly allowance, for such was not customary. Money was more probably sent at irregular intervals, and on request.

The accounts of Mary Todd's life in Springfield do not show that she dressed extravagantly. Her clothing was appropriate, but it was not indicative of "money to burn." In one of Frances Wallace's statements [1] about the Lincoln-Todd wedding and the white silk dress someone said her sister wore are these sentences: "Mrs. Lincoln never had a white silk dress in her life till she went to Washington to live. After I was married I gave her my white satin dress and told her to wear it until it got soiled, but then to give it back to me. She was not married in it. It was too soiled. She may have married in a white Swiss muslin, but I think not. I think it was delaine or something of that kind."

After their wedding Mr. and Mrs. Lincoln boarded at the Globe Tavern, for four dollars a week; next they moved into a rented house on Monroe Street; and after that they bought a simple, inexpensive house. During the first decade of married life there were financial worries. Lincoln helped his father's family with some contributions, and he paid off the New Salem debts. He supported his own family. He was playing the political game, and that was, and is, expensive for an honest man with high standards. His earnings at the bar were not large, and he held a paying office only once, and that for but two years. I. N. Arnold [2] estimated Lincoln's income from his law practice at from two thousand to three thousand dollars a year, saying that he had a very large, and it might have been a very lucrative, practice, but that his fees were ridiculously small. Two to three thousand dollars a year was the annual income according to William H. Herndon,[3] who knew better than anyone else. It is also the figure given by J. F. Newton.[4]

Lincoln was a frugal, thrifty man; he met his obligations

[1] Bibliography, No. 181.
[2] Bibliography, No. 4, p. 83.
[3] Bibliography, No. 75a, p. 447.
[4] Bibliography, No. 127, p. 43.

and in addition put away some money. There are records that show him lending money comparatively early in his married life. The account which he ran at Smith's store, and which can still be seen in Springfield, includes such items as cloth, buttons, and thread and indicates that Mrs. Lincoln made the children's clothes as well as some of her own and Mr. Lincoln's, and that they lived modestly and sensibly. That she had a reputation in Springfield for being careful is shown in the letter written by her cousin Mrs. Grimsley, from Washington, in which Mrs. Lincoln is said to be living frugally there, as she did in Springfield. Newton says:[1] "During the first four years after he left Congress he was often hard pressed for money." Oliver R. Barrett does not think that Mrs. Lincoln suffered any privation in this period. I agree with him, at least to this extent: the deprivations of the period were not considerable enough to have left any harmful effects on her personality. They probably did Mrs. Lincoln more good than harm. There must be some more plausible origin of her money hunger than this.

In the decade between 1851 and 1861 the Lincoln finances improved considerably. Dr. William E. Barton says that "the financial pressure eased up." This is reflected in the family expenditures. The Lincolns were entertaining and giving even elaborate parties. They could not keep up with the Edwardses in such matters, but they were somewhat in the game. This called for more money to be spent on the household, and also for finer clothes and more of them. A second story was build on the house, and other additions were made; some town real estate was purchased. Except the Bloomington property, all of this real estate was still included in the Lincoln estate in 1865. There was more money to loan. In this period there were good fees and retainers. The Parker and the Todd estates were settled and they added something, though it was not a great amount. There are reasons for thinking that Lincoln made a little

[1] Ibid.

more than he spent during each year of the period. His friends Arnold and Whitney say that when he went to Washington he had accumulated ten thousand dollars. This estimate was conservative, at least. Herndon, however, quotes Lincoln as saying, in 1858:[1] "I am absolutely without money now even for household expenses."

Just as in the previous decade, we fail to find in the experiences of these ten years any adequate explanation of the money hunger which characterizes Mrs. Lincoln's conduct between 1865 and 1875. It is natural to suppose that Mrs. Lincoln had desires for the finery she saw other women wear, and to spend as they spent, and in the "Springfield tradition" there are statements that she spent a good deal on clothes and personal adornment. All of this has some weight, but it does not give enough basis for a quality that became so dominant.

As Mrs. Lincoln laid her plans for Washington, she knew that her husband was to have one uphill fight and she was to have another. His party was new to Washington, and there was prejudice against it there. She must not hamper him by letting Washington regard her as uncouth or, worse still, as a frump. On the other hand, if she could win Washington society, she would be able to help him win his battles. This story needs no chart for women readers, nor is it new matter for husbands. She had the society manner; she knew form and ceremonial; she knew polite conversation. She needed clothes and jewelry, and with those she felt that she could hold her own or better. They must be good clothes and of the latest style.

In January 1861 she went to New York, and there began the foundation for her major trouble. She bought what was necessary for her campaign, as she saw it. Her brother-in-law the Springfield merchant was there to advise her and otherwise to help. She had the advice of New York merchants who knew the Washington game better than she

[1] Bibliography, No. 75a, p. 447.

did. When she finished buying, her bill called for a larger sum of money than she had and more than she felt she could ask her husband for or even tell him of. Just here she made her second crucial mistake, in keeping from her husband all knowledge of her debt. Her first error was one of judgment; her second was that and something more.

Mrs. Keckley[1] was quoting Mrs. Lincoln's arguments in explaining why she piled up her enormous debt. She wrote that Mrs. Lincoln was very much aware of the dignity of her position as Mistress of the White House, and of the need that she should make a proper display of dresses and jewelry. Soon after she arrived at the White House, she sent for Elizabeth Keckley, who, she had heard, was an excellent dressmaker and reasonable in her prices. After driving some close bargains Mrs. Lincoln engaged Mrs. Keckley to make sixteen dresses. Subsequently, she kept her busy working overtime, trying to make dresses as fast as she bought material. Work as hard as she would, Mrs. Keckley never could catch up; the supply came in too fast. After the President's death Mrs. Lincoln said the Republican politicians must pay those bills. She had contracted them because, as the wife of the first Republican President, she had to make a proper showing.

In spite of her efforts, the social battle went against her. She decided that one way to improve her chances was to buy more clothes and jewelry — another error in judgment. By now the bills had reached a figure that made it difficult for her to see a way out. Very good business men have gradually become mired financially, with no recognition of financial danger until suddenly they have discovered themselves trapped with no hope of escape. Now she had genuine financial worries, and there was that most trying complication — her husband did not know, and a confession might have to come. The foundation of a money urge was appearing. Many a good business man has known the experience of

[1] Bibliography, No. 85, pp. 28, 144, 147.

having one exhibition of bad business judgment lead to another and then to a succession of them. Finally Mrs. Lincoln's debts mounted, Mrs. Keckley says, to seventy thousand dollars, nearly as much as her husband's salary as President for three years. Mrs. Lincoln's thinking was fast getting to the point where " bad judgment " is not the term that best fits it. Worry over the debts, and anxiety about her husband's reaction, were being piled on top of disappointments in social recognition, the bitterness of political animosities, and the emotions due to loss of relatives and friends in the Civil War.

Then came the plan for a second term. She saw in that her salvation. Certainly it gave her a breathing-spell, a ray of hope; and, in so far as it did, her decision to help bring it about was good judgment. How it was going to save her, one cannot easily see. Viewed from this standpoint, her judgment was still poor. Every business man, however, has seen cases in which luck or inventiveness or originality or something opens a way out of situations that seemed hopeless. We think of business men who have accepted such chances and won as being "brave," "courageous," "willing to take a chance," and as having both rare judgment and keen foresight. If they take the chance and lose, opinion does not deal so pleasantly with them.

With the assassination of Lincoln, down went his wife's house of cards.

On September 12, 1865 Mrs. Lincoln wrote Judge David Davis, relating a conversation she had had with her husband in March, at City Point. The war was being won, peace was in sight, and four more years of position and power were to be their lot. He apparently relaxed and became domestic, confiding, and forthright, as he had been before the pressure of the presidency had made it well-nigh impossible for him to be Lincoln the husband. He told his wife of his yearning for peace and quiet, of his desire, finally, to be buried in a silent, country churchyard; then he spoke of his finances. She wrote of what Lincoln had told her: he had saved his money until he had enough capital so that the expense of living could be borne by the interest from his investments; he hoped to save all of his salary for the four years between 1865 and 1869.

Upon his death Lincoln's estate went into court, and Judge Davis was appointed the administrator. Since there was no will, and Tad was a minor, we can follow the family finances quite well during the next seven years. Judge Davis's reports were made periodically. They are official and public records, copies of which are in the Illinois State Historical Society Library, where I have studied them. Illinois law provides that the children receive the real estate, and Mrs. Lincoln's share was limited to one third of the stocks, bonds, and other personal property of her husband's estate. The real estate consisted of the homestead in Springfield, one town lot in Lincoln, one hundred and twenty acres of farmland in Crawford County, Iowa, and forty acres in Tama County, Iowa. The report of the Committee on Pensions, United States Senate, Fortieth and Forty-first Congresses, reads: "The report of her husband's estate shows that it inventoried $110,000 in bonds and stocks, and Mrs. Lincoln's portion was $36,765.60. Her yearly income from the estate was given at $1,700." The usual figures given elsewhere range from $1,700 to $2,000 a year.

Here was the situation that confronted her: She owed somewhere between $27,000 and $70,000, and she had $36,765.60 with which to pay the debt; or, not paying the debt, she had a yearly income of $1,700, the interest on her bonds. Outright payment of the debt by her was impossible. Her $1,700 a year income was not enough for her to live on and make any payment on the debt. She could not expect much help from her sons; Tad, the minor with his property in the hands of the court, had the same annual income as she, and Robert was not established in a profession or in business. Congress gave her $22,000 of her husband's salary for the year. She used some to pay on the debt and a part to live on, but most of it went to buy the house in Chicago, which cost her $18,000. Let us say that all of this should have gone to paying her debts; at least, she should not have used any of it to buy a house. But would it have been wisdom to throw all of the money into a hole that it would not nearly fill?

Buying the house proved to be poor judgment. She sold it for $20,000, it is true, making $2,000 on the investment; but she found its upkeep so expensive that she could not afford to live in it, and during the eight years she owned it, the rent received did not much more than pay taxes, upkeep, and interest on investment. This purchase might be called something worse than poor judgment, but many a business man, lawyer, or even court has viewed leniently a widow's efforts to acquire a home.

Mrs. Lincoln's dilemma was great. She tried to get the merchants to take back most of the material they had sold her, it is said; but they could not see the business advantage of doing so. In the last half of 1865 an effort was made to collect money to pay Mrs. Lincoln's debts. The several letters from Mrs. Lincoln to Mr. Williamson and others show her very anxious to have this movement succeed. There is no record that any money was collected in this particular drive, though it is generally thought that political associates of her husband helped in the final settlement of the debts. Meanwhile she offered some of her dresses and jewelry at private sale, but few came forward to buy.

Then came the awful mistake of the attempted auction. Most of the responsibility for this mistake should be borne by others, but Mrs. Lincoln was a willing party to it, abetted it, and schemed and planned to make it go. Mrs. Keckley said that in money matters in the White House days Mrs. Lincoln was "penny wise and pound foolish." Even stronger terms must be used to designate the blunder of the proposed auction. This episode probably increased rather than diminished the debts, though not to any considerable extent.

Not long after that, and before her petition to Congress for a pension, the debts had been settled somehow and they no longer harassed Mrs. Lincoln.

The settlement of the debts left her with $1,700 a year income for herself, and a like amount for Tad. Judge Davis's accounts show that she pooled her income and his, but in spite of this they found it difficult to pay household expenses, bills for clothing, and tuition and educational expenses for the boy. The correspondence shows that the administrator worked diligently, but without entire success, to keep the accounts within the technicalities of legal requirements.

About a year after the end of the auction fiasco, the question of a pension for Mrs. Lincoln was raised. When the Committee on Pensions made its report, it claimed to think that Mrs. Lincoln had an estate of $60,000. The members knew all about the debts; they knew she had been confronted with a debt said to be $70,000, and that some of her money had gone for that. Men on that Committee had probably contributed to the fund that helped finally to pay off the debt—one of the senators referred to a subscription for her. Senator Tipton, who was conducting the opposition, alluded to the proposed auction as having contributed to her assets. He knew it had not, and he should have known that it actually added a little to her liabilities. They charged her with bad faith, but, while her course is not wholly defensible, it was fully as above-board as theirs. She finally received a pension of $3,000, and that, with her $1,700 income from the estate, put her in a very comfortable financial position.

Judged by the result, this strife for a pension showed wisdom on Mrs. Lincoln's part. But her efforts to accomplish the end and especially the letters she wrote—the method she employed—subjected her to criticism. Her correspondence in pushing her claim was voluminous, and many of her letters dealing with the matter are available now. In these letters she often showed bad taste. She was persistent, intrusive, and often unfair. Her urge for money had become pathologic.

In 1870 Mrs. Lincoln's pension of $250 a month was begun. Tad was of college age, the hostile comment on Mrs. Lincoln quieted, and early in the next year they came home from Europe. One year after payments of the pension began, Tad died.

When Tad Lincoln died, he was still a minor, and consequently his estate was under the control of the Sangamon County courts and Judge Davis as guardian and administrator. The reports of the administrator, as shown by the court record, set forth that Tad owned liquid assets worth, at face value, $37,065.16, principally in United States gold bonds. Judge Davis reported that the estate also owned a half-interest in three pieces of real estate, which were under the management of Robert T. Lincoln. The latter filed a sworn statement that the real estate was rented for very small annual rentals, that at Lincoln bringing in only forty dollars a year. Mrs. Lincoln appears to have received one half the bonds, or $18,532.58; she "made no claim to interest in the real estate." [1]

From 1872 to 1875 Mrs. Lincoln had enough income to free her from financial worries. In 1874 she is said to have written a will, but later to have destroyed or lost it. In 1875 her estate went into court, and from that time until the fall of 1876 we again learn of her finances from the court records.[2]

In December 1875 Robert Lincoln asked the approval of the court in giving Mrs. Lincoln at Springfield the many trunks and boxes of clothing once stored at Milwaukee and Chicago. A similar petition related to a box of jewelry. One box is said to have been filled with keys.

In June 1876 Robert Lincoln reported her estate as worth $68,750. Her income for the year was $11,140.35. Some

[1] Bibliography, No. 153. [2] Records, Cook County, Illinois, Court.

of this income, $4,264.38, was used to buy bonds to be added to the principal. Some of it was used to pay bills for lace curtains and other merchandise purchased before the first trial. The merchants had taken back part of the goods and credited the account with $549.83, and probably there were other credits of which there is no record. If the congressional appropriation of $22,000 be added to the amount Mrs. Lincoln received from her husband's estate, the sum practically equals the amount of the estate when it was placed in charge of Robert Lincoln in 1875. In this ten years she had spent her income from all sources, or most of it, but she had not used any of the principal. She had been extravagant at times and somewhat unwise in money matters, but she had been clear enough mentally not to spend any part of her principal.

When N. W. Edwards testified that she had lived within her means in 1875 and 1876, he told the truth. From 1865 to 1875 she had bought insanely and lavishly, and she had had a mad urge for money; but she had kept within her means. If Mrs. Lincoln's mentality were to be measured by that standard alone, then the only period in which she was unbalanced would be between 1861 and 1865.

"Mary Lincoln, financier," date 1865, was bankrupt; "Mary Lincoln, financier," date 1875, was solvent—good enough for a heavy loan at any bank.

In 1882 Congress increased Mrs. Lincoln's pension to $5,000 a year, and gave her $15,000 in addition with which to meet her pressing obligations, of which, incidentally, she then had none. In explaining the increase in Mrs. Lincoln's estate between 1876, when Robert Lincoln relinquished his control as conservator, and 1882, when he became administrator, the addition of this flat sum of money and the greater monthly pension payments for about half a year must be taken into account.[1]

Upon the death of Mrs. Lincoln her financial affairs again

[1] Bibliography, No. 128, July 18, 1882 (New York City Library).

became a matter of court record.[1] On October 4, 1882 Robert T. Lincoln filed an inventory of his mother's estate showing a value of $77,555. The final and complete inventory, settlement, and report were filed on November 6, 1884, showing an inventory of $84,035. Robert Lincoln swore ". . . that the personal estate of Mary Lincoln will probably amount to the sum of $90,000." Between 1876 and 1882 the estate had increased from about $70,000 to about $90,000. It is true that during this time she had the help and wise counsel of Mr. Edwards, Judge Davis, and other friends, but not all of the virtue of the performance should pass to them. She was alone in Europe for four years, for one thing. In 1875 they thought she could not manage her property. The answer is the bankruptcy of 1865, set against the inventories of 1865, 1875, and 1882.

"Mary Lincoln, financier," 1882, was a solid, substantial enterprise on a splendid financial basis and entitled to an A-1 rating by Dun or Bradstreet.

This statement is something more than fair to Mrs. Lincoln, in that it implies great business acumen. To make it square with the facts, certain exceptional sources of income must be taken into consideration.

Congress gave her two sums of money — $22,000 at one time, and $15,000 at another. She received a pension of $3,000 for several years, and of $5,000 for several months. And the heavy debt was somehow satisfied without great reduction of Mrs. Lincoln's capital; the portion she paid was far short of the amount of the debt. To have a correct estimate of her financial ability we should count among her liabilities only so much of the debt as she paid.

Mrs. Lincoln's investments were practically all gilt-edged. Her husband owned some of dubious value when he lived in Springfield, but his savings as President went into government bonds. Mrs. Lincoln's share of her husband's estate

[1] Book 9 of Inventories, p. 418; Probate Record, No. 24, p. 572; County Court, Sangamon County, Illinois.

was in securities of this type, and whatever she added to it was of the same kind. In 1866 she wrote to N. Brooks[1] asking him if he could sell "some Nevada claims and also a petroleum claim" which she then owned. Brooks says that among her holdings were certain wildcat stocks sent to her in her days of prosperity. She knew the breed and she tried to get them out of her strong-box.

Finally, the period 1865 to 1882 taken as a whole was one in which investments increased in value. This was especially true of the government bonds and other high-grade securities such as she owned. The great panic of 1873 and several lesser panics wiped out a multitude of fortunes; many rich men were impoverished. These were passing episodes, however, the recession of waves. The period was really one of great growth in fortunes, in national wealth, in industry and commerce, and, most of all, in the power of money. Mrs. Lincoln had inherited the best of all securities, and she had retained and added to them. The inventory value of a given security was greater in 1882 than in 1865. Her investments were in her country's future, and she sat by and saw them increase in value.

It all sums up thus: Mrs. Lincoln at times spent money lavishly and prodigally, but she never spent enough to disturb or endanger her principal or to hazard her financial future.

Worry about finances was an outstanding factor in the breakdown of her personality and mentality. Thought of money shaped many of her mental vagaries and peculiar activities after 1861, and especially between 1865 and 1871. She showed very poor financial judgment between 1861 and 1865, when her relations with the New York merchants are viewed solely in that light; but in 1865 her financial judgment was good. It was also good after 1875, a period of legally established insanity.

[1] Bibliography, No. 25, p. 124.

CHAPTER TEN

The Help and Harm of Politics

He that leadeth into captivity shall go into captivity; he that killeth with the sword must be killed with the sword.

— REVELATION xiii, 10

It were good, therefore, that men in their innovations would follow the example of time itself, which indeed innovateth greatly, but quietly and by degrees scarcely to be perceived.

— FRANCIS BACON

CHAPTER TEN

The Help and Harm of Politics

POLITICS WERE THE LADDER ON WHICH MRS. LINCOLN climbed to the summit of her ambition, and they were one of the agencies that precipitated her downfall. Lincoln's politics, and the relation of his wife to them, are a theme worthy of more space than can be given here. The only aspects considered at any length are the effects on Mrs. Lincoln of certain political battles.

Elizabeth Norris [1] gives several illustrations of Mary Todd's Whig partisanship in her youth. When she went to Springfield, she merely transferred herself from one political atmosphere into another.

When Abraham Lincoln married into the influential Todd family in Springfield, his friends thought he had strengthened himself politically. Superficially considered, this did not prove to be correct. In the early forties he wrote some of his friends in New Salem that, while the people in Sangamon County had rejected him, he was happy in thinking that those who had known him longest and best—the people of New Salem and Menard County—were loyal to him. This was written twelve years after he had arrived in New Salem. Twelve years later still, he was to learn that his old section had deserted him politically, never to return—not even when he needed them so badly in 1862 and 1864.[2]

[1] Bibliography, Nos. 72 and 73.

[2] The facts as to the results of the several elections in Illinois in which Lincoln

Considered more carefully, this charge of aristocracy which cut Abraham Lincoln so deeply — as we know because he wrote of it more than once — was of service to him politically. It meant that his old Democratic and southern Illinois affiliations were breaking. Had these persisted, he would never have been President; as they dissolved, he made new ties and found new supporters in the north end of the state. These were the foundations on which his political fortune after 1856 was built.

Lincoln's political experiences between 1842 and 1860 tried his mettle continuously. A man with less wisdom, shrewdness, and patience would have been eliminated very early. In the first half of the period he won but one contest, and that only by an agreement between a group of three men, that each would have a try at one term in Congress. It is true that his other contests were hopeless because he was running as a Whig in a state that always voted the Democratic ticket. Neither his successes nor his failures had particular significance for either him or his wife. In the second decade of the Springfield period Lincoln continued to lose his political battles, the state being still consistently Democratic. The great event of supreme political importance to him was the death of the Whig party and his transfer to the Republican party.

Mrs. Lincoln was a better Whig, with more Whig background, than her husband. Her Lexington connections of one kind and another helped to convert him from a Whig on Illinois issues to a nationally minded Whig. In this period her political acumen prevented her husband from making two tactical mistakes of great moment. More than one biographer, basing his opinion on the events of this period, has said that Mrs. Lincoln had more political wisdom, fore-

---

had a political and personal interest were found in the following sources: T. C. Pease (Bibliography, No. 146); A. C. Cole (Bibliography, No. 43); the *Daily News Almanac*; the *New York Tribune Almanac*. These sources supply some facts that are not matters of general information. My conclusions are based on these facts.

sight, and intuitive knowledge of men than her husband. She is credited by William H. Townsend[1] with having contributed indirectly to most of Lincoln's interest in and knowledge of slavery, at any rate. Mrs. Lincoln went with her husband into the Republican party whole-heartedly and without reservation. Dr. William E. Barton wrote:[2] "Mrs. Lincoln declared truthfully that when her husband left the old Whig party and joined a new party opposed to the extension of slavery she encouraged him to make no half-way matter of it."

After the election of 1856 Mrs. Lincoln wrote her half-sister Emilie Todd Helm:[3] "The election resulted very much as I expected, not hoped. Although Mr. Lincoln is, or was, a Frémont man, you must not include him with so many of those who belong to that party, as Abolitionist. In principle he is far from it. All he desires is that slavery should not be extended. . . . The Democrats in our state have been defeated in their governor so there is a crumb of comfort for each and all. What day is so dark that there is no ray of sunshine to penetrate the gloom?"

The election of 1860 meant a great deal to Mrs. Lincoln. It demonstrated Lincoln's foresight in cutting away from his old southern Illinois supporters and taking up with the people of the north end of the state. In this election he carried Illinois because of that northern support, despite the disaffection of southern Illinois, including his old counties, Sangamon and Menard. His views carried the north end of the state again in 1862 and also in 1864, the south end still being in the opposition. Mrs. Lincoln shared in the satisfaction which this confirmation of his judgment brought, but this was no more than a minor in its effect on her personality. The exultation at the realization of her hopes was a powerful stimulus to that part of her make-up which we designate as drive.

[1] Bibliography, No. 176, p. 136.
[2] Bibliography, No. 11.
[3] Bibliography, No. 73, p. 124.

The events of the presidential period had a different effect. The politics were more bitter than any she had ever known. To the ordinary animosities were added those of war politics. The politics of the period, while very harassing to Lincoln, were highly educational and even wholesome to him. Both his intellectuality and his personality were benefited by them. On the other hand, they were baneful to his wife. Senator Cameron linked politics with society as the leading agencies in tearing her down.

Two of the many political battles of 1861 to 1865 especially concerned Mrs. Lincoln.

In 1864 she was intensely interested in Lincoln's re-election. If he failed, she saw no way out of her financial difficulties, for one thing. For another, re-election would vindicate her husband. The war would be over, and life in Washington should be more pleasant for both of them. The re-election of Lincoln may be considered one of the molding forces in her life, as had been the success of 1860. The victory revived Mrs. Lincoln's interest in life. Under its stimulus her personality recovered from its period of introversion, isolation, and resentment. She regained her normal drive.

Mrs. Lincoln was the victim of some political battles, largely within her husband's party and many of them not fought until after his death. For these there were many causes, but none approximated in importance the issue of re-union or reconstruction. That issue Lincoln foresaw in the very beginning, and he laid his plans early. He could not foresee how long it was to continue, how far-reaching it was to be, or how the animosities it engendered were to operate to the hurt of his family.

Lincoln had an unusual capacity for seeing into the future. It was not supernatural, as some have said, but the result of a capacity to learn; of open-mindedness, clear reasoning, vision, and common sense. When he was debating with Douglas, he saw beyond the senatorial contest to the presidential election of 1860. Had those debates been covered by a present-day reporter rather than by a man of the Joseph Medill type, and in 1932 instead of seventy-odd years before, the headlines might have been: " Lincoln Puts Douglas on the Spot." When it came to making a new Mason and Dixon's line, Lincoln was far-seeing enough to move it from Pennsylvania to Tennessee. When it came to writing an Emancipation Proclamation, Lincoln knew how to do it — even to dividing Louisiana into three parts, like all Gaul, and Virginia into two.

And Lincoln knew more about reconstruction in March 1861 than we know seventy years later. He never asked Congress to declare war. He started with the theory that the objective was to reconstruct the Union. He launched his war on that theory; on that he fought and won it.

When the question was fighting the war and providing machinery and money for it, " Old Thad " Stevens behaved like a wheel-horse; not even Stanton or Seward pulled better than he. But whenever the question of reconstruction bobbed up, " Old Thad " was at once fighting against, not with, Lincoln, and he was able to draw in with him more than one prominent war statesman. By the end of 1864 the time had come to plan the reconstruction campaign. By February 1865 the campaign was under way. Stevens had the House, and that was hopeless. Sumner must be captured; in him lay Lincoln's hope for the Senate. Sumner was assigned to Mrs. Lincoln. She was to get him for the trip to City Point. On that trip Lincoln hoped to win him over. Grant was to have a part in the program; he was to handle the old soldiers, perhaps with some help from Sherman. Alexander H. Stephens was to be the arm for the South.

Toward the end the Cabinet knew about it and, so far as is known, all approved at that stage, though they had rejected it cold when Lincoln had first asked them to consider it.

It was not until Andrew Johnson was President and had met a few times with his Cabinet that he learned the plan and became a convert to it. In a short while the Lincoln reunion policy was known as the Johnson reconstruction policy. The old Thad Stevens army of opposition to the Lincoln reunion policy was still aligned in hostility to it under its new name. Johnson lacked the political sagacity of his predecessor and permitted the interjection of new issues. What was even more vital, he failed to capitalize Lincoln's responsibility for the plan. The bitter impeachment battle resulted.

Allan Nevins [1] has written convincingly in proof of the similarity in essentials of the Lincoln reunion policy, as he terms it, and what is more commonly known as the Johnson reconstruction policy; and the dissimilarity of both to the reconstruction policy of Thad Stevens and his associates.

C. H. McCarthy [2] understood the Lincoln plan to be essentially that of Johnson — or, rather, the Johnson plan was essentially that of Lincoln and diametrically opposite to that of Stevens. But in his opinion the Lincoln plan was not complete in detail at the time of the assassination.

However crude we may now consider Lincoln's plan, it should not be forgotten that with him the paramount consideration was the overthrow of the Confederacy. It was not without its advantages: it aimed to restore with as little technicality and innovation as possible the Union of the Fathers; with some exceptions, the natural leaders of Southern society were to participate in the work of reorganization; and the author of this simple plan approached his difficult task in a generous and enlightened spirit.

McCarthy analyzed not only the Lincoln plan, but the reaction to it of several of the states, and expressed his confidence in Lincoln's ability to make it succeed, saying: [3] "His uniform success in dealing with other embarrassing questions appears to justify the opinion that he would not have failed altogether in solving the greater problem presented by the return of peace."

[1] Bibliography, No. 126, p. 51.
[2] Bibliography, No. 116, pp. 496–7.
[3] Ibid., p. 406.

It is a reasonable inference that A. C. Cole agrees with the Nevins and McCarthy opinion, that the Johnson policy of reconstruction was in principle the Lincoln policy of re-union; for he wrote:[1] "It seemed that Johnson inherited the elephant" — a characterization which indicates the author's opinion that the question might have been destructive to Lincoln, as it proved to be to Johnson. However, says Nevins:[2] "The secret rejoicing of the radicals when Lincoln fell was the rejoicing of men who knew that he would almost certainly have been too strong for them."

The impeachment proceedings against President Johnson had their political foundation in the battle over reconstruction, although the contest itself was over secondary developments. The animosities that these proceedings, as such, engendered were largely within the Republican party.

Mrs. Lincoln was caught in the aftermath, at least twice. In 1867, when the proposed auction episode was attracting so much newspaper notice, the politicians were "in a frame of mind." Bitterness and hatred were in the air. Just when the politicians' nerves were at their rawest, Mrs. Lincoln made her mistake. When the vitriolic anger of Thurlow Weed and other politicians and political editors was poured out, it fell on her head — and there was no protection for her.

Next came the congressional battle over the pension. This lasted eighteen months, from first to last — mostly latent, but flaring up periodically. It occupied space in the newspapers, as well as time in the Senate. In the debate everyone who mentioned Abraham Lincoln did so with praise, but many of those who spoke of Mrs. Lincoln spoke with disparagement. There were whisperings and innuendoes.

This debate began in the Fortieth Congress, before the same Senate that had tried the impeachment case. In the action finally taken in the Forty-first Congress, there were twenty-seven senators voting who had also voted on the

[1] Bibliography, No. 43, p. 138. [2] Bibliography, No. 126.

charges for removal on the impeachment; there were thirteen senators still in the Senate who had sat on the impeachment trial, but who did not vote in the pension matter, being recorded as absent. Of the senators who voted to sustain the President, only one voted for Mrs. Lincoln, and six against her. Of those who voted to depose the President, fourteen voted for Mrs. Lincoln, and six against her; fourteen others who voted in the impeachment proceedings had dropped out of the Senate. Of the senators new to the Forty-first Congress, fourteen voted for Mrs. Lincoln, and eight against her. During the debate the charge was made that the Democrats would vote for Mrs. Lincoln. The outcome showed that they had voted against her; they had voted for Johnson. They were for President Lincoln's policy of reconstruction, but against his widow. Seven tenths of those who had voted against Lincoln's policy voted for his widow, and three tenths against her.

This evidence seems to show that there was not much direct relation between the votes on these two matters. I do not claim that the partisanship for or against the one carried over into the consideration of the other, as such, to any determining extent. It is my contention that the bitter personal feeling, the hatred, and the partisanship developed in the impeachment proceedings and trial determined the votes of many among both those for the pension bill and those against it.[1]

Certain dates given in juxtaposition will help in the understanding of these relationships. The fight between President Johnson and Thad Stevens and his allies began in the spring of 1865. The wardrobe-auction episode occurred in September 1867. President Johnson was tried by the Senate in May 1868. Mrs. Lincoln's application for a pension was

[1] My conclusions as to the relations between the Lincoln reunion policy, the Johnson reconstruction policy, the debates and votes on the impeachment of President Johnson, and the bill to pension Mrs. Lincoln are based on: Allan Nevins (Bibliography, No. 135); C. H. McCarthy (Bibliography, No. 125); and the daily reports of congressional proceedings as found in the *Congressional Globe* (*Record*), 1867–71.

filed in January 1869, and the pension was voted in July 1870.

Of the forces that dethroned Mrs. Lincoln's reason, none except the death of her husband and children outranked the two political conflicts between 1866 and 1870: the projected auction episode, and the pension fight.

CHAPTER ELEVEN

Was Religion A Help?

If we are told a man is religious, we still ask: What are his morals? But if we hear at first that he has honest morals and is a man of natural justice, we seldom think of the other question — whether he is religious or devout.

— SHAFTESBURY

CHAPTER ELEVEN

Was Religion A Help?

THE TODD FAMILY IN LEXINGTON WAS A RELIGIOUS household, but not puritanical or devoutly following church forms and exercises. Among the forbears of Betsy Humphreys Todd were ministers — some of them of the New England variety — but the home was not run as a New England preacher ancestor might have exacted. In Lexington the family was Presbyterian. The adults attended that church with the customary regularity, and the children went both to Sunday school and to church.

In Springfield Mary Todd was an Episcopalian. She was married by an Episcopal rector. After the death of Edward the family transferred its allegiance to the Presbyterian church, and Mrs. Lincoln attended this church until the family left for Washington. In Washington, also, the Lincolns attended the Presbyterian church. The funeral exercises for Lincoln, both in Washington and in Springfield, were under Presbyterian direction.

After leaving Washington, Mrs. Lincoln did not engage in any church activities or manifest any great interest in church affairs. The funeral exercises for Tad in Chicago were conducted by a Baptist clergyman, but those in Springfield by a Presbyterian. Mrs. Lincoln's funeral sermon was preached by Dr. Reed, pastor of the Presbyterian church in Springfield.

This easy transference of allegiance from one church to

another might indicate that Mrs. Lincoln had not studied the creed of any church closely or had not accepted any one as superior to the others. She probably knew little about church tenets and changed from one to the other in accordance with the preferences of the household in which she happened to be living. It is generally accepted that her change of membership from the Episcopal to the Presbyterian church was because of Lincoln's appreciation of the sermon preached by the Presbyterian minister at Edward's funeral.

Nor is there evidence that Mrs. Lincoln studied, or even read, her Bible, as Mr. Lincoln did so frequently. She did not quote it in her letters, nor did she make reference to Biblical history or characters.

But Mrs. Lincoln was religious, in spite of these paradoxes in her observances. Her conversation and writing gave evidence of a fundamental belief in God. She frequently referred to God and His influence on the lives of men. Such statements as that God had protected her husband from harm showed her belief that God participated in the affairs of individual men.

While her character and behavior were influenced to only a slight extent by the organized church, her religious ideals were responsible to a far greater extent for her acts and her attitudes.

The religious influence, if it may be called such, which dominated her later life more than any other was spiritualism. She and Lincoln were somewhat under the influence of spiritualists before they went to Washington. In that city the contacts were more frequent and the influence was greater.

In the last century and a half there have been several revivals of spiritualism and, naturally enough, these have tended to come in times of war. The great waves of emotion which characterize war, the deaths of loved ones, the transition from one world to another without that preparation of the emotions of those left behind which a death from disease gives opportunity for, recognition of forces beyond the control of men — all this creates a soil in which spiritualism flowers.

In 1861 public circles in Washington were very much under the influence of the spiritualist cult. Many men of prominence were convinced or half-way persuaded. It was into such an atmosphere that the Lincolns came. There was a something in Lincoln's make-up which made him listen with a good deal of sympathy to what the members of this sect said. In Mrs. Lincoln an unwillingness to surrender her children to death supplied a strong urge to take up spiritualism. Her acceptance of enough of it to keep her in supposed touch with Willie after his death is evidenced by Mrs. Helm's diary. She again indulged in "spiritualistic visitations" after her husband's death and, somewhat, after Tad's. It appears to be true, however, that she was less in touch with spiritualists, and had fewer "visitations" after the last of the three deaths than after the other two, though Dr. Danforth told of some séances she participated in.

Just how close Mrs. Lincoln and, for that matter, President Lincoln were to the spiritualists' organization is not easy to ascertain. There are books, pamphlets, and newspaper articles on the subject, but they leave one very much in the dark. There are no records signed by them and no written documents proving that they ever had any connection with the organization. We have no difficulty, however, in finding notices of visits by spiritualists in Chicago, Batavia, Springfield, and Washington. That these people were received and conversed with, there can be no doubt. But about it all there was always mystery. Names are seldom given, and addresses never. The allusions are to "mysterious visitors" and "unknown men."

N. Brooks [1] credited Elizabeth Keckley with putting Mrs. Lincoln in the hands of a fraudulent spiritualist, who in

[1] Bibliography, No. 25, p. 64.

1862 served as a medium through whom Mrs. Lincoln supposedly held converse with Willie.

To sum up the effect of religion on Mrs. Lincoln's personality: Her youthful grounding in religion contributed to her character, as well as to her behavior, and influenced her personality favorably. In the periods of storm and stress in her adult life, religion was not of great service to her. It was not a haven in which she took refuge, nor a rock on which she stood. It was not an instrument which she used, either as a shield or as a spear. The only religion, or near religion, which affected her emotionally in her great trials was spiritualism, and that did her more harm than good.

CHAPTER TWELVE

The Influence of Society

It is an old saying — A blow with a word strikes deeper than a blow with a sword.

— DEMOCRITUS

CHAPTER TWELVE

The Influence of Society

IN WRITING OF THE EFFECTS OF SOCIETY ON MRS. LINCOLN, I am referring to that which the society editor deals with, and not to the " society " of the sociologist. The possibility of being misunderstood has caused some society editors to seek to avoid trouble by calling the social group with which they deal " polite society." The connotations have prevented this term from finding acceptance. Some have tried " aristocracy " and other terms which imply exclusiveness, but in a democracy it is dangerous to use such words in connection with the name of anyone who depends on the people for support. In 1845 [1] Lincoln was writing letters and showing other signs of anxiety because the adjective " aristocratic " was being applied to him.

Society did much for Mrs. Lincoln when she was in the constructive phases of her evolution. Then came the period of destruction, wherein it did its best to annihilate her.

Mary Todd was born into no mean social atmosphere. She inherited the position in Kentucky of two generations of Todds, Parkers, and Porters. She knew the homes, the parents, and the young women of the best social circles in the Blue-Grass country. She spent years training for society and worked zealously to perfect herself in its arts. She was like a racehorse that was being prepared and pointed. For some reason, doubtless a good one, she did not make a social

[1] Bibliography, No. 9, p. 275.

début in Lexington, though she probably went to such parties as it was customary for a " sub-deb " to attend.

It was in Springfield that Miss Todd had her social career. She made her début under the powerful auspices of the Edwards-Todd clan, and she participated in all the social and socio-political functions of the vigorous new state capital. She crowded into three years all of her social experiences as a matrimonially inclined young woman.

Society was her friend in these years. If we accept the theory that she had an introvert personality, no part of the education of Mary Todd was of greater benefit to her than that of these three years of young womanhood, because they required association with others.

During the first part of Mrs. Lincoln's married life in Springfield, society neglected her in a way that caused those who knew her when she first came to Springfield to wonder. But she was a busy woman — occupied with her babies, her husband, and her home; and she did not have much time to mope. Had there been fewer duties, the harm done by the social neglect would have registered more.

In the later years of her married life in Springfield, society was more of a factor. Emilie Todd, afterwards Mrs. Helm, made her a long visit, and this helped the renewal of social relations with the acquaintances of the old days, and the making of new friends. After that, the Lincolns themselves gave some large parties, and participated in the social functions of the Executive Mansion. Springfield was doing its part in the education of Mrs. Lincoln for the position of Mistress of the White House.

The first heavy debit against society in Mrs. Lincoln's account-book is that found among the Washington entries. Several of her biographers, and those who knew her best, gave her social ambitions as in the van among her great hopes and aspirations. She went to Washington giving evidence that she knew her social opportunity had come, and that she was ready to throw her great capacity for drive into achieving success. The drubbing Washington society gave her — the social ostracism — was part of her great frustration — the greatest that had ever come to her.

A careful reader of W. O. Stoddard's [1] story concludes that he placed this disappointment in the front rank of those forces which broke down Mrs. Lincoln's personality. Senator Cameron, addressing the United States Senate,[2] charged Washington society with a full measure of responsibility.

Between her arrival in Chicago in 1865 and her departure for Europe in 1868, society ignored Mrs. Lincoln, but that did not harm her. In Washington she had had hopes, cherished ambitions, and dreamed dreams; social pre-eminence was among her desires. In Chicago she dreamed nothing; hope had been abandoned; society now had neither rewards nor punishments for her. Her mind was running to plans for financial security, and she was indifferent as to the rest of the world. In Europe, from 1868 to 1871, she wrote letters to old society friends and occasionally referred to them in her letters, but what was in her mind, as her letters reveal, was the possibility of their helping her to get a pension. Adam Badeau [3] wrote that he pitied her because of her loneliness in London, but there is no acceptable evidence that she cared what people did or thought, except as this bore on the pension bill or as it related to Tad. In this period she was very much introvert and restless, and social interests would have been of great help to her personality.

Chicago society continued to ignore Mrs. Lincoln after 1871, and she returned a typical introvert response. She lived among strangers almost altogether between 1871 and 1875. She wrote to no one. She lived in hotels and alone except for companion nurses.

She was in Waukesha in 1874, in search of health; and the accounts tell us of trips to the spring and long, lonely walks, but not a word of social intercourse or of friendliness toward her. She was in Florida in the winter of 1874,

[1] Bibliography, No. 168. [2] Bibliography, No. 45. [3] Bibliography, No. 6.

at least, and she must have looked in on society a little because she wrote her impressions of Southern social life — in a very detached way, almost as though she were among some foreign people, observing them and writing of them.

She was still more of an introvert, or schizoid,[1] in Springfield after 1875, and in France in the same period. Society was quite willing to pay no heed to her, and she was more than willing to be left alone. She saw almost no one except the members of her family and a few old friends, and if she wrote letters, I know of none that has been found.

To the tragedy of Mary Lincoln society made just one major contribution — the Washington experiences. But that was enough.

---

1 "Resembling schizophrenia, a term applied by Bleuler to the shut-in, unsocial, introspective type of personality." Bibliography, No. 48.

CHAPTER THIRTEEN

The Physical Phases of Her Personality

Mental and physical perfection are fundamentally connected and will, when the present causes of incongruity have worked themselves out, be ever found united.

— HERBERT SPENCER

CHAPTER THIRTEEN

The Physical Phases of Her Personality

THE SOURCES OF INFORMATION ABOUT MRS. LINCOLN'S appearance — her facial lines and angles, expression, size, stature, shape, and posture, all combined to make what is called, colloquially, "looks" — are of two sorts: pictures of her, and written descriptions by a number of writers.

The only pictures of Mary Todd prior to her marriage are the two or more portraits painted by Katherine Helm, based on a daguerreotype which may have been taken in 1839 or possibly earlier. There are no other pictures for twenty years, so far as I have discovered. Some photographs must have been taken between 1850 and 1860, but I have not been able to identify them. Between 1861 and 1865 many were taken, and a letter to Brady shows that Mrs. Lincoln exercised critical control over the taking of these and over their promulgation.

The group pictures of the Lincoln family were generally fabricated, but the individual pictures assembled to make the combinations were genuine. After 1865 the supply of pictures diminishes almost to the vanishing-point. I have found none taken later than 1871.

There are several descriptions of Mrs. Lincoln's looks and carriage. Elizabeth Norris wrote of Mary Todd as she was at about the age of thirteen to sixteen. Miss Helm's description[1] of Miss Todd, and her paintings of her at

[1] Bibliography, No. 73.

eighteen to twenty years, were doubtless criticized by members of the family who knew Mary in her younger years.

There are several descriptions of her appearance as a young woman in Springfield society, and during the years of married life in Springfield. The society writers of Washington tell of her appearance, and also of her dress and jewelry, in 1861 to 1865. Between 1865 and 1882 what is written relates more to her appearance as to health than to her looks.

AS A CHILD

Mrs. Norris wrote of her appearance:[1] "She had clear, blue eyes, long lashes, light brown hair with a glint of bronze, and a lovely complexion. Her figure was beautiful, and no old master ever modeled a more perfect arm and hand. Even as a schoolgirl in her gingham dress she was certainly very beautiful."

AS A YOUNG WOMAN

Miss Helm's description of Mrs. Lincoln as she was in 1840 is entitled to some consideration. It came from one of her family, on whose knowledge it was based. Besides, Miss Helm is a painter of portraits, and her best-known works are the portraits of her aunt. "Mary," said Miss Helm,[2] "although not strictly beautiful, was more than pretty. She had a broad, white forehead, eyebrows sharply but delicately marked, a straight nose, short upper lip, and an expressive mouth curling into an adorable, slow-coming smile that brought dimples into her cheeks and glinted long-lashed, blue eyes. . . . Spirited carriage of her head. . . . Plump round figure . . . intelligent bright face . . . lovely complexion . . . soft brown hair."

Reproductions of two of the three portraits of Mary

---

[1] Bibliography, No. 73, p. 52.   [2] Ibid., p. 73, and Bibliography, No. 72.

Todd painted by Miss Helm are found in her biography of her aunt,[1] and one in Townsend's *Lincoln and His Wife's Home Town.* These pictures show a good-looking, wholesome, healthy girl with fine features and an excellent carriage; a good neck, shoulders, and arms. The eyes are quite light in color, and the amount of the white ball showing is about right. The individual features are good. At the same time the combination is not one that would entitle her to the distinction of being called beautiful, without the use of a qualifying word. In no account of Miss Todd's appearance do we find her described simply as "beautiful."

AS A WIFE

E. B. Washburne informs us[2] that I. N. Arnold was a friend of Abraham Lincoln's from 1840 to 1865, and he was acquainted with Mrs. Lincoln until 1875, at least. Arnold describes her as: "Of medium height, and form rather full and round; a dark brunette with a rosy tinge to her cheeks, eyes gray-blue, hair abundant, and dark brown in color." This description probably applied to Mrs. Lincoln as Arnold saw her when he was being entertained in the Lincoln home in Springfield. This was principally about 1855.

H. B. Rankin wrote of Mrs. Lincoln, as she impressed him in 1856 or thereabouts:[3] "In personal appearance Mrs. Lincoln was not strikingly commanding, nor was she considered handsome. . . . Her features, not of a strictly regular or beautiful type, were yet pretty when viewed in connection with her complexion, her soft brown hair, and her clear blue eyes. She was not of a conventional type. She had a plump, rounded figure and was rather short in stature. Physically, mentally, emotionally she was the extreme opposite of Mr. Lincoln."

In what was written of Miss Todd in her young

[1] Bibliography, No. 73.

[2] Bibliography, No. 4, p. 69.

[3] Bibliography, No. 149, p. 160.

womanhood, we find no reference to shortness or plumpness. Most women expect to get stout after the age of thirty, and Mrs. Lincoln lived up to this expectation. The descriptions of her written after 1850 all include some reference to shortness and plumpness. This impression, which most people had of her, was partly due to contrast with her long, lean husband and partly to the styles. In 1860 dresses made the wearers appear latitudinous. But a part of Mrs. Lincoln's apparent dumpiness was due to the individual and not to the height of her husband nor to her clothes. She was stout, and her features carried a definite impression of fatness. And, as she became stouter, the descriptions of her became progressively less appealing to the vanity of a woman.

One writer described Mrs. Lincoln when she entered Washington life as "ugly." Ben Perley Poore limited his criticism of her at her first reception to a statement that she wore a wreath of flowers "which did not become her."[1] Genevieve Forbes Herrick wrote:[2] "Abraham Lincoln and a short lady at his side, in blue and white checked silk, held their first reception." Dr. William E. Barton, though he doubted its accuracy, gave a story[3] to the effect that, as they started for the reception room, Lincoln announced: "Ladies and gentlemen, here is the long and the short of the Presidency." "The long," said Barton, "was six feet four. The short, five feet nothing. . . . But Mary Todd Lincoln walked proudly beside the tall man whom she always said she married in full faith that he would one day be President, 'because, you know, he really isn't handsome.'"

I have been able to find only one report which spoke of Mrs. Lincoln in this period as being pretty, or even handsome. Most of the reports describe her clothes, her manners, or the way she carried herself — anything but her looks.

Elizabeth Keckley described Mrs. Lincoln as follows:[4] "I

[1] Bibliography, No. 141, p. 116.
[2] Bibliography, No. 77.
[3] Bibliography, No. 11.
[4] Bibliography, No. 85, p. 28.

saw a lady inclined to stoutness. She was about forty years of age. . . . She had a beautiful neck and arms, and low dresses were becoming to her."

Stoddard said she was "a pleasant looking woman, well educated, and with a renown for keen wit."

Senator James Harlan, the father of Mrs. Robert T. Lincoln, described Mrs. Lincoln at the first inauguration as being: "Fair, of about medium height, but, standing near her husband, by comparison seemed short." [1]

Miss Helm, writing of the same period,[2] said she was still strikingly youthful and attractive in appearance. She was "fair and forty," but not fat, as she weighed only a hundred and thirty pounds. "Her hair, a lovely chestnut, with glints of bronze, had as yet not a gray thread. Her beautiful shoulders and arms gleamed like pearls. She held her head high, slightly tilted back, possibly because she had so tall a husband to look up to. She was not tall, but seemed shorter than she really was by the side of her towering husband. More than merely pretty, she was both brilliant and fascinating." Miss Helm's is much the most flattering description of her aunt's appearance in 1861 to 1865 that has come from any source. Julia Taft Bayne,[3] however, described Mrs. Lincoln in 1861 as being "nearly beautiful."

Some time after 1876 Mrs. Lincoln lost flesh. Her relatives in Springfield describe her as being thin as well as short. They give her weight in that period as a hundred and ten pounds or even less. B. F. Stoneberger describes her as small and thin, almost wizened. The New York description of her as she returned from Europe in 1880 would indicate that she was senile in appearance. At that time she was "little and thin, wrinkled and gray, and she looked like an old woman."

---

[1] Bibliography, No. 73, p. 167.
[2] Ibid. p. 175.
[3] Bibliography, No. 17, p. 8.

HER FEATURES IN DETAIL

An analysis of Mrs. Lincoln's size, weight, posture, and features throws some light on her mentality and her personality.

Her head was large and broad. The cranium was so large that it indicated a brain of extra size and weight for the size and weight of its owner. Her method of combing her hair — parted in the middle, carried laterally to expose the brow, and then downward to cover the upper two thirds of the ears — accentuated the height and size of the brow and the size of the face. The dark color of the hair threw her prominent white forehead into further contrast. The combination of head and upper part of the face marks Mrs. Lincoln as of an intellectual type. This does not mean that all intellectuals have heads and upper faces of this type, but it does indicate a probability that she was an intellectual woman.

There are none of those prominences of the face which, when present, indicate enlarged sinuses, but which are usually credited to something else — such as overhanging brows. The space between Mrs. Lincoln's eyes and between her eyebrows was broad. The eyebrows make one think there might have been "tricks of the trade" even in that day.

Mrs. Lincoln's mid face tells us less about her type, especially if we limit this region to the features between the brows and the upper lips. Her eyes were blue. Miss Helm's portrait gives the eyes an expression of directness and frankness, the keynote of the picture. In photographs taken in later years there is not the same domination of the whole by the expression of the eyes. While some of this difference in appearance is due to other causes, a part of it results from the pose, and a larger part from the relative size of the aperture of the lids. In the three portraits that Miss Helm painted, the eyes are never looking toward the spectator;

in the photographs the tendency was to take the face even more in profile. Mrs. Lincoln's later pictures do not indicate that her eyes were prominent. They appear to be somewhat small and inconspicuous features in a broad, fat face. Whatever the cause may have been, the effect was that her face lost one of its best features—the expression of her youthful eyes— as she acquired age.

Mrs. Lincoln's nose was her poorest feature. A glance at her profile and near-profile pictures gives an impression of pug-nose. A closer look shows that the pug-nose effect was due to poor development of the bony part of the nose in the eye-and-bridge region rather than to an upturning of the tip. The lower part of the nose is better developed. When her features began to be changed by the deposition of fat, this lower segment of the nose received more than its quota, and no other change did more to rob her of her good looks. She ultimately became fat-nosed.

Her cheek-bones were not high. In this region, as in the lower forehead, there was no indication of large sinuses. But if the mid section of the face, especially its bony framework, did not cause the mid face to push as far forward as the forehead and chin, it was broad enough—in fact, too broad. Most of the suggestion of breadth of face, however, is found only in the later pictures, and resulted from the fattening process.

Just as Mrs. Lincoln's "brain-box," forehead, and upper face proclaimed her an intelligent woman, the lower part of it stamped her as aggressive and determined. The configuration of the upper part of the face is determined by bony formations, the pattern being dependent on the need of space for brains. That of the lower part is determined by muscles and fat, as well as by the development of the upper and lower jaw-bones. Except in her youthful portraits, it is her mouth that dominates Mrs. Lincoln's features. Her lips were not broad and sensuous; in fact, they were not quite heavy enough— without being thin-lipped. Had they shown a little more vermilion, she would have been better-looking. The distinguishing feature of her mouth was that it formed a straight line, curving neither upward nor downward, and her lips closed firmly. The upper lip was a trifle too broad because her nose was a little too short. Her lower jaw and chin were well developed. Her teeth met well, neither jaw protruding. She was not iron-jawed, nor was her chin square.

If the face above the tip of the nose be covered by the hand, the part remaining in view appears to be rather overdeveloped. Much of that appearance was due to fat. But after allowing for that, the well-developed bones and the firm, strong muscles indicate that the possessor of that face knew what she wanted when she wanted it, and intended to get it if she could.

Every picture shows a broad, sweeping curve or wrinkle extending from the nose region outward, passing below the eminence of the cheek, skirting round the corners of the mouth, and losing itself on the upper part of the lower jaw. The angles of the mouth are pulled downward ever so slightly, and the muscles, skin, and tissues are set in that position. This is the only suggestion of wrinkles that the pictures show. Wrinkles of the face, at least those which precede the criss-cross wrinkles of very old age, are the result of persistent muscle-pulling. Had Mrs. Lincoln been a chronic laugher, that broad face-curve would have been more pronounced, and it would have pulled upward toward the top of the curve. Secondary upward curves would have developed around the corners of the mouth. As it was, this large curved wrinkle was of the type so frequently found in rather serious men whose features are a little too heavy. Had Mrs. Lincoln been more fun-making, the corners of her mouth would have had a different slant. Had she had a sense of humor, or better enjoyed a good joke, she would have had a rather different squint around her eye regions, and radiating wrinkles across the temples would have resulted.

In her entire face there was not one bad feature. Nor were her features out of level or out of harmony and balance. When she was young, she came very near being pretty, even strikingly so. Probably at every period of her life she was prettier than she was regarded. Her features were not of the type that give more than a fair break to their possessors. There was a little too much face, and her brow was rather too prominent. The eyes showed not quite enough of the "clinging" type to prejudice in her favor. But it was, above all, the firm mouth and strong under jaw, the expression of the face from the nose down, that would make her appear inferior to others in good looks.

The change in Mrs. Lincoln's face that robbed it of its beauty was largely the result of the fattening process. As time passed and she stored up fat, it was her lot to have an undue amount deposited in her face. This coarsened her features and emphasized the effects of maturity.

It is unfortunate that there is no photograph of Mrs. Lincoln taken after her weight had fallen to a hundred and ten pounds, and her trials had caused muscle wrinkles to develop here and there. The chances are that she then regained something of her youthful good looks. At least her features were less heavy and coarse.

When fat is absorbed in the neck region, longitudinal wrinkles appear. Probably in her time of emaciation her neck lost its beauty. But the face may have become more attractive. It is the expressions of emotions, determination, joy, and sorrow that register on the face as wrinkles; the absorption of face fat is of secondary importance. As the wrinkles came out around her eyes and mouth, and as certain features became less large, the likelihood is that she gained more in looks than she lost.

Mrs. Lincoln's neck was always good. It was not even bad when she was stoutest. Her dresses usually showed her neck well.

Her arms were also good. The Springfield *Journal* said

she was a woman of great strength, meaning resistance, endurance, persistence, and determination, rather than muscle strength. There are pictures of her, however, which show arms that might have had strong muscles.

Her hands were small and very shapely. This indicates that her feet, as nature made them, were of the same type. The hands and feet are composed predominantly of bone, and the general type of the one is followed by the other. But talking of her feet is pure speculation. In that age women's feet were used to stand on.

I have found no very definite statement as to Mrs. Lincoln's height. We read that she was not short as compared with other women. She stood erect. Her posture was good. The probability is that she was taller than she gave the impression of being. No weight over a hundred and thirty is recorded, but she must have weighed more than that part of the time. The impression she gave was of an underheight, overweight woman — at least, after 1855 and until about 1876.

Her movements were quick and suggestive of aggressiveness. She spoke a little rapidly.

Students of Mary Lincoln's personality should not overlook the lessons which a close study of her face, head, and physical characteristics convey.

CHAPTER FOURTEEN

Her Mental and Personality Qualities

The mind is its own place, and in itself
Can make a heaven of hell, a hell of heaven.

—Milton, *Paradise Lost*

CHAPTER FOURTEEN

Her Mental and Personality Qualities

THERE IS NO POPULAR INTEREST IN MRS. LINCOLN'S intellectual ability. She wrote no books, and no state documents are attributed to her. She was not a professional woman, nor a leading light in anything. She was no Queen Elizabeth, Queen Victoria, Cleopatra, Madame de Staël, nor even a Dolly Madison. She did not engage in intrigue, and she made no impression on public affairs. Her name will go down in history as that of a wife.

There would be no popular interest in her as a wife except that she was the wife of Abraham Lincoln, the most studied and the most frequently portrayed man — in American public affairs, at least. Even though she was the wife of Lincoln, she might have escaped exceptional public interest but for certain things that were said about her. Those of her qualities that are discussed relate to her personality rather than to her intellectuality. The peculiarities of her behavior resulted from her emotions rather than from her thinking.

Popular interest in her continued to the end of her career, even in those years after her husband had died and she was living a private life in retirement, where her behavior was interesting because it was peculiar. Here, again, the interest was in the personality rather than in the intellect, because her conduct was determined by an insanity of her emotions, rather than of her mind.

To make the distinction between thinking and feeling, between emotional acts and those dominated by intellect, between intelligence and personality, and to hold these distinctions always clearly in mind, is not an easy matter.

The distinction that Webster makes is as follows:[1] "*Personality.* That which constitutes distinction of person; distinctive personal character; individuality. *Personality* implies complex being or character having distinctive and persistent traits, among which reason, self-consciousness, and self-activity are usually reckoned as essential."

"*Mentality.* Mental endowment or acumen; mental power; mind considered as a characteristic."

The definition of "mentality" given by the Oxford Dictionary is:[2] "Intellectual quality, intellectuality."

The term "personality" is used here in a broad sense. It includes intellectuality (which, in turn, includes intelligence and mentality). It also includes emotional reactions, personal appearance, facial expression, carriage. Its major heads are physical, intellectual, and emotional. There are many minor heads, such as character, taste, likability, energy, aggressiveness, habits, graciousness, and many others. In Mrs. Lincoln the greatest interest attaches to her emotional reactions. That which set her apart all through the years of her adult life was her personality, and particularly that part of it which related to her emotional reactions. From the reputed contact of the child Mary with Henry Clay, to the end of Mrs. Lincoln's days, the impressions she made on people related principally to the emotional. She had likes and dislikes, and these begot likes and dislikes in others. She had animosities, and these were paid back in the same medium.

[1] Bibliography, No. 185. [2] Bibliography, No. 124.

YOUTH

Mary Todd at about eight years of age is described by William H. Townsend [1] as: "A sprightly but curiously complex little creature, high-strung, headstrong, precocious, warm-hearted, sympathetic, and generous; fond of birds, flowers, party dresses." We do not know where this very careful investigator found the basis for this estimate. If she was fond of flowers and birds at the age of eight, she lost that fondness before she reached twenty-eight. Neither she nor Mr. Lincoln showed a fondness for flowers in Springfield or in Washington.

Frances Wallace wrote: [2] "Neither Mr. nor Mrs. Lincoln loved the beautiful. I have planted flowers in their front yard myself to hide nakedness, ugliness, etc. . . . have done it often and often. Mrs. Lincoln never planted trees, roses . . . never made a garden; at least, not more than once or twice."

Katherine Helm, who did not know her aunt, but who knew of her from her own mother and other members of the family who did, uses these descriptive terms about Mary Todd: [3] "Very studious. . . . Far in advance of other girls of her age in education. . . . A mind that enabled her to grasp and thoroughly understand [this is Mrs. Norris's statement]. . . . The life of the school . . . companionable . . . vivacious. . . . In this Kentucky period she was imperious, impatient, and tending to revolt."

WOMANHOOD

Emilie Todd Helm, who was at home when Mrs. Lincoln visited Lexington in 1847 and 1848, who visited Mrs. Lincoln in Springfield in 1856 and in Washington in 1862, and

[1] Bibliography, No. 176, p. 51.
[2] Bibliography, No. 182, p. 289.
[3] Bibliography, No. 73.

who had the further advantage of discussing her half-sister with their close relatives, gave this estimate of her:[1] "She was singularly sensitive. She was also impulsive and made no attempt to conceal her feelings; indeed, it would have been an impossibility had she desired to do so, for her face was an index to every passing emotion. . . . Without desiring to wound she occasionally indulged in sarcastic, witty remarks that cut like a Damascus blade; but there was no malice behind them. She was full of humor, but never unrefined. Perfectly frank and extremely spirited, her candor of speech and independence of thought often gave offense where none was meant."

J. F. Newton wrote of her:[2] "Mary Todd, a Kentucky girl of distinguished lineage, highly cultured, compact of brilliance, coquetry, and wit. . . . Lincoln had not met such a woman before, and he was captivated by her cleverness, vivacity, and beauty."

Some of the qualifying statements about her as a young woman are: " . . . as spirited, accomplished, and self-confident a young woman as Springfield had ever seen";[3] " . . . brilliant, witty, highly educated, ambitious, spirited, with a touch of audacity."[4]

Of the exhibit material awaiting analysis none surpasses some letters which she wrote to friends and social acquaintances. These reveal a young woman of education and a good letter-writer. She was vivacious and witty. Her letters were filled with gossip, mostly very kindly, but some of it critical. Plainly, her mind ran to people and social events. She was interested in what was happening and what was being said. These letters, when compared with those written to friends in later years, are seen to lack some of the grace, form, and ceremonial of the later products, but they show that the interest she had in people was just as characteristic in 1840 as it was in 1870 and in the years between.

[1] Bibliography, No. 72.
[2] Bibliography, No. 127.
[3] Bibliography, No. 170, p. 243.
[4] Bibliography, No. 172, Vol. I, p. 173.

We can accept that, then, as an ingrained quality of her mind.[1]

Extracts from three letters written to Emilie Todd, later Mrs. Helm, in 1856, illustrate well this quality of Mrs. Lincoln's mind — her interest in personalities and events. She wrote:[2] "Colonel Warren gave a bridal party to his son, who married Miss Birchall. . . . Miss Dunlap is spending the winter with her sister, Mrs. Mc, looking very pretty, but the beaux do not appear so numerous as the winter you passed here. . . . Dr. and Mrs. Brown, also Mr. Dwight Brown and his wife, are residing here. . . . I saw Elizabeth this afternoon. . . . Julia and Mrs. Baker are in Peoria at the fair, from thence go to St. Louis. . . . Julia has nothing but her dear husband and silk quilts to occupy her mind. How different the daily routine of some of our lives! . . . Nothing pleases me better than to receive a letter from an absent friend, so remember, dear Emilie, when you desire to be particularly acceptable, write me one of your agreeable missives and do not wait for a return of each from a staid matron and, moreover, the mother of three noisy boys. . . . Reminds me of your question relative to Lydia M. The hour of her patient lover's deliverance is at hand. They are to be married privately, I expect. . . . Some of us who had a very handsome dress for the season thought it would be in good taste for Mrs. Matteson, in consideration of their being about to leave their present habitation, to give a general reception. . . . This fall, in visiting Mrs. M., I met a sister of Mrs. Maginnis, a very pretty, well-bred woman from Joliet. . . . Frances Wallace returned two or three days ago from her visit to Pennsylvania. . . . Mr. Edwards's family are well. . . . Mr. Baker and Julia are still with them. Miss Iles was married some three weeks ago. . . . Mr. Scott is frequently here playing the devoted to Julia.

[1] The Peoria letters owned by Oliver R. Barrett and Logan Hay are also good illustrations of Mrs. Lincoln's gossipy tendencies.

[2] Owned by Miss Helm. Bibliography, No. 73, p. 120 ff.

. . . I suspect the family would not be averse to him. . . . Charley R. was on a visit to him in Lexington. . . . He, it is said, is to be married this winter to Jennie Barrett, a lovely girl. Mr. R. took tea with us an evening or two since and made particular inquiries about Mother. Still as rough and uncultivated as ever, although some years since married an accomplished Georgia belle with the advantage of some years in Washington."

In the writings about her social life she is described as having been talkative, bright, and an excellent conversationalist, so long as she was allowed to pick her own ground. Her talk was almost altogether about people and events — personalities and gossip. She was not especially good at the exchange of social chatter, but when it came to saying clever things or reciting some event in which she could imitate someone, she was a source of great merriment. She had plenty of wit, but she was without humor. She could make others laugh, and was very fond of doing so, but she was not a good laugher. No one has ever pictured her with a twinkle in her eye, and her pictures never show the crow's-feet at the outer corner of the eye, nor the upturned corners of the mouth, which comedians know mean mirth.

Her wit was cutting at times, and sometimes what she said hurt. Her mimicry also made some enemies for her. A fair estimate is that she was admired more than she was liked.

She did not "mother" her beaux nor flatter them by simulating an interest in them. She dazzled rather than warmed them. Her conversation was not flattering nor soothing to those on whose ears it fell. She was not a "clinging vine." No sap-headed boy left her presence certain that he was a Daniel Webster, or a "mute, inglorious Milton." No boy loved her from the same impulse that made him love his mother. The reaction to her in society was composed far more of admiration — and even wonder — than it was of sympathy, friendliness, and affection.

Ward H. Lamon describes Mrs. Lincoln as ". . . high-bred, proud, brilliant, witty, and with a will that bent everyone else to her purpose. Her tongue and her pen were equally sharp." [1]

J. W. Weik, following Herndon, as he nearly always did, wrote: [2] " She was an excellent judge of human nature; a better reader of men's motives than her husband. . . . A shrewd observer. . . . She coveted place and power . . . wanted to be a leader in society, and her ambition knew no bounds. . . . She was devoid of patience, tolerance, and self-control."

Dr. William E. Barton uses the following terms: [3] " Passionate, high-strung, extremely temperamental, ardent, quick to fly into a passion, and as ready to get over it. . . . She never did anything by halves. She either loved or hated, and she did it with intensity."

EMOTIONALISM

Emotionalism is a part of the picture of Mrs. Lincoln, from the earliest record we have. Until her marriage there were few limitations and fewer restraints. When exacting interests, such as those of wifehood, motherhood, and the cares of the household, began to limit Mrs. Lincoln, and life started to multiply restraints, certain peculiarities of her personality began to come to the fore. They had been present all the time, but hitherto they had not been discordant or out of harmony. Now they commenced to be sources of disharmony. The spirit which so many admired in the girl grew to be in the woman the temper which made enemies. The gossip which in the girl was harmless enough now aroused unpleasant gossip in return. The tendency to criticize, to mimic, to make fun of people — while it made her no friends, but was even admired in her schoolgirl days

[1] Bibliography, No. 99, p. 238.
[2] Bibliography, No. 186, pp. 94–7.
[3] Bibliography, No. 11. Also No. 9, Vol. II, p. 410.

— now was provocative of enmities. The out-of-the-ordinariness which in the young girl caused laughter, entertained, and was esteemed brilliant, now became proof of abnormal personality. The quality in the young person was the same as that in the older, except that it had grown stronger or, coming back to the harmony simile, louder. But the setting was not the same. Dissimilarity in setting and in degree caused the quality to be looked on differently.

WHAT MR. LINCOLN MAY HAVE THOUGHT

Charles F. Gunther, who began collecting Lincoln relics while Mrs. Lincoln was still alive, bought objects of interest to Chicago and to her during the years when she was resident in that city. Mr. Barrett says that some of these were brought to Mr. Gunther by Mrs. Lincoln herself, and others she sent by messenger. Among the articles purchased by Mr. Gunther and later sold to Mr. Barrett was a book, *The Elements of Character,* by Mary G. Chandler,[1] on the title-page of which was written: " Mary A. Lincoln." The handwriting is Mr. Lincoln's, and the supposition is that he wrote " A. Lincoln " in the book, and subsequently prefixed " Mary " to it. Marks were found on the margin of various pages. On the fly-leaf Mr. Gunther had indicated the location of these marginal lines and had written that they were made by Mr. Lincoln, which information he, presumably, received from Mrs. Lincoln.

It is reasonable to infer that Lincoln saw that his wife was not getting along as well as she might. He had been somewhat disturbed over the way she had taken Edward's death. He had other reasons for thinking that all was not going well with her. He may have sensed that some of the trouble lay in her personality, although in that day psychologists knew but little on that subject. He was a politi-

[1] Bibliography, No. 31.

cian, and a skillful one, and every politician is a good practical psychologist, whether he knows it or not. Lincoln knew as much about applied psychology as the professors did.

As he read this book, he probably decided that his wife could read it with advantage. It had something that she needed. Let us examine it analytically, looking for light on what Lincoln thought of his wife's personality, of her qualities that might be bettered, and of suggestions as to how to better them.

There is a chapter on character, most of which is given over to statements of the author's opinions on what is not character. She held that character is a spiritual development, for which in the end one will receive the rewards and the punishments to which it is entitled. "But if we do not succeed in attaining true health, wealth, and power, the responsibility is all our own."

On page 10, in the same chapter, this is marked: "A wisely trained character never stops to ask, What will society think of me if I do this thing or leave it undone?" The spirit of the passage and its setting is: "Hew to the line, let the chips fall where they may."

Another marked passage in this chapter (though not listed by Mr. Gunther) reads: "If we would train character into genuine goodness, we should observe whether evil in ourselves or in others offends us because it is opposed to the will of God. If the former be the case we shall find ourselves angry; if the latter, we shall be sorrowful. Anger is, in its very nature, egotistic and selfish."

A marked paragraph on page 36 refers to children who are governed by their affections. (Preceding chapters had been concerned with children governed by imagination, and with others governed by thought.) "There is still a third class of a calmer aspect. Its members may not shine so brightly, but there is more warmth in their rays. They will not learn so much nor so rapidly as some, but their whole being is permeated by what they know. They are constantly studying the relations of the things they learn to each other and to life."

One marked paragraph almost supplies a prelude for that conversation of Lincoln and his wife in 1862 when he told her she was allowing her likes and dislikes to warp her judgment of people: "We are all of us perpetually liable to gross self-deception by thus transferring in fancy our love or our hate for the consequences of vices or virtues to the vices or virtues themselves. If we made this transfer in fact, we should at once set about gaining the one and putting away the other; but so long as we believe that sin dwells within us without our consent and approval, we become daily more and more the servants of sin."

Among the sentiments, many of them epigrammatic, which Lincoln did not emphasize by marking, are the following: "There are some who think much of the vices of life, but always in relation to their neighbors. . . . The centuries that have passed have, many of them, been darkened even to blackness by insane endeavors to write creeds of man's devising, in letters of fire and blood upon the nations. Now men rush to the opposite extreme and mistake licentiousness in belief for liberty of conscience. . . . We know that a determined will works wonders in overcoming the defects of the body, and it can do even more in overcoming the defects of the mind. . . . Jealousy, envy, discontent, and love of scandal are among the earliest products of an idle mind. . . . We all, perhaps, know that saying, and yet need to be reminded, that a bad president stands lower in the scale of being than a good town officer. If improper motives are allowed to have sway, a person soon becomes confirmed in the habit of gossiping — a habit that degrades the intellect and the heart. . . . The heart never suffers alone for the indulgence of any wrong passions. The intellect and the passions ever sink as well as rise together. . . . Of all the powers of wit, sarcasm is the lowest. There is nothing easier than ridicule, nothing requiring a weaker head or a colder heart. . . . Sarcasm is a weapon we are almost sure to find constantly used by the gossip. . . . The fine lady of the well-bred class may be polished to the last degree when, arrayed in silks and laces, she glides over the rich carpets of the drawing-room; and yet, with her servants at home, she is possibly less the lady than they; or, worse still, the fine lady married to a fine gentleman of a character similar to her own, in the privacy of domestic life carries on a civil war with him, in which all restraint of courtesy is set aside. . . . Indifference, ill-temper, selfishness, envy, and arrogance — all positive vices — are the characteristics that ultimate themselves in ill manners."

WAS MRS. LINCOLN JEALOUS?

There is very little evidence that Mrs. Lincoln was jealous of Abraham Lincoln's attentions to women, and certainly no man ever gave his wife less cause. I am not in a position to make any contribution to the controversy now waging as to Lincoln's fondness for erotic stories, but in his conduct toward women he did nothing to provoke criticism. His conduct was above reproach.

There are three or four witnesses who testify that Mrs. Lincoln was jealous. One of these was William H. Herndon. Another was Elizabeth Keckley, who said:[1] "Mrs. Lincoln was extremely jealous of Mr. Lincoln."

A few illustrations are given by General Badeau, one of which was partially confirmed by other witnesses to the occurrence. General Badeau writes of a fit of violent temper in which Mrs. Lincoln indulged on March 26, 1865, when she was visiting the army at the front with the President. This outbreak he ascribed to her jealousy over her husband's attentions to a Mrs. Griffin. She stopped the vehicle in which she and Mrs. Grant were riding, and tried to get

[1] Bibliography, No. 85, p. 124.

out. This was very embarrassing to Mrs. Grant. " She was absolutely jealous of poor ugly Abraham Lincoln," wrote General Badeau.[1]

General Horace Porter, who was also in the hack, wrote a story[2] about Mrs. Lincoln's outbreak, but he attributed it to the jolting she got from the team trotting over a corduroy road.

Other instances of Mrs. Lincoln's jealousy were given by Badeau. " She was jealous of Mrs. Orne for riding horseback with Lincoln. . . . She became frenzied. . . . She called Mrs. Orne bad names . . . tried to have General Orne removed. . . . During all this visit similar scenes were occurring. Mrs. Lincoln repeatedly attacked her husband in the presence of officers, and I never suffered greater humiliation and pain. . . . General Sherman was a witness of some of these episodes and mentioned them in his memoirs."

General W. T. Sherman does mention at least one of these episodes.[3] He tells of discussing it with Captain Barnes, who was also a witness. However, he does not give jealousy as the reason for Mrs. Lincoln's outbreak.

General Badeau quotes Mrs. Stanton as saying that she did not visit Mrs. Lincoln. She refused to go to Ford's Theater with President and Mrs. Lincoln the night of the assassination unless General and Mrs. Grant would go. " I will not sit without you in the box with Mrs. Lincoln," Mrs. Stanton is quoted as having said to Mrs. Grant. The context of this quotation indicates that General Badeau thought Mrs. Stanton was actuated by fear of Mrs. Lincoln's jealousy of her husband.

This is all the evidence I know of that jealousy of her husband was one of the bad qualities of Mrs. Lincoln's

---

[1] Bibliography, No. 6. (This letter is in the New York Library, and is marked "Ford Collection." It is from General Adam Badeau, dated January 8, but with no year. It may have been 1875.)

[2] Bibliography, No. 142, pp. 412, 414.

[3] Bibliography, No. 159.

personality. I do not think there is enough proof to sustain the charge. Too many frank people, eager to find unkind things to say, made no reference to Mrs. Lincoln as jealous — even what might be termed normally so.

In the main, the influences which operated on Mrs. Lincoln's personality prior to 1861 were constructive, while those of the succeeding years were destructive. In each period there were subordinate forces as well as those that dominated, and in between there was a border zone in which the groups were nearly of equal importance.

We may say, roughly, that after she went to Washington, the destructive forces were in the ascendancy. In that life the strain on her personality became immeasurably greater. It was her twilight zone. Most of the analyses of her personality written by those who knew her then dealt with her shortcomings; though some who wrote were close enough to see and to write of qualities that the herd knew little of. Of these W. O. Stoddard was the only one with good opportunities for observation, coupled with a background of understanding. An old Illinois friend and political supporter of her husband, he was serving as a private secretary to the President, in charge of personal as distinguished from political relations, and in daily contact with Mrs. Lincoln for almost four years. He wrote of her good mind and her other good qualities, and he also told of her personality and the difficulties it raised for herself and others. This he did in a frank, straightforward way — understandingly and kindly.

It is difficult to say just when Stoddard got the opinions and matured his own views, as expressed in the next statement quoted.[1] His book did not appear until 1884, but it deals with the 1861–4 period and is written in the present tense. It seems probable that he set down his views at the time he was writing of, but that he made additions

[1] Bibliography, No. 168, p. 62.

and subtractions before publishing them, twenty years later.

" At first it was not easy to understand why a lady who could be one day so kindly, so considerate, so generous, so thoughtful, and so hopeful could upon another day appear so unreasonable, so irritable, so despondent, even so niggardly, and so prone to see the wrong side of men, women, and events. It is easier to understand it all and to deal with it after a few words from an eminent medical practitioner."

This can only mean that some time prior to 1864 a physician recognized Mrs. Lincoln's trouble and told Stoddard what it was, and that thereafter he was able to recognize the limits of her responsibility. Could others have known as much as Stoddard did, history would have been kinder to Mary Lincoln.

F. B. Carpenter has very little to say about Mrs. Lincoln. He gives one story [1] of an exchange of repartee with Secretary of War Stanton, which serves to show her spirit and her quickness of wit. What, for our purposes, is more important, this sally is an illustration of the type of witticism which made Mrs. Lincoln so many enemies.

Mrs. Keckley made several statements of her opinion of Mrs. Lincoln's mentality; [2] among these: " She was shrewd and far-seeing."

The impression which Julia Taft Bayne [3] got of Mrs. Lincoln was that of a kindly, loving, and very considerate woman, although she gives at least two minor instances in which Mrs. Lincoln took advantage of her position as First Lady to get for herself dresses, ribbons, and other articles of adornment that belonged to other people. At one time, seeing on the hat of Mrs. Bayne's mother, Mrs. Taft, some ribbon which she fancied, she connived to get it off. The request quite flabbergasted Mrs. Taft and she was disposed to refuse and resist, even to the extent of sitting on her hat.

[1] Bibliography, No. 28, p. 201
[2] Bibliography, No. 85, pp. 136, 204.
[3] Bibliography, No. 17, p. 43.

In her indignation, she told Mr. Taft of the astounding request. He recognized that women in good society do not pull ribbons out of other women's hats, but this case was different. Mrs. Lincoln lived in the White House. Mrs. Taft did not sit on her hat, and Mrs. Lincoln got the ribbon. This, and other similar incidents, caused Mrs. Bayne to write: "Mrs. Lincoln wants what she wants when she wants it, and she accepts no substitute."

Mrs. Bayne gives another occurrence which tells us something else of Mrs. Lincoln. On this occasion she told young Julia of Edward, her son who had died more than ten years before. She grew very emotional in her recital of Edward's good qualities and of the circumstances of his death. Soon she was crying hysterically, just as though his death had but recently occurred.

Mrs. Lincoln had a mind far above the average quality as regards capacity for observation, for ability to read and in other ways acquire information, and for analysis. Her mind was of the introvert type, but with great determination, force, and drive. She had a good memory and an adequate use of words. Her judgment was about as good as that of the average person, and she was not without wisdom. She had more than the usual insight into motives — what is called "intuition." She could foresee, but otherwise her imagination was not above the average.

Her rating on other qualities which, added to mentality, went to make up her personality, is as follows:

Her society manners were exceptionally good. Her personal appearance, features, facial expression, stature, build, and posture were in her favor. She had physical as well as social grace. She was emotional, with the qualities of a person given to obeying the emotions. She responded unhappily to restraint. She evoked admiration, envy, and jealousy more than she did friendliness, fraternal spirit, sympathy, and love. She liked to shine; she did not care to warm, or, if she did, she did not know how. She had character and the idealism and basic religious feeling of the people of breeding and character from whom she sprang, but she was not consistent in observing religious forms. She was a virtuous, domestic woman, with the principles of such women.

The weak points of her mind were: too great seriousness and an inability to laugh at herself; capacity to ridicule others, but not herself; lack of humor. Except for her husband and children, her family affections were not strong. She did not have an artistic sense, nor love of beauty for beauty's sake, in either color, form, or sound. "She wanted what she wanted when she wanted it," and she could not stand failure to get it.

Great weaknesses of her personality, in addition to those indicated in their contrast relations, were: inability to withstand restraint; a tendency to hysteria; and a disposition to disregard the point of view and feelings of others, to give offense, to resent criticism, to give way to anger, to remember hurts, to be revengeful. Jealousy was a minor in her make-up, but envy was a major.

No psychologist nor psychiatrist has ever stated the matter better than did Samuel Butler, nor could anyone summarize Mrs. Lincoln better than did that wise philosopher when he wrote: [1] "All our lives long we are engaged in the process of accommodating ourselves to our surroundings; living is nothing else than this process of accommodation. When we fail a little we are stupid. When we flagrantly fail we are mad. A life will be successful or not, according as the power of accommodation is equal to or unequal to the strain of fusing and adjusting internal and external chances."

[1] Bibliography, No. 27.

CHAPTER FIFTEEN

On the Rocks

With curious art the brain too finely wrought
Preys on itself and is destroyed by thought.

— Churchill

Woe! woe! to all who plunder from the immortal mind
Its bright and glorious crown.

— J. G. Whittier

CHAPTER FIFTEEN

On the Rocks

It is never easy to say when twilight ends and night begins. For our purposes we class Mrs. Lincoln's mind as insane after 1865, and what follows in this chapter bears particularly on its disturbed qualities.

THE TYPE OF HER INSANITY

None of the physicians [1] who testified when Mrs. Lincoln was on trial were specialists in mental disorders. In consequence, they made no effort to diagnose the type of their

[1] The physicians who attended Mrs. Lincoln were all men of standing. Dr. N. S. Davis was born in New York in 1817, graduated in medicine in 1834, and came to Chicago to become a professor in Rush Medical College in 1849. He is commonly known as "the father of the American Medical Association." In 1875 he was the most prominent medical man in Chicago. Dr. H. A. Johnson, born in 1822, was graduated from the University of Michigan in 1849, and from Rush Medical College in 1852. He and Dr. Davis were among the founders of the Chicago Medical College. For many years he was a member of the Chicago Board of Health. Dr. R. N. Isham was also a prominent physician. He was born in 1831, and was graduated from Bellevue Hospital Medical College in 1854. He was in charge of the Marine Hospital for several years and, in addition, was an associate of Drs. Davis and Johnson on the Chicago Medical College faculty. Dr. S. C. Blake was city physician of Chicago from 1865 to 1867. Dr. R. M. Paddock lived in the south-western corner of Cook County, in the direction of Joliet. Dr. T. W. Dresser was born in 1837. He was graduated from the Medical University of New York City in 1864. Dr. R. J. Patterson, born in Massachusetts in 1816, was graduated in medicine in 1842. He founded the Bellevue Place Sanatorium at Batavia, Illinois, in 1867, but before that he had been connected with hospitals for the insane such as the Ohio Insane Hospital, Indiana Insane Hospital, and Iowa Insane Asylum. He was an associate of Drs. Davis, Johnson, and Isham on the faculty of the Chicago Medical College. Dr. Willis Danforth was born in 1826 and was graduated at the Rock Island Medical College in 1849. For several years he was Professor of Surgery and Gynecology at the

patient's insanity. They swore briefly that she was insane, irresponsible, and unable to manage her property.

Dr. T. W. Dresser, her family physician for years and the son of the minister who married her and Mr. Lincoln, wrote:[1] "While the whole world was finding fault with her temper and disposition, it was clear to me that her trouble was a cerebral disease." He meant that he knew her to be insane, but beyond that he did not go in his diagnosis.

One of the physicians who testified, Dr. Willis Danforth, gave a description of her behavior in some detail, but made no attempt to interpret the meaning of her symptoms. He described hallucinations of sight and hearing, and various others, including delusions of persecution.

After her death, the Chicago *Times*[2] had a story of her mental disturbance which contained the following information:

"She became possessed of some peculiar whims. One was that she would suddenly come to poverty and want. She could not be shaken out of this belief even though she admitted that she owned $60,000 in bonds and she had no debts. Another queer fancy she had was for accumulating window curtains. While staying at a hotel in Chicago, with no prospect of ever again keeping house, she had piled up in her room over sixty pairs of lace curtains. When her mind was instable she rarely bought articles singly. When she purchased dress-goods, it was by the bolt, lace curtains in

Chicago Homeopathic College. At the time he attended Mrs. Lincoln, in 1872 and thereabouts, his office was at 1224 Wabash Avenue (old number), Chicago. About 1880 he moved to Milwaukee. Dr. Charles Gilman Smith was born in Exeter, New Hampshire, in 1828; was graduated from Harvard University in 1847, went to Philadelphia for his medical education, and was graduated from the University of Pennsylvania in 1851. He settled in Chicago in 1853. Drs. Davis, Johnson, Isham, Danforth, and Smith testified in the 1875 trial. Dr. Blake was on the jury. Dr. Paddock was on the jury in the 1876 trial. Dr. Smith also attended Tad in his last illness, and Drs. Davis and Johnson were consultants. Dr. Danforth attended Mrs. Lincoln at times between 1872 and 1875. Dr. Patterson was in charge of Mrs. Lincoln at Batavia. Dr. Dresser attended her in Springfield.

[1] Bibliography, No. 75c, p. 351.

[2] July 17, 1882.

pairs, watches in threes. On one occasion it was the entire stock of one article." This is confirmed by accounts from other sources.

In Eddie Foy's narrative of his life,[1] there appears some evidence from his mother as to Mrs. Lincoln's symptoms, after 1871 and before 1875. He wrote: "Mother was employed as a sort of nurse, guard, and companion to Mrs. Lincoln." He fixed the period as beginning in February 1872 by relating the period of employment to the date of Jim Fiske's death. Continuing, he said: "Mrs. Lincoln had always been a woman of rather unusual disposition. After her husband's assassination she fell into deep melancholy and after her son Tad died, she suffered from periods of mild insanity. She had many strange delusions. At these times she thought gas was an invention of the devil and would have nothing but candles in her room. At other times, she insisted on the shades being drawn and the room kept perfectly dark. Mother was with her at Springfield most of the time but made one or two Southern trips with her in winter. The position was a trying one and Mother gave it up twice, but each time the kinsmen induced her to come back after she had had a short rest. She remained with Mrs. Lincoln until toward the close of the latter's life, when that unfortunate lady became so much unbalanced that the family thought it best to place her in a private sanatorium."

On August 28, 1875 Dr. Patterson wrote a letter,[2] addressed to the editor of the Chicago *Tribune,* giving an account of Mrs. Lincoln while in the sanatorium. "She is certainly much improved, both mentally and physically, but I have not at any time regarded her as a person of a sound mind. . . . I heard all the testimony at the trial and saw no reason to doubt the correctness of the verdict. I believe her now to be insane. . . . The question of her removal has received careful consideration. . . . The proposition having been made that she should go and live with her sister,

[1] Bibliography, No. 60.

[2] Bibliography, No. 83, September 1, 1875.

I at once said if she should do this in good faith I should favor it. . . . In accordance with this, Mr. Lincoln [Robert] made efforts to transfer her to Springfield. . . . It is well known that there are certain insane persons who need what, in medico-legal science, is termed ' interdiction,' which does not necessarily imply restraint. If time should show that Mrs. Lincoln needs only the former, all will rejoice to see any possible enlargement of her privileges. . . . I am still unwilling to throw any obstacles in the way of giving her an opportunity to have a home with her sister. But I am willing to record the opinion that, such is the character of her malady, she will not be content to do this, and that the experiment, if made, will result only in giving the coveted opportunity to make extended rambles, to renew the indulgence of her purchasing mania, and other morbid mental manifestations. . . ." Returning to her behavior more directly, he said: "She will not remain indoors except by her own choice more than two or three waking hours of any day. She receives calls from ladies of her acquaintance in Batavia and may return them. She has been called on by General Farnsworth and by some of her relatives from Springfield."

On July 2, 1875 the *Illinois State Journal* copied a story from the New York *Tribune,* which was written by a special correspondent and gives evidence of stating Dr. Patterson's opinions, as follows: "No restraint other than a prudent supervision is necessary. At present her derangement exhibits itself mainly in a general mental feebleness and incapacity. No encouragement is held out that Mrs. Lincoln will ever become permanently well."

Dr. E. Swain, a dentist and Civil War veteran who lived near by, called on Mrs. Lincoln at the sanatorium. He reported that she was under the delusion that she was still in the White House.

A reporter who visited the sanatorium, because of reports that had grown out of the Bradwell correspondence, also wrote that Mrs. Lincoln was under the delusion that she was still in the White House, and that Mr. Lincoln was with her. At times they were alone together, she thought, and over him she exercised a motherly care. At other times public receptions were being held, or important visitors were being entertained. She complained of rappings on the wall, and of people talking in the next room. She had many hallucinations and not a few fixed delusions. She showed irresponsibility in her purchases made in Aurora. She was allowed to drive through the beautiful surrounding country, and she called on some of the neighbors and was visited by them in turn.

After Mrs. Lincoln's release from Batavia and until her death she behaved differently. A change had come over her and she was quite unlike her former self. She was no longer aggressive or offensive; she fought no battles, indulged in no hysteria. She did not purchase goods wildly nor show other evidences of prodigality. She traveled but twice, and both trips showed judgment. Her long, quiet stay in Pau, away from emotions and people who excited them, was wise in its conception and in its execution. Her trip to New York was for a purpose. But these incidents, occurrences, and attitudes do not mean that mental soundness had been attained; they mean that Mrs. Lincoln had acquired the ability to yield to restraint—self-restraint and restraint by others. She continued to have hallucinations and delusions, to be at once a miser and a spendthrift (though both qualities were restrained), to cherish grudges against her family and friends, to keep in a dark room, and to avoid life. Even more significant, they confirm the opinion that her personality was of the introvert type.

This introvert type of personality disturbance Mrs. Lincoln manifested in a striking way from the time she was released from the sanatorium until her death, in 1882. It is true that the European record is most fragmentary, but such information as there is indicates that Mrs. Lincoln lived the life of a hermit. What is said of her in Springfield goes to prove that she lived away from everybody and everything after she returned from Europe.

In 1882 there was some evidence of slowly developing dementia. Laura C. Holloway says:[1] "During the last few months of her life she was most of the time little cognizant of what was taking place about her."

MONEY

When Mrs. Lincoln's sanity was passed on legally, the feature of her mental disturbance which her son and his lawyers had largely in mind was unsound judgment in financial matters. In the ten years preceding this trial Robert had felt some responsibility for his mother and her affairs, and it was this phase of her behavior that had occasioned him most worry. He knew that it had been the cause of the auction and the pension episodes; and the bitter experiences of these had greatly impressed his young mind. Much of the evidence presented at the first trial, and practically all of that brought out in the second, related to Mrs. Lincoln's ability to manage her property.

Nothing in Mrs. Lincoln's history prior to the middle or latter part of her Springfield residence throws any direct light on this quality. As to the Springfield days, there are a few references to frugality, combined with a tendency to spend money somewhat extravagantly on dress.

About a month before the family was ready to leave Springfield, Mrs. Lincoln did something that has been interpreted as being the first indication of mental disturbance. This was going to New York "to make purchases for the White House." Katherine Helm says[2] she went, and for the purpose indicated. The Cleveland *Herald* carried a news item that Mrs. Lincoln and party had passed through that city *en route* to New York. On January 17 Mrs. Lincoln wrote to Judge David Davis from New York. On Janu-

[1] Bibliography, No. 80, p. 544. [2] Bibliography, No. 73.

ary 24 she was back in Springfield. Beyond doubt the purpose of the trip was to shop, but it is not certain that she bought anything for the White House except, possibly, some curtains. Probably " the purchases for the White House " might better have read: " purchase of dresses to be worn in the White House."

Much more significant are those financial tangles in which Mrs. Lincoln was involved after she got to Washington, coupled with the reports of coexistent parsimoniousness and prodigality.

Elizabeth Keckley's narrative is supplemented by evidence from other sources. After due allowance has been made for carping, there remains enough proof to establish the fact that Mrs. Lincoln, between 1861 and 1865, was most foolishly extravagant and at the same time decidedly near, close, or frugal.

Between 1865 and 1871 the mania for getting money drove her into embarrassing situations. It caused her to write letters in which she fawned and pleaded for help and in which she was also very uncomplimentary and unfair to those who failed to meet her exactions. In this period she indulged in some extravagances. Occasionally the character of these indicated insanity, as was testified at the trial. After 1871 the mania for money-getting was not particularly manifested, and after 1875 the extravagance in buying and other spending was less in evidence. Frugality now developed into miserliness and dominated the mind of Mrs. Lincoln on its financial side.

An illustration of the nature of her imbalance is supplied by a controversy which she precipitated in 1881. Mrs. Lincoln was advised by Dr. Lewis A. Sayre to get a maid or nurse, because of her crippled condition caused by the Pau accident. She replied that she could not afford one; her means were limited to her pension of $3,000; she formerly had had an income of $1,400 from her husband's estate, but she had lost that.

This interview started an unfortunate discussion. The Springfield (Illinois) *Journal*[1] quoted Jacob Bunn as saying his bank ". . . held in trust for her bonds worth $60,000, the interest on which is $2,120 yearly. This is in addition to her pension. While she was in Europe she spent all her income, frequently drawing it in advance. But since then she has saved $5,000. She now has a capital of $65,000 and her yearly income is $5,300." Mr. Bunn's statements were more than conservative.

The three-cornered fight in her mental make-up between the desire to get, the desire to spend, and the desire to hoard had lasted for nearly forty years. Sometimes one combatant was on top, sometimes another. In the final stretch miserliness held the field of battle.

Mrs. Lincoln inherited her financial type of mind. In her childhood she and her teachers must have failed to catch the meaning of the Tenth Commandment, and thus she missed something she greatly needed. Her financial mental qualities had no opportunity to show themselves prior to her marriage. The influence of her husband's prudence helped to develop the frugality feature of her complex. Anticipated social demands of the White House caused her to remove the restraints from her desire-to-spend quality. Her urgent need of money between 1865 and the beginning of her pension was responsible in that period for the complete dominance of the mania for getting money. When she received her pension in 1871, acquisitiveness, extravagance, and frugality resumed their interrupted contest. The testimony given at the trial made her aware of the error of her extravagance, as well as its futility, and after that miserliness had no difficulty in dominating this field of her mind.

This complex of mania for money, extravagance, and miserliness — paradoxical as it appears to laymen — is well known to psychiatrists. It is present in many people

[1] July 18, 1882.

who are accepted as normal. In Mrs. Lincoln I think the majority of psychiatrists would hold that it was developed to the point where it did not prove actual insanity; that, at most, it made of her not more than a border-line case. All would agree as to the disintegrating effects of her worries over financial insecurity.

EMOTIONALISM

Mrs. Lincoln inherited a considerable degree of emotionalism, though in her forbears it was generally under control and was not developed beyond the capacities of the individual. Elizabeth Norris's account [1] indicates that emotionalism was so prominent in Mary Todd as to be foreboding.

The first account of a manifestation which was serious in itself was that which followed the death of Eddie. (Dr. William E. Barton did not think it was of great import at that time.) The deaths of Willie, Tad, and Mr. Lincoln were responsible for outbreaks that were of great influence. These prolonged hysterical outbreaks were not manifestations of a diseased mentality, and it is not as such that they are given prominence in the portrayal of Mrs. Lincoln's behavior.

When she mourned as she did, she was influenced partly by the customs of her day and partly by her upbringing. We must judge her by the customs of her times, and not by those of ours.

Lyle Saxon quotes [2] from the diary of Lestant, who described life in Louisiana in 1850. In a part of the diary he deals with mourning customs and emotional exhibitions of women, as follows: "The painful tale was told my aunt, who immediately fainted, and during the day had many fainting fits, which followed each other in rapid succession. Her grief was great, and her cries and lamentations so

[1] Bibliography, No. 72.

[2] Bibliography, No. 155, pp. 234–6.

painful that everyone present could not but sympathize with her, and in the whole house the whites and blacks were bathed in tears. . . . Her grief continued. For the next week she went from collapse into collapse."

The tragedies in Mrs. Lincoln's life occurred only twelve and fifteen years after the period of which Lestant wrote, and Mrs. Lincoln followed a method of mourning generally in vogue during her youth. She wore deep-mourning clothes and mourning jewelry, wrote on black-bordered paper, and talked and wrote of her dead from 1865 until she died. She followed almost the same method for three years prior to 1865. This was not greatly out of line with the customs of the time.

Nor is our boasted twentieth century civilization above the influence of environment on mourning methods. There are circles in which wild and hysterical mourning is the rule, and quiet acceptance of death raises questions. We have seen the poor impoverish themselves by extravagant expenditures on funerals; and recent history is replete with stories of barbaric splendor at the grave-side of murderers, racketeers, and other social outcasts.

The significance of Mrs. Lincoln's mourning was twofold. It tended to wear down such emotional stability as she possessed; it was a cause of her trouble, and not a manifestation. And it demonstrated a lack of equilibrium, stability, and poise. This lack was shown in the tantrums of her childhood. There were other outbreaks of temper at other times. It was this quality, becoming more and more evident, that caused Lincoln to tell his wife in Washington that she was letting her prejudices and her dislikes spoil her political judgment. The crowning manifestations of her resentment of frustration were her emotional outbreaks upon the deaths of her husband and two children.

Yet while Mrs. Lincoln had temporary periods of great emotionalism during her years of insanity, this quality was not a continuing or characteristic symptom.

HALLUCINATIONS AND DELUSIONS

Since hallucinations were so prominent in the composition of Mrs. Lincoln's disturbed mind, and since these were not due to the use of drugs, we must look for an explanation to two causes: one, her type of mind; two, the experiences of her life.

Hallucinations are almost normal with a considerable percentage of children. The psychiatrists recognize what they term the eidetic type of mind. Stedman's *Medical Dictionary* defines " eidetic " as: " Relating to the power of visualization of objects previously seen or imagined. An eidetic person is one possessing this power to a high degree." Children of this type are given to realistic day-dreams in which they see people and scenes with great particularity and detail. They are credited with lying about these visions with a coolness and assurance that cause parents and courts great apprehension. It is, to a degree, a phenomenon of childhood. Not much training is required to bring these eidetic children out of the danger zone and to land them in a state of assured normalcy. The specialists in children's behavior say, however, that this eidetic type continues to manifest itself throughout adult life, though not in vagaries of vision. Persons of the type have photographic memories, remember poetry well, can reproduce what they see or hear in art or music. Some of them become spiritualists, and some develop hallucinations.

No one tells of any ancestor from whom Mrs. Lincoln might have inherited eidetic qualities, nor is there any story of her youth or childhood that shows her to have an eidetic constitution. Emilie Todd Helm's diary [1] contains the first reference to Mrs. Lincoln's hallucinations. This related to manifestations in 1863.

It was certain that Mrs. Lincoln was very much under the influence of spiritualists and spiritualism. Her words, as

[1] Bibliography, No. 72.

Mrs. Helm quotes them,[1] were evidently based on spiritualist dogma and creed. They were not the creations of a disordered brain, and, not being so, they lose much of their significance. An ability to agree with an unsound belief, or to accept it as a religious creed, may indicate a lack of well-balanced judgment, but it is not proof of mental unsoundness. In Mrs. Lincoln, as is so often the case with spiritualists, wishful thinking was the chief reason for acceptance.

At the time of Mrs. Lincoln's trial the significance of spiritualism and its possible relation to insanity was under discussion in medical circles. It was in this period that Dr. W. A. Hammond,[2] the leading psychiatrist of the times, wrote a book entitled *Spiritualism and Allied Causes and Conditions of Nervous Derangement.* Dr. Patterson was certainly acquainted with Dr. Hammond's views, and Dr. Danforth, who also said much about Mrs. Lincoln's visions, may have known of it. Dr. Hammond was of the opinion that spiritualism was both a cause of insanity, and a manifestation of mental unsoundness that at least bordered on the pathologic. The rather general acceptance of the Hammond view in 1875, and for several years thereafter, militated against Mrs. Lincoln.

"WANDERLUST"

Dr. Patterson based his opinion that Mrs. Lincoln was irresponsible partly on her " wanderlust."

Prior to 1861 Mrs. Lincoln traveled very little, when all things are considered. She went to Springfield and back to Lexington in 1837. In 1839 she returned to Springfield and stayed there steadily for twenty-two years, with the exception of one trip to Niagara, one to Washington, two or three visits to her family in Lexington, and one or two short trips. Between 1861 and 1865 she developed something of a mania for travel — her foot " itched for the

[1] Bibliography, No. 72. [2] Bibliography, No. 68.

road," in the parlance of the hobo. She indulged this " foot-itch " enough to bring harsh criticism.

Between 1865 and 1871 she went to New York on business once, and she visited her husband's grave in Springfield. She went to health resorts several times. Most of the time she had no home and stayed in hotels at resorts nearly as much as she stayed in them in Chicago. On the first trip to Europe she kept Tad in school, but she moved about somewhat extensively and frequently.

After 1871 and until 1875 she appears to have wandered most of the time. In several instances, however, her visits were in search of health. Between September 1875 and October 1876 she stayed closely in her sister's home in Springfield. Then came the second trip to Europe. She appears not to have traveled much during those four years in Europe. Her two visits to New York after 1880 were for the purpose of securing expert orthopedic advice.

The conclusion is that Dr. Patterson over-emphasized Mrs. Lincoln's desire to travel in his diagnosis and prognosis.

Mrs. Lincoln's personality was the basis of her trouble, and part of this was the result of inheritance. A larger part was due to her education — formal and informal, youthful and adult, school and life. Her undoing was the reaction between her personality and the experiences of her life. C. L. McCollister says:[1] " There appears to be a limit to the amount of mental stress and physical strain that every individual is capable of bearing, determined not only by the inherent qualities of the individual, but also by the environmental conditions during the formation period of early life."

Mrs. Lincoln's insanity was an emotional disturbance. It was not until she was approaching the end that she developed any considerable degree of dementia. Hallucinations

[1] Bibliography, No. 117.

and delusions, over-emotionalism, lack of poise and stability, poor judgment proceeding from prejudices and dislikes, a paradoxical combination of miserliness and extravagance, and an urge to travel were symtoms of her disorder. More important than these symptoms, in ascertaining the type of her insanity, was her habit of shutting herself in and excluding the world, particularly when she failed to accomplish what she wanted. This was the more significant because, mixed with this quality, were aggressiveness and determination, both very prominent in her behavior at times. She had an introvert personality, and she developed an insanity which was of the emotions, now called "involutional."

WHEN DID SHE BECOME INSANE?

There is no accepted definition of insanity. Courts have one definition, physicians a second, and lay people a third. Not infrequently one court will decide that a person is insane, while a second court will come to a contrary decision. Physicians show the same lack of agreement. It is not to be wondered at that persons who wrote of Mrs. Lincoln differed as to when she became irresponsible.

W. O. Stoddard saw that something was wrong soon after 1861. The Chicago *Times* wrote of her:[1] "She had always been of a nervous temperament. After her husband's assassination she appeared always to be weighed down with woe, and after the shock of Tad's death was added, she showed marked symptoms of insanity. Many of her old-time friends say she showed signs of insanity as far back as 1860."

It is true, as the *Times* said, that it had been suggested that she was insane before she went to Washington. Some of the "Springfield tradition" said she was mentally unbalanced in the second decade of the Springfield era. These,

[1] July 17, 1882.

however, were just gossipy stories and were never seriously considered.

Jane Gray Swissheim wrote:[1] " I think she was never entirely sane after the shock of her husband's murder; but on most subjects she was entirely clear."

Lloyd Lewis says[2] that Abraham Lincoln gave Mrs. Lincoln's mental state as one reason for having Robert continue in college rather than go to war. His words are: " Since her sanity was always a matter of tender concern to her husband, he had feared that her reason would topple over if he [Robert] had been exposed to the dangers of war." This implies a fear of insanity in 1861.

The Chicago *Tribune* states:[3] " This death [Tad's] following that of her husband and, more remotely, that of two other children, has been a fearful blow to Mrs. Lincoln. Her physician [Dr. C. G. Smith] dreads that it may produce insanity, though he is hopeful of averting so sad a calamity." The Chicago *Tribune*,[4] the day after the first trial, traced her insanity to the death of her husband, saying the death of Tad was a contributing cause.

Robert T. Lincoln[5] regarded his mother as unbalanced as early as October 16, 1867. On that date he wrote Mary Harlan, who later became his wife: " My mother is on one subject [money] not mentally responsible. . . . It is hard to deal with one who is sane on all subjects but one."

Eddie Foy, basing what he wrote on what his mother told him, set the date of onset as 1871.[6] His mother, in turn, was repeating what she had heard from Mrs. Lincoln's physicians, family, and friends.

Laura C. Holloway sets the date of onset as 1865, saying:[7] ". . . from the time of Mr. Lincoln's death . . . a mental wreck . . . would never recover."

[1] Bibliography, No. 169, July 18, 1882.
[2] Bibliography, No. 101, p. 29.
[3] July 18, 1871.
[4] May 20, 1875.
[5] Bibliography, No. 73, p. 267.
[6] Bibliography, No. 60.
[7] Bibliography, No. p 80, pp. 539 ff.

H. C. Whitney[1] was of the opinion that Mrs. Lincoln was not responsible for her acts after April 1865.

F. F. Brown quotes the Hon. A. G. Riddle as agreeing with this, in these words:[2] ". . . the national calamity which unsettled her mind, as I always thought."

I. N. Arnold fixes the date of Mrs. Lincoln's mental aberration as 1871:[3] "After 1871 Mrs. Lincoln, in the judgment of her most intimate friends, was never entirely responsible for her conduct. She was peculiar and eccentric and had various hallucinations." He describes her mental attitude and conversation in the summer of 1865, however, as being quite normal.

If called upon to decide between these several opinions, I would say that Mrs. Lincoln was irresponsible after April 1865, and that between 1861 and 1865 she should not be held accountable for some of her actions.

[1] Bibliography, No. 190.
[2] Bibliography, No. 26.
[3] Bibliography, No. 4, p. 433.

CHAPTER SIXTEEN

Mutual Influence

Few great men have flourished who, were they candid, would not acknowledge the vast advantage they have experienced in the earlier years of their careers from the spirit and sympathy of woman.

— DISRAELI

A pearl becomes red by the nearness of a rose.

— SANSKRIT

CHAPTER SIXTEEN

Mutual Influence

When Mary Todd met Abraham Lincoln she was over twenty years old, and he was over thirty. When they were married, she was nearly twenty-four years old, and he was well on towards thirty-four. In the interval of more than three years there was a period of about eighteen months in which he saw very little of her. Their married life lasted nearly twenty-two and a half years, during which time they became the parents of four boys. Together they bore the sorrow caused by the death of two of them. They enjoyed together the training and upbringing of these children, one to four years, two to twelve, one to twenty-two.

Abraham Lincoln gave his wife opportunity. Through him she came to be Mistress of the White House. He was responsible for her acquaintance with many great men and women. He was a politician with great acumen, and she, too, was politically minded. Together they met defeats and celebrated victories. Discussing this theme, one might be justified in an excursion into these fields and many others, but that would raise more questions than can be settled.

Several of their objectives were held in common. That he influenced her through his intellect and his personality needs no argument. It can be accepted as a fact, and the only question to argue is as to the limits and bounds of that influence. That she influenced him can also be accepted. The questions to be discussed, then, are: How? In what qualities? Within what limits?

When two such different, even divergent, types of mind as those of this husband and wife are mated for more than twenty years, there must be adjustments.

Dr. William E. Barton wrote:[1] "Abraham Lincoln and Mary Todd were divinely constituted to make each other uncomfortable, and it is fortunate that they were made so. . . . She helped him to become a great man by not making him too comfortable. Some men do not know how much they have to be thankful for in this regard. . . . Mr. and Mrs. Lincoln were not always happy together, but their lives supplemented and enlarged each other. . . . They took each other for better or for worse and they, and the world, were better for it."

Mrs. Lincoln's mind crystallized early; Mr. Lincoln's, late. Lincoln could learn from almost anyone; Mrs. Lincoln, after maturity, could not learn much from anyone. His was a type of mind that offers large possibilities for adult education; hers was of the opposite type.

Lincoln's mind did not have great influence in shaping that of Mrs. Lincoln. This is not saying she did not learn from him, for she did. She was never a patient, forbearing, forgiving woman — that she could not be as long as she retained confidence in herself. She did acquire, however, a little of these qualities, as perhaps the following incidents may show.

She disliked Jacob Bunn and wrote about him in anger to Elizabeth Keckley, but she restrained her irritation and met him graciously. She had some tiffs with the Mathers and, remembering that they had fought her husband politically more bitterly than she thought they should have done, she refused to allow Lincoln's body to be buried in the ground bought for the purpose from the Mathers. And yet when she returned to Springfield, she went one day to the Mather

[1] Bibliography, No. 11.

home, wearing her deep widow's weeds, to show the family that she was willing to forget and be friends. She did not like William H. Herndon, but in 1866 she wrote him an appealing, kindly letter, in response to a letter asking for an interview, and she saw him when she went to visit her husband's grave, greeting him in friendly fashion.

She learned something of Lincoln's patience and forbearance, but not much. Whatever business capacity she had she must have learned from him, because previously she had had no business experience, and between 1865 and 1882 she showed considerable business ability. Certainly she learned politics and a measure of statecraft from her husband. However, summing up all we know, and applying what is known of psychology, the conclusion is that Lincoln did not succeed in greatly changing his wife's personality or her mental type. He tried when he gave her Mary G. Chandler's book. Doubtless he tried all his married life, but Mrs. Lincoln was of a type not easily changed.

INFLUENCE OF MRS. LINCOLN'S MIND AND PERSONALITY ON THOSE OF HER HUSBAND

The time has not come to write an adequate thesis on the mind of Lincoln. What is written now cannot be final or convincing; we need more information, but above all we need closer analysis of that we have. Dr. Barton was at least investigating this aspect of Lincoln, but either he did not mature his opinions or he had not found time to record them.

An investigation would necessarily include a study of Lincoln's anatomy and physiology, his body type, features, beard; his ways of thinking and talking, his ability as a lawyer, his position on political questions; a close analysis of all speeches (similar to that Barton made of the Gettysburg address), messages, and writings. It is to be hoped that someone will conduct to a conclusion some such comprehensive study of the mind of Abraham Lincoln.

Meanwhile the purpose in writing these pages, which do not logically belong in a study of Mrs. Lincoln's personality, is to put on record as much of an answer as I have found to one of the questions with which the study began.

A study of the influence of Mrs. Lincoln on her husband's personality should begin with some understanding of his inherited qualities.

The members of his family, and even Lincoln himself, had the habit of aligning themselves with the wife's clan — not a matriarchy, but a habit having some suggestions of that. Let us start the story with Thomas Lincoln.

By the time Tom Lincoln had settled down in Elizabethtown, Kentucky, he had cut away from the Lincolns, and only a few times thereafter did he encounter any of his own blood except his children. When he met Nancy Hanks, she was living with her aunt. After he married, his family affiliations were with the Hanks family. When they moved from Kentucky to Indiana, Nancy's uncle, aunt, and cousin went with them. All of these Hankses, except Dennis, died and were buried in Indiana by the side of Nancy and her daughter. When Tom and his household, including Dennis Hanks, moved to Illinois, they went to the home of John Hanks, in Macon County.

After Abraham moved to Sangamon County, he had no family life until he married Mary Todd. After that he rarely saw any of the Hankses, and he never saw any of the Lincolns, except for a few visits to his parents, an occasional contact with Dennis, and a few brief visits with some of his own very distant cousins. Is it to be wondered at that almost no one knew of any Lincoln kin he had, and that few of the Lincolns knew that the Abraham Lincoln of Illinois, nominated for president in 1860, was of the Kentucky family of that name, not to mention that he was one of the Virginia and Massachusetts Lincolns?

When Lincoln married, he followed the example of his father and joined his wife's clan. There were many Todds in Illinois. Among those in Springfield were Mary Todd's three sisters; her uncle, Dr. John Todd, and his family; her cousins, Judge John T. Stuart, Judge Stephen T. Logan, and Congressman John J. Hardin. There were the husbands, wives, and children of all of these and, possibly, a number of other less prominent relations. This was a large clan and a powerful one. It did much to promote the fortune of Lincoln, one way or another — and it also hampered him. Certainly his wife's people, if not his wife, modified Lincoln by the unconscious influences of family association.

Lewis M. Terman, of Stanford University, is quoted as saying:[1] "Extensive tests over years indicate husbands are prone, after marriage, to take on certain of the characteristics of their wives and to surrender certain of their attributes." Mary Day Winn writes:[2] "Psychologists tell us that marriages in which woman is the dominating half show a higher percentage of success than those which are the other way round. . . . The higher the husband rises in the scale of achievement, the more power he will probably let his wife assume in the family. Compare the relative standing of the wife in the ditch-digger's home with her position in that of the corporation president's." And then Miss Winn quotes James L. Clark:[3] "The rear-seat status in the family is an indication of strength rather than weakness."

The acceptance of this doctrine would make it possible to hold that Mrs. Lincoln was the dominating member of the firm of Abraham and Mary Lincoln, without committing *lèse-majesté*. But the facts will not justify the conclusion.

If we set side by side the Lincoln of 1839 and the Lincoln of 1865 and compare them point by point, detail by detail, we realize that potent influences were at work in this twenty-six-year period. I doubt if in all history there is an illustration of greater change in personality, mentality, and culture

[1] Bibliography, No. 193. [2] Ibid. [3] Ibid.

where the person under comparison was thirty years old at the beginning of the observation. No single agency was responsible for the change in Abraham Lincoln, and certainly I would not undertake to show that Mrs. Lincoln was entitled to a great deal of the credit. There were certain turning-points in Abraham Lincoln's life, and whoever or whatever was exerting much influence during these episodes can be said to be in a measure responsible for the changes that resulted.

Albert J. Beveridge [1] regards the Shields duel episode as one of these turning-points, if he does not think it of even greater importance than this designation implies. He says: "Thus ended the most lurid personal incident in Lincoln's entire life, the significance of which in his development is vital." Ida Tarbell [2] agrees with Beveridge as to the importance of this affair; at least, in great measure. If Beveridge's view be accepted, Mary Todd deeply influenced Lincoln, because she was the cause of that incident. I am of the opinion that, while the Shields duel episode changed Lincoln's political methods, it had no profound influence on his mentality. Early in his life he was a good deal of a country bumpkin, and not infrequently he wrote anonymous letters that contained buffoonery. The Shields duel episode was the somewhat dramatic and embarrassing event which ended Lincoln's indulgence in clowning.

There is one suggestion that surpasses that of Beveridge in its implications. It is that when Lincoln married Mary Todd, there was an end to his periodic melancholia; or, better, a mastery over it — a mastery which pulled its teeth and made it harmless. The suggestion comes from John G. Nicolay, who wrote: [3] "His marriage to Miss Todd ended all those mental perplexities and periods of despondency from which he had suffered more or less during his several love-affairs, extending over nearly a decade. Out of the keen

[1] Bibliography, No. 18, p. 353.
[2] Bibliography, No. 170, p. 243.
[3] Bibliography, No. 133, p. 69.

anguish he had endured he finally gained that complete mastery over his own spirit which Scripture declares to denote a greatness superior to that of him who takes a city. Few men have ever attained that complete domination of the will over the emotions, of reason over passion, by which he was able, in the years to come, to meet and solve the tremendous questions destiny had in store for him."

In connection with these statements Nicolay discussed the Ann Rutledge and the Shields duel affairs. Evidently he thought the peculiar melancholia was a temporary phase of the Lincoln make-up and was one of the by-products of his urge for mating. It was impersonal, as far as the woman was concerned, and manifested itself during the Ann Rutledge, Mary Owens, and Mary Todd affairs and other Lincoln associations with women. He regarded it as biological.

The " Lincoln blues " have been the subject of much discussion. Dr. Barton, who investigated the subject more insistently than anyone else, was of the opinion that periodic melancholia was an inherited trait of the Lincoln family, and was known among them as the " Lincoln blues." He interviewed cousins of Abraham Lincoln, who told him they had the same personality fault as did other Lincolns, and that it was something of a family peculiarity. They did not say that it was peculiar to any period of life, or that it was related to the mating urge. Barton certainly had read Nicolay at the time he interviewed the Lincoln cousins, but he seems to have missed the suggestion that the melancholy was related to the mating urge.

Dr. J. H. Kellogg, accepting the opinion of Judge Stuart, attributed the periods of depression from which Lincoln suffered to obstinate constipation and the frequent use of large doses of calomel. Others have ascribed the attacks to malaria — then endemic in the Illinois country, as well as in Kentucky and Indiana — from which Lincoln is known to have suffered. Others have attributed it to bad teeth; and still others, to bad feet.

Karl Menninger[1] classes Lincoln as a cyclic personality, the melancholia being the depression stage of this type of personality. It is not true that Lincoln had no return of these attacks after his marriage, as might be inferred from what Nicolay said. Menninger probably thinks the attacks were finally overcome, because he takes the position that the Lincoln cyclic personality was trained into a greater " evenness."

J. F. Newton[2] quotes Nicolay and John Hay as ascribing these fits of depression to the general mental depression of pioneers fighting battles against privation and disease. He quotes William H. Herndon as thinking three causes were operating simultaneously: heredity, mourning for the lost Ann Rutledge, and the unhappiness of his home. And then he gives his own opinion, which was: " His sadness was largely due to his temperament." Most Lincoln biographers say Lincoln's blues were far from ending with his marriage.

Beveridge says[3] that melancholia was Lincoln's most striking personality characteristic when he was practicing law on the circuit between 1840 and 1860, basing his opinion on incidents and opinions supplied by such intimate associates as Leonard Swett, Judge David Davis, H. C. Whitney, Herndon, and Matheny. In fact, he quotes Matheny as saying that, when Lincoln " first came amongst us," he was anything but melancholy, and the characteristic was later acquired. This we know is also a mistake.

F. F. Brown[4] gives attacks of melancholy as having been frequently observed in Washington after 1861.

Marriage did not cure Lincoln of his melancholia, and no one can claim such a cure as a result of the influence of his wife. On the other hand, there is so much evidence that Lincoln was subject to these attacks prior to his marriage that we need not pay attention to the charge made by more than one person that Mrs. Lincoln was the cause of them. It is true that after his marriage he never fled when in bad

[1] Bibliography, No. 119.
[2] Bibliography, No. 127, pp. 316, 328, 329.
[3] Bibliography, No. 18, p. 521.
[4] Bibliography, No. 26, p. 543.

"spells," as Herndon says he did after Ann Rutledge's death and after the break with Mary Todd. But if, in time, there was a difference in his reaction to the melancholy tendency as the years rolled by, it was because with age, and perhaps marriage, he had more responsibilities and he gained poise and self-control. Much as we should like to think that marriage cured Lincoln of his blues and, therefore, to his wife is due some part of the credit, there are too many facts and opinions that interpose.

THE EFFECT OF AN UNHAPPY HOME

Herndon wrote:[1] "Mrs. Lincoln's fearless, witty, and austere nature shrank instinctively from association with the calm, imperturbable, and simple ways of her thoughtful and absent-minded husband." He makes the statement that Lincoln's home life was unhappy, and he says it in more ways than one. It was his opinion that the irascibility of Mrs. Lincoln caused her to quarrel with her husband, to tongue-lash him considerably; and, at times, caused him to leave the house to secure peace. He tells of Lincoln's staying weekends in circuit towns, absenting himself from home, eating cheese and crackers in the office; and he retails gossip of quarrels.

J. W. Weik's opinion[2] on the domestic discord of the Lincoln family is a combination of that of Herndon, Davis, Milton Hay, and Matheny — all of them intimate friends of Lincoln, who doubtless talked over the question with each other more than once, particularly after Herndon's lectures had become the occasion of forensic battles on the streets, in the homes, and elsewhere in Springfield. This combined or consensus opinion was then somewhat modified by Weik, who had done much investigation on his own account. It was, in substance, that domestic discord and a lack of peace and

[1] Bibliography, No. 75c.

[2] Bibliography, No. 186, pp. 89–93.

harmony in his home caused Lincoln to cultivate people wherever they could be found; to stay in his office and study; to work rather than follow a natural inclination to loaf comfortably and happily at home.

Oliver R. Barrett[1] holds about the same opinion. In elaboration of the theme, he says that Mrs. Lincoln taught her husband patience; how to accept what he could not alter. Had it not been for her and what she taught him, he could never have invited Stanton and Chase into his Cabinet, or stood them after they got there. Had his home been quieter and more comfortable spiritually, he would have visited less, made fewer acquaintances, read less.

Lloyd Lewis accepts this opinion also, saying:[2] "The woman Lincoln loved, and who loved him, had a fiery, scolding way that could be managed only with tolerant persuasion. . . . Instances like this seem typical of Lincoln's genius for management. He guided the electorate as he handled his wife."

These opinions as to the domestic relations of the Lincolns mean that Mrs. Lincoln's influence worked to Mr. Lincoln's advantage, though working contrary to his comfort and peace of mind.

The following may be stated as general laws: Too much comfort and satisfaction in the home tends to contentment and stagnation. The man who is very popular, who fits in very well, whose personality wins for him without effort, is liable to accept his winnings and to become inactive and unprogressive. Conversely, misfit conditions, within limits, promote that preparation and industry through which growth is at its best.

That Mrs. Lincoln had more ambition than her husband, as well as more drive and aggressiveness, is rather generally accepted. Newton wrote:[3] ". . . guided also by his ambitious little wife, who had been most unhappy during his

1 Personal statement.
2 Bibliography, No. 101.
3 Bibliography, No. 127, p. 58.

subsidence." Whitney's opinion was: [1] "The nation is largely indebted to her for its autonomy, I do not doubt. As to the full measure thereof — God only knows."

In support of the view that Mrs. Lincoln influenced her husband to be ambitious, Henry B. Rankin wrote: [2] "Above all, she had the most constant and enduring faith in Lincoln's political future, and tried by every means in the range of her unusually inspiring and vigorous personality to assist her husband in season and — some of her friends thought — out of season, when she saw Lincoln's ambition beginning to fail." Ward H. Lamon wrote: [3] "From that day to the day of the inauguration she never wavered in her faith that her hopes would be realized." And, again, Newton said: [4] "While not lazy, he was disposed to loaf and he needed the prodding of his gifted and aspiring wife. Had he married Ann Rutledge, or some other gentle country girl, he would not now be known to fame."

We can accept the view that Mrs. Lincoln had more ambition and aggressiveness than her husband, since it is fully in accord with what we know of the psychology of each. The combination of her superior possession of these two qualities, with her husband's foresight, wisdom, and genius for influencing and winning men, was a great one and in the end proved irresistible.

What information have we as to Mrs. Lincoln's influence over her husband during his incumbency of the presidency? How much of the Lincoln statesmanship, the Lincoln national policies, was the result of his wife's arguments, opinions, and influence? Elizabeth Keckley [5] leads us to think that her influence in this period was trivial. Lincoln was so impressed by his wife's emotionalism that he had lost confidence in her ability to weigh men fairly. His time was too fully occupied, and his attention too much engaged for him

[1] Bibliography, No. 190.
[2] Bibliography, No. 149, p. 122.
[3] Bibliography, No. 99, p. 221.
[4] Bibliography, No. 127, p. 322.
[5] Bibliography, No. 85, p. 104.

to talk seriously and at length with his wife, even if he had not found out that her emotionalism was ruining her judgment. The Lincoln policies, plans, and methods of the presidential period were Lincolnesque. They give no evidence of his wife's influence.

One of Herndon's estimates of Lincoln's mind was:[1] "Such was Lincoln's will. Because on one line of questions — the non-essentials — he was pliable, and on the other he was as immovable as the rocks, have arisen the contradictory notions prevalent regarding him. It only remains to say that he was inflexible and unbending when it was necessary to be so, and not otherwise. At one moment he was pliable and expansive as gentle air; at the next, as tenacious and unyielding as gravity itself."

As a politician Lincoln's mind was Fabian. Politicians have a Fabian psychology. They rise or fall, survive or perish, according to how accurately they diagnose time, place, and people, and act in accordance with the diagnosis. The Lincoln mind, in certain of the exigencies to which it was subjected, was as hard as rock. On some occasions it was resilient, soft, yielding; on others, it was granite-like. When a mind of this type is long in contact with a mind of Mrs. Lincoln's type, it is the more resilient and pliant one that best stands the friction.

Lincoln's outstanding mental characteristic was wisdom. His judgment was clear and cold. The decisions of Mrs. Lincoln were too much swayed by her likes and dislikes, prejudices, and other emotions to be designated as wise, or based on good judgment.

Summing it up, I cannot think that on matters of importance — or, in the long run, on many of lesser importance — Mrs. Lincoln's mind influenced that of her husband to any great extent.

---

[1] Bibliography, No. 75a, p. 609.

CHAPTER SEVENTEEN

Health

Till, like a clock worn out with eating time,
The wheels of weary life at last stood still.

— Dryden

CHAPTER SEVENTEEN

Health

THERE IS NO INFORMATION ABOUT MARY TODD'S HEALTH prior to the time she met Lincoln. The story of her Lexington life indicates, in a general way, that she was in excellent health, well nourished, and bubbling over with vitality. She may have had her share of childhood infections, because she was immune to scarlet fever, diphtheria, typhoid, and smallpox when these diseases invaded her own household. The Lincoln family infections [1] were in the persons of her children and husband. She lived to be sixty-three years of age and appears to have been sound in all her organs to the day of her death, unless diabetes was an exception. To a limited degree this may have meant that she had not suffered severely from diphtheria, scarlet fever, rheumatism, and some other diseases that often leave their marks on the vital organs. Also, to a limited degree, this argues that she may have acquired her immunities by the exposures of life—those that slowly confer protection rather than precipitate into disease.

[1] Abraham Lincoln, writing in the late fifties to his Kellogg kin, spoke of the Springfield family as well as the Cincinnati family having scarlet fever. The Kellogg child that was supposed to have the disease was Franklin Pierce Kellogg, born in 1852, who wrote me (April 4, 1931): "I do not remember any scarlet infection except hives when about age seven (1860). School epidemic gave me holiday from a schoolmarm, but my cousin Ed Smith (son of my half-aunt, of Springfield, Ill.) about that date had the scarlets."

HEADACHES

The first reference to any ill health that Mrs. Lincoln had related to headaches. On April 16, 1848 Lincoln wrote his wife a letter[1] from which the following is quoted: "And you are entirely free from headache? This is good — considering it is the first Spring you have been free from it since we were acquainted. I am afraid you will get so well and fat . . ." trailing off into a jest. The letter was written from Washington, where Lincoln was serving in Congress, to Lexington, where his wife and two children were visiting.

What does this quotation mean? Plainly, he was replying to a letter in which his wife had written that she had suffered no headaches. He said that she had had the disorder "since we were acquainted," which means 1840. "It is the first Spring you have been free from it. . . ." "Free from it" means that she had the headache habit — at least, that she had frequent attacks. They must have been limited to the springtime, or else they were much less violent and disabling at other seasons. Evidently he is doubtful about this being an end to the trouble, as she must have written in her letter she thought or hoped. He knew too much about the course of the headache habit, and about the nature of his wife's, to agree quickly that there were to be no more.

Mrs. Lincoln's further history confirmed her husband's doubt in the matter. From that time forward, the records that refer to the more intimate details of Mrs. Lincoln's affairs contain references to repeated headaches. This continues to be true until 1867.

If we can accept the negative evidence on the headache habit as meaning that there were no headaches prior to 1839, we have this habit developing in a woman about twenty-one years of age, becoming more disabling after

[1] Collection of Oliver R. Barrett.

marriage, and persisting until she is a little beyond fifty years of age. About all the evidence there is indicates that Mrs. Lincoln had some form of sick headache, or migraine, and probably a form that is more frequently encountered among women than men. It is in some way related to the sex organs and, many times, to sex life. It becomes less disabling after the menopause, the headaches recur less often, and the affliction eventually discontinues.

GENERAL COMPLAINTS

Mrs. Lincoln's letters from 1850 until her death — at least all that have been found — are filled with allusions to her poor health. She seems not to have been very ill, or ever to have had any definite disease, but she was usually complaining of some symptom or other or some sickness. She appears to have had the habit which many women and some men have of writing and talking about their symptoms and their illnesses.

In her letters written from Washington, Chicago, and various other places — many of which are in the North — she complains of chills and fevers. Because some of these places are not malarial now, we cannot say that they were not malarial then.

The references to poor health were a prominent theme in Mrs. Lincoln's letters written between 1861 and 1865, and almost a major in those written between 1865 and 1875. Dr. Willis Danforth's testimony relates to physical as well as mental illness, particularly about 1873. The two groups of disorders were traveling hand in hand. When she was in St. Augustine, Florida, in January 1875, she was sick in bed for three weeks. Her illness was severe enough to make the services of a nurse necessary.

In 1869 Mrs. Lincoln developed a persistent cough and evidently considered that she had "weak lungs." Her physicians may have agreed with her. In September 1870 she wrote to Mrs. Robert Lincoln from Leamington, England: [1] " I am coughing so badly I can scarcely write. In Liverpool I was so ' completely sick.' . . . This is the first day I have sat up. . . . My physician says I must go to a drier climate. . . . My health is again beginning to fail, as it did last winter." On January 13, 1871 she wrote from London to Mrs. Shipman: [2] " I get myself coughing most disagreeably." This may have been a transient bronchitis of no great importance. However, Tad's last illness may have been an effect of it. In the early spring of 1871 he developed a pleurisy that may have been tubercular.

One of the findings of the jury at the first trial was that Mrs. Lincoln was " not subject to epilepsy." I have found no evidence to the contrary. Mrs. Lincoln never had any symptoms of major epilepsy, nor any suggestion of minor epileptic manifestations. Her mind did not have the characteristics accepted as those of the epileptic mind. Nor is there any evidence of epilepsy in her family tree. The allusion to this disease may have been required by law, or in response to a suggestion found in the printed form supplied by the court.

THYROID TROUBLE

In her youth Mrs. Lincoln was sometimes overactive. This might have been the result of hyperthyroidism. In her later life — before the loss of weight which occurred as her final years approached — she appeared short and fat. After 1876 she did not often leave her room; her life was very inactive.

Photographs are, commonly, well touched up before being given out, and therefore may be misleading. In medical clinics specializing in thyroid troubles, the photographs of the patients kept in the files are " untouched." Some of Mrs. Lincoln's pictures — those taken toward the evening of her

[1] Bibliography, No. 73, pp. 271–98. [2] Ibid., p. 289.

life — are indicative of myxœdema. (Note the picture facing page 341.) This possibility is increased by the symptoms and attitudes recorded above. Myxœdema is a thyroid-minus condition, or hypothyroidism, which develops rather frequently in middle-aged women. It causes obesity, physical torpor, and mental slowness.

Beyond these indications there is no evidence that Mrs. Lincoln had any thyroid trouble, and such evidence as is cited is not of much value.

HALLUCINATIONS AND WHAT THEY SUGGEST

Mrs. Lincoln's mental illness was characterized by hallucinations. She saw persons who had no existence, and she heard sounds that were not. This quality of mind — manifested first in 1862, frequently shown in 1865, and very much in evidence in 1875 and thereafter — raises the question whether she used drugs, since bromides and other sleep-producing drugs, opiates, and whisky tend to promote hallucinations. No proof is forthcoming. No part of the record shows that she used drugs, and inquiry among those who might have known has not revealed anything.

The disposition which Mrs. Lincoln is known to have developed is suggestive of the long-continued use of sedatives of the bromide family. A woman of today, with her symptoms, probably would have tried bromides and more than one other sedative of that group. Here, too, proof is lacking that Mrs. Lincoln used any bromides or barbituric group drugs, and no one says that she did. Proof that Mrs. Lincoln used opiates is entirely lacking.

The members of the Lincoln household were abstemious in the purchase and use of liquors. Some have charged that Lincoln was a drinking man, citing as proof purchases for the household. Students of Abraham Lincoln have investigated these charges and report them without foundation.

Such infrequent purchases of alcoholics as were made for the household were for domestic purposes, and neither wife nor husband was ever a drinker.

DIABETES

There are many reasons for thinking that Mrs. Lincoln had diabetes during the later years of her life, perhaps after 1875. Symptoms of diabetes may have caused her to leave for France in October 1876. Pau was then a noted health resort, though not especially renowned for the treatment of diabetes. While in Pau, she drank Vichy water, and that has enjoyed some reputation in connection with this disorder. She drank these waters, but they did her no good. "However, I was not very much in need of them save for the continual running waters, so disagreeable and inconvenient," she is quoted as saying. The recurrent attacks of boils, the reference to "continual running waters," and the use of Vichy are suggestive of diabetes. Though hitherto a fat woman, her weight fell to a hundred and ten pounds — also suggestive of diabetes.

THE FALL AND ITS CONSEQUENCES

Mrs. Lincoln's fall from a step-ladder, in Pau, caused her to return to America and to her sister's home. It kept her in bed for a number of weeks and no doubt occasioned considerable pain. After returning to Springfield she went to New York twice for treatment.

The New York *Graphic* [1] carried the following story of her illness: "The chief injuries she sustained by this fall manifested themselves in an inflammation of the spinal cord and a partial paralysis of the lower part of her body. For these injuries she twice consulted Dr. Lewis A. Sayre of this city. In October 1881, she came to New York to see Doctor

[1] July 18, 1882.

Sayre for the second time, taking rooms at the Clarendon Hotel. About January, 1, 1882, Doctor Sayre said: 'I found she could not walk safely without the aid of a chair and even then she was liable to fall at times.' Later, Mrs. Lincoln moved to a water-cure establishment on 26th Street, where she remained under Doctor Sayre's care until March, when she returned to Springfield, but little improved in health."

Dr. Sayre's diagnosis indicated a severe injury. Yet none of the stories relative to Mrs. Lincoln's life between March and July 1882 make reference to any after-effects of this injury.

FINAL ILLNESS AND DEATH

In 1882 Mrs. Lincoln was again suffering from boils, and all the witnesses agree that she was very much underweight. She remained in seclusion most of the time, in an artificially lighted room. There is testimony that her mind showed evidence of loss of quality. The summer of that year was intensely hot and dry, and this added greatly to Mrs. Lincoln's discomfort.

That she was a sick woman her relatives could see, but they had no suspicion that death was near. It is true that she often talked of dying, but the family had heard similar expressions from her more than once and had come to disregard them.

On Friday, two days before the final issue, she became distinctly worse. Some of the accounts indicate that on that day she was in less pain from her boils — at least she complained less — and at times she was heavy mentally — probably no more than semi-conscious. As to what happened in the sick-room on the next day there is not entire agreement.

The following is the account of her last illness and death as given in the *Illinois State Journal:* [1] " Within the past few days Mrs. Lincoln has been suffering from an attack of boils

[1] Monday, July 17, 1882.

which caused her great pain and, no doubt, greatly increased her nervousness. On Friday, last, she was up and walked across the room. Again, on Saturday, she walked across the room with a little assistance; but she grew worse later in the day and about nine o'clock in the evening experienced a paralysis which seemed to involve her whole system, so that she was unable to articulate, to move any part of her body, or to take food. She soon afterward passed into a comatose state and so continued, breathing stertorously up to 8.15 P.M., Sunday, when she died."

This was substantially the story telegraphed over the United States and carried in a majority of the newspapers which took notice of the passing of Mrs. Lincoln.

Dr. T. W. Dresser's death certificate read that she died from "paralysis." Generally speaking, the word "paralysis" is very loosely used. It might refer to any one of several kinds of apoplexy, to diabetic coma, to unconsciousness due to drugs or poisons, or to general paralysis of the insane, called paresis. Dr. Dresser clarified the certificate with the statement, given to William H. Herndon,[1] that he meant apoplexy. There was no necropsy.

Mrs. Lincoln did not have general paresis, and her unconsciousness was not due to drugs or poisons. The description of her death, as given in the newspapers, is confirmatory of Dr. Dresser's opinion that the immediate cause of death was apoplexy, probably due to the rupture of a blood vessel in the brain.

There is considerable suspicion of diabetic coma, in some degree, during the last week of her life. Nor do the newspaper accounts of her last three days preclude the possibility that this was the immediate cause of her death. Apoplexy merely seems to be the better explanation. However, there is no contradiction between diabetes, and even diabetic coma, and apoplexy.

Mrs. Lincoln was in her sixty-fourth year, and that is just

[1] Bibliography, No. 75a, p. 434.

in the middle of the apoplexy period. She may have had, and probably did have, diabetes. That disease damages the blood vessel walls in a way that no other disease surpasses. Proof of that is the frequency of diabetic gangrene. It is probable that if Mrs. Lincoln had diabetes her disease had damaged the walls of the blood vessels of her brain.

Mrs. Lincoln died on Sunday night, July 16, 1882, in the home of her sister Mrs. Edwards. The funeral was delayed until her son, Robert, then Secretary of War, could reach Springfield from Washington. The funeral services were held in the parlor in which she had been married.

Governor Cullom issued a proclamation in which he ordered all public activities suspended during the funeral exercises, and asked all business houses and all citizens to unite reverently in honoring Mary Lincoln for her own virtues and out of respect to the memory of her husband. The Mayor of Springfield proclaimed a suspension of business and commended her virtues. Her body was borne from the Edwards home to Oak Ridge Cemetery by Governor Cullom and other leading citizens, while Springfield did her honor. At last she was at rest by the side of her husband and her children.

The newspaper comment of the Springfield papers appears kindly and even reverent. The Chicago papers were equally considerate. The Chicago *Times,* so often bitter in its attacks on Lincoln, joined in the tributes to his widow. The newspapers everywhere seemed willing to cover her memory with a mantle of charity. In Springfield gossip appeared to be stilled and dislikes forgotten; envy and enmity were at an end; old enemies and old friends joined in respectful tribute.

The years have passed. Those who knew her — friend and foe — have died. But tradition lives. And tradition has not been kind, or even just.

CHAPTER EIGHTEEN

Justice

He hath shewed thee, O man, what is good; and what doth the Lord require of thee, but to do justly, and to love mercy, and to walk humbly with thy God?

— MICAH vi, 8

CHAPTER EIGHTEEN

Justice

WE, AS A PEOPLE, LIKE FAIR PLAY. WE BOAST OF OUR ability to give everybody a show in spite of prejudices — in spite of everything. Willingness to give the oppressed a chance to state their case and make their plea is a part of the Magna Charta — in fact, its very essence — and runs through all that is based thereon. On this principle is founded our system of jurisprudence. This is what the American public meant when it fought the Civil War and freed the slaves. It was what the political leaders of Mrs. Lincoln's period were talking about in their speeches, and what they were writing about in their papers.

We men regard ourselves as chivalrous. We profess a readiness to give a woman an even break. At least, we claim to be willing to do so if the woman is not in direct economic competition with us. Perhaps we are less chivalrous since the passage of the Nineteenth Amendment, but even now we would resent the charge that we are unfair to a woman in distress.

Have the American people been fair to Mrs. Lincoln? Have we, men or women, been willing to give her a day in court? Have we men been chivalrous toward her?

Here is Isaac N. Arnold's answer:[1] "The abuses which a portion of the American press so pitilessly poured upon the head of Mary Lincoln recall that splendid outburst of

[1] Bibliography, No. 4, pp. 439–40.

eloquence upon the part of Burke, when speaking of the Queen of France. 'Little did I dream that I should live to see such disasters fall upon her in a nation of gallant men; a nation of honor; cavaliers. I thought ten thousand swords would have left their scabbards to avenge even a look that threatened her with insult. But the age of chivalry has gone.' May I also remind you of the words of the Earl of Oxford to the Duke of Burgundy, when the latter spoke coarsely of Margaret of Anjou. 'My lord, whatever may have been the defects of my mistress, she is in distress and almost in desolation.' "

W. O. Stoddard had the gift of prophecy when he gave utterance to the following:[1] " People are picking up all sorts of stray gossip relating to asserted occurrences under this roof [the White House], and they are making strange work out of some of it. It is a work they will not cease from. They will do it to the very end so effectively that a host of excellent people will one day close their eyes to the wife's robe with her husband's blood. There will be in that day a strange blindness and brutality concerning the awful shock produced by an infernal murder. Then charity and chivalry alike will be forgotten in the sneering comments which will follow the remaining days of a disturbed mind and a shattered nervous system. Even the shadow of the tomb itself will, at last, not be regarded as a sufficient curtain to prevent an unjust judgment from peering and looking back to this time, and reading in it nothing but the prurient scandals of this feverish war time."

Howard Glyndon wrote:[2] " I think her extravagances of behavior, her hallucinations, her sufferings of mind and body have not met with that respect, that respectful silence and sympathy from the American Press and people, which the distinguished services of her husband to his country gave them a right to command. Her erratic behavior has been commented upon in a spirit which will not show well when all

[1] Bibliography, No. 168, p. 63.

[2] Bibliography, No. 61.

the events connected with her life have become history. I feel satisfied that in a few years Mrs. Lincoln will be thought of with the sincerest pity and that there will be a prevailing regret that the foibles and weaknesses of an unoffending woman, whose mind was shaken, as well it might be, by the sudden calamity which unhinged the whole nation, have not been less offensively dealt with."

At some time in 1875 General Adam Badeau wrote:[1] "The verdict that her mind was diseased relieved Mrs. Lincoln from the charge of heartlessness, of mercenary behavior, and of indifference to her husband's happiness. The pitiful story of Miramar casts no slur on Maximilian's Empress, and the shadow of insanity thrown across the intelligence of Mrs. Lincoln relieves her from reproach and blame."

J. F. Newton wrote:[2] "She was never popular as the First Lady of the Land, but that is no reason why her unfortunate traits should be emphasized to the neglect of others which were not only more numerous, but more lovely and winning. Pitiful was her grief after the last great tragedy which so shattered her mind that she was never herself again. Yet to the end she was pursued by a prying press in a manner so unmanly, so unchivalric, that one can find no words severe enough for rebuke."

Dr. William E. Barton said:[3] "But if we are unintentionally cruel to our Presidents, what shall be said of the manner in which we treat their wives. Who among them has escaped idle curiosity and even spiteful slander? . . . No woman who has occupied the White House, unless possibly the wife of Andrew Jackson, has suffered such merciless slander. The time has come when it should be possible to tell the truth concerning Mary Todd Lincoln."

If Abraham Lincoln had been able to foresee the harshness of the world toward his widow in the years of her

[1] Bibliography, No. 6.
[2] Bibliography, No. 127, p. 323.
[3] Bibliography, No. 9, p. 409.

tribulations and sorrows, the following words by Mary G. Chandler [1] would have precipitated an attack of melancholy: "A few generations ago there was a spirit which armed itself with fagot and axe in order to destroy those who held opinions in opposition to the dominant power. The axe and fagot have disappeared but, alas for human nature! The spirit that delighted in their use has not wholly passed away; the flame and the sword it uses now are those of malignity and hatred; it does not scorch nor wound the body, but only burns and sears the reputations of those whom it assails."

The science of behavior has developed far enough now for a sense of fair play to support a demand for less condemnation of Mrs. Lincoln between 1861 and 1871; you and I should be as understanding and sympathetic as Stoddard was after he had received the physician's opinion. Who today would condemn Mrs. Lincoln for her behavior in the last seventeen years of her life? If anyone does, he marks himself as uninformed and unfair.

[1] Bibliography, No. 31, p. 23.

Bibliography

Bibliography

1. *American Encyclopedia of Biography*, Vol. IV. J. T. White & Co.
2. *Anti-Jackson Bulletin*. Lexington, Kentucky, 1828.
3. ARNOLD, I. N.: *History of Abraham Lincoln and the Emancipation of the Slaves*. Clarke & Co., 1867.
4. ARNOLD, I. N., *Life of Abraham Lincoln*, third edition. Jansen, McClurg & Co., 1885.
5. Aurora *News Beacon*, July 21, 1923.
6. BADEAU, GENERAL ADAM, in New York *World*, January 8 (1875?).
7. Bard family. Chronicles of the, *Kittochtinny Magazine*, Vol. I, 1905. Chambersburg, Pennsylvania.
8. BARTON, WILLIAM E.: "Abraham Lincoln and New Salem," *Journal of the Illinois State Historical Society*, Vol. XIX, Nos. 3–4.
9. BARTON, WILLIAM E.: *Life of Abraham Lincoln*. 2 vols. Indianapolis: Bobbs-Merrill Co., 1925.
10. BARTON, WILLIAM E.: *Lincoln at Gettysburg*. Indianapolis: Bobbs-Merrill Co., 1930.
11. BARTON, WILLIAM E.: "Mr. and Mrs. Lincoln." *Woman's Home Companion*, February 1930.
12. BARTON, WILLIAM E.: "The Lincoln of the Biographers," *Transactions of the Illinois State Historical Society*, 1929.
13. BARTON, WILLIAM E.: "The Making of Abraham Lincoln and the Influence of Illinois in his Development," *Transactions of the Illinois State Historical Society*, 1921.
14. BARTON, WILLIAM E.: *The Soul of Abraham Lincoln*. New York: George H. Doran Co., 1920.
15. BARTON, WILLIAM E.: *The Women Lincoln Loved*. Indianapolis: Bobbs-Merrill Co., 1927.
16. Batavia *Herald*.
17. BAYNE, JULIA TAFT: *Tad Lincoln's Father*. Boston: Little, Brown & Co., 1931.
18. BEVERIDGE, A. J.: *Abraham Lincoln*. Vol. I. Boston: Houghton, Mifflin Co.
19. Bloomington *Pantagraph*, August 26, 1930. Bloomington, Illinois.

20. Boggess, A. C.: *The Settlement of Illinois, 1778–1830*, Vol. V. Chicago Historical Society, 1908.
21. Bowers, Claude G.: *The Tragic Era*. Boston: Houghton, Mifflin Co., 1929.
22. "Border History, Narrative Notes and Conversation with Judge Levi Todd, 1851," Library Wisconsin Historical Society.
23. Bradford, Gamaliel: *Wives*. New York: Harper & Bros., 1925.
24. Bradford, Gamaliel, in *Harper's Magazine*, September 1925.
25. Brooks, N.: *Washington in Lincoln's Time*. New York: Century Co., 1895.
26. Brown, F. F.: *The Everyday Life of Abraham Lincoln*. Chicago: Brown & Howell Co., 1914.
27. Butler, Samuel: *The Way of All Flesh*.

28. Carpenter, F. B.: *Six Months at the White House*. Hurd & Houghton, 1866.
29. Carr, H. A.: *Personality*. Longmans, Green & Co., 1925.
30. Chandler, Josephine Craven: "Lincolns in Springfield," *National Republic*, February 1931.
31. Chandler, Mary G.: *The Elements of Character*, fourth edition. Crosby, Nichols & Co., 1856.
32. Chicago *Daily News*.
33. *Chicago Daily News Almanac*.
34. Chicago *Journal*.
35. Chicago *Mail*.
36. Chicago *Post*.
37. Chicago *Post and Mail*, July 13, 1875.
38. Chicago *Times*.
39. Chicago *Tribune*.
40. Clark Manuscript, Draper Collection, Wisconsin Historical Society.
41. Clemmer, Mary Ames: *Ten Years in Washington: Life and Scenes at the National Capitol as a Woman Sees Them*. Lloyd D. Worthington, 1876.
42. Cole, A. C.: "The Era of the Civil War, 1848–1870," *Centennial History of Illinois*, Vol. III. Illinois Centennial Commission, 1919.
43. Cole, A. C.: "Lincoln and the Presidential Election, 1864," *Transactions of the Illinois State Historical Society*, 1917.
44. Colman, Edna M.: *Seventy-five Years of White House Gossip*. Garden City: Doubleday, Page & Co., 1925.

45. *Congressional Globe* (*Record*), 40th and 41st Congresses.
46. Cook County, Illinois, Lunatic Record of County Court.
47. *Cultivator*, N. S. II, 1845. Quoted by U. B. Phillips.

48. DORLAND: *The American Medical Dictionary*, fifteenth edition.
49. Draper Collection, Wisconsin Historical Society.
50. Durrett Collection, University of Chicago.

51. EAMES, CHARLES M.: *Historic Morgan and Classic Jacksonville*. Jacksonville: *Daily Journal*, 1885; printed by *Daily Journal* Steam Job Printing Office.
52. EDWARDS, MRS. ELIZABETH: Narrative. Lamon copy of Herndon MS. Huntington Library and Art Gallery, Pasadena, California.
53. ELLETT, MRS. E. F.: *Court Circles of the Republic*. Philadelphia Publishing Co., 1872.
54. ELLIS, HAVELOCK: *Philosophy and Conflict*. Boston: Houghton, Mifflin & Co., 1919.

55. Fayette County (Kentucky) Circuit Court, August term, 1859, Louisa Todd, Plaintiff, versus Levi O. Todd, Defendant. Filed July 12, 1859.
56. FEARON, H. B.: "Sketches of America," *Niles' Weekly Register*, VIII. London, 1819.
56a. FEARON, H. B.: *Sketches of America*. London, 1818.
56b. FEARON, H. B.: *Sketches of America*. Cleveland, 1906.
57. FELL, JESSE W.: "Incidents Connected With Lincoln Autobiography." Photostat copy in Union League Club Library.
58. FERGUSON, W. J.: "Lincoln's Death," *Saturday Evening Post*, February 12, 1927.
59. FORDHAM, E. P., in *Niles' Weekly Register*.
59a. FORDHAM, E. P.: *Personal Narrative*. Cleveland: A. H. Clark Co., 1906.
60. FOY, EDDIE and HARLOW, A. E.: "Clowning through Life," *Collier's Weekly*, December 25, 1926.

61. GLYNDON, HOWARD: "The Truth about Mrs. Lincoln," *Independent*, August 10, 1882.
62. GOLTZ, C. W.: *Incidents in the Life of Mary Todd Lincoln*. Sioux City, Iowa: Deitch & Lamar Co., 1928.
63. GORDON, L. L.: *From Lady Washington to Mrs. Cleveland*. Boston: Lee and Shepard, 1889.

64. GRAYSON, CARY T.: "Health of the Presidents," *Ladies' Home Journal*, May 1927.
65. GREEN, T. M.: *Historic Families of Kentucky*. Chicago: Robert Clarke & Co., 1889.
66. GREENVILLE, S. C., *News*.
67. GRIMSLEY, MRS. ELIZABETH TODD: "Six Months in the White House," *Journal of the Illinois State Historical Society*, Vol. XIX, Nos. 3–4.

68. HAMMOND, W. A.: *Spiritualism and Allied Causes and Conditions of Nervous Derangement*. London: H. K. Lewis, 1876.
69. HARRIS, W. T.: *Remarks made during a Tour through the U.S.A., 1817–1819*. London, 1821.
70. *Headlight*, 1879.
71. HEINL, FRANK J.: "Newspapers and Periodicals in the Lincoln-Douglas Country, 1831–1832," *Journal of the Illinois State Historical Society*, Vol. XXIII, No. 3.
72. HELM, MRS. EMILIE TODD: "Mary Todd Lincoln," *McClure's Magazine*, 1898, Vol. II.
73. HELM, KATHERINE: *Mary, Wife of Lincoln*. New York: Harper & Bros., 1928.
74. HENDERSON, ARCHIBALD: *The Conquest of the Old Southwest*. New York: Century Co., 1920.
75. HERNDON, W. H., and J. W. WEIK: *Abraham Lincoln*. First printing, 3 vols., Chicago: Belford, Clarke & Co., 1889.
75a. HERNDON, W. H., and J. W. WEIK: *Abraham Lincoln*. First edition, second printing, Springfield, Illinois. Herndon's Lincoln Publishing Co., 1922.
75b. HERNDON, W. H., and J. W. WEIK: *Abraham Lincoln*. Second edition, 2 vols., New York: D. Appleton & Co., first printing, 1892.
75c. HERNDON, W. H., and J. W. Weik: *Abraham Lincoln*. New York: A. & C. Boni, 1930.
76. HERR, REV. HANS: *Genealogic Record of Herr Family*. Lancaster, Pennsylvania, 1908.
77. HERRICK, MRS. GENEVIEVE FORBES: "Democracy's Drawing-room," Chicago *Sunday Tribune*, December 16, 1928; February 9, 16, 23, 1929.
78. HOLDEN, RAYMOND: *Abraham Lincoln, the Politician and the Man*. New York: Minton, Balch & Co., 1929.
79. HOLLAND, J. G.: *Life of Abraham Lincoln*. Gurdon Bill, 1866.
80. HOLLOWAY, LAURA C.: *The Ladies of the White House*. Philadelphia: Bradley & Co., 1885.
81. HOMER, HENRY, *Address*, Springfield, 1928. Privately printed.

82. *Illinois State Historical Society, Journal of the*, September 1922.
83. *Illinois State Journal.*
84. *Illinois State Register*, 1882.

85. KECKLEY, ELIZABETH: *Behind the Scenes.* New York: G. W. Carleton & Co., 1868.
86. *Kendall County Record.*
87. *Kendall County Record and Batavia Herald.*
88. *Kentucky Gazette.* Lexington, Kentucky.
89. (*Kentucky Monitor*) *Western Monitor.* Lexington, Kentucky.
90. *Kentucky Observer.* Lexington, Kentucky.
91. *Kentucky Observer and Reporter.* Lexington, Kentucky.
92. *Kentucky Reporter.* Lexington, Kentucky.
93. *Kentucky Statesman.* Lexington, Kentucky.
94. *Kittochtinny Magazine*, Chambersburg, Pennsylvania, 1905 (see No. 7).
95. *Knox's Springfield City Directory*, 1857–8.
96. KOEHLER, G.: "The Establishment of Lotteries in Illinois for the Purpose of Raising Fund to Improve the Public Health." *Transactions of the Illinois State Historical Society*, 1928.
97. KOERNER, GUSTAV: *Memoirs.* Cedar Rapids, Iowa: Torch Press, 1909.

98. LAMON, W. H., Copy of Herndon Manuscript, Huntington Library and Art Gallery, Pasadena, California.
99. LAMON, WARD H.: *The Life of Abraham Lincoln.* Boston: J. R. Osgood & Co., 1872.
100. LAMON, W. H.: *Recollections of Abraham Lincoln.* Washington: Dorothy L. Teillard, 1911.
101. LEWIS, LLOYD: *Myths After Lincoln.* New York: Harcourt, Brace & Co., 1929.
102. LEWIS, LLOYD: "When Tad Lincoln had 'A Girl' in Chicago," Chicago *Daily News*, Midweek Section, February 5, 1930.
103. Lexington (Kentucky) *Herald.*
104. Lexington (Kentucky) *Intelligencer.*
105. Lexington (Kentucky) *Public Advertiser.*
106. LINCOLN, ABRAHAM: Autobiographical statement of 600 words, made to Jesse W. Fell, December 1859. Photostat copy in Union League Club Library.
107. LINCOLN, ABRAHAM: Letter to Mrs. Lincoln, April 16, 1846,

owned by Oliver R. Barrett, *Collier's Weekly*, February 11, 1928.
108. LINCOLN, MARY: *A Letter to Her Cousin, Elizabeth Grimsley, September 29, 1861*. Privately printed, 1917, H. E. Barker.
109. LINCOLN, MARY: Letter to Mrs. Orne.
110. LINCOLN, MARY: Letter to Mrs. White.
111. LINCOLN, MARY: Letter from somewhere in Europe, no address. Property of O. W. Hannah, Kenilworth, Illinois.
112. LINCOLN, MARY: Letter to Mr. Williamson.
113. LINCOLN, ROBERT: Letter to Rev. Henry Darling, November 15, 1877. Collection Chicago Historical Society.

114. Marysville *Eagle*. Marysville, Kentucky.
115. MASTERS, EDGAR LEE: *Lincoln, the Man*. New York: Dodd, Mead & Co., 1931.
116. MCCARTHY, C. H.: *Lincoln's Plan of Reconstruction*. New York: McClure, Phillips & Co., 1901.
117. MCCOLLISTER, C. L., in *Bulletin*, Massachusetts Department Mental Diseases, Vol. XIV, 1930.
118. MELISH, JOHN: *Travels in the United States, 1806–1809*. Philadelphia, 1812.
119. MENNINGER, KARL: *The Human Mind*. New York: Alfred A. Knopf, 1930.
120. MORROW, HONORÉ WILLSIE: "Lincoln's Last Day with his Wife" (two letters of Mrs. Lincoln's, 1865), *Cosmopolitan Magazine*, February 1930.
121. MORROW, HONORÉ WILLSIE: *Mary Todd Lincoln*. New York: Morrow & Co., 1928.
122. MORROW, HONORÉ WILLSIE: "The Woman Lincoln Loved," *Cosmopolitan Magazine*, May 1927.
123. MORSE, JOHN T.: *Abraham Lincoln*, American Statesmen Series. Boston: Houghton, Mifflin Co., 1893.
124. MURRAY, SIR JAMES A. H. (editor): *A New English Dictionary*. Oxford.

125. *National Reporter*, "Lincolns in Springfield," February 1931.
126. NEVINS, ALLAN: *Lincoln's Plans for Reunion*, Abraham Lincoln Association Papers. Springfield, Illinois: Abraham Lincoln Association, 1931.
127. NEWTON, J. F.: *Lincoln and Herndon*. Cedar Rapids, Iowa: Torch Press, 1910.
128. New York *Daily Graphic*.
129. New York *Daily Tribune*.
130. *New York Tribune Almanac*.

131. New York *World*.
132. NICOLAY, JOHN G., and JOHN HAY: *Abraham Lincoln: A History*. 10 vols. New York: Century Co., 1890.
133. NICOLAY, JOHN G., *A Short Life of Abraham Lincoln*. New York: Century Co., 1902.
134. *Niles' Weekly Register*.

135. OGLESBY, GOV. R. J.: Letter to, from Mrs. A. Lincoln, written June 11, 1865. In possession of Hon. John Oglesby, Elkhart, Illinois.

136. PATTERSON, DR. R. J.: Letter about Mrs. Lincoln, *Illinois State Journal*, September 1, 1875.
137. PEASE, T. C.: "Illinois Election Returns, 1818–1848," *Illinois Historical Collections*, Vol. XVIII; Statistical Series, Vol. I.
138. PEASE, T. C.: "The Story of Illinois," *Centennial History of Illinois*, Vol. II. Chicago: A. C. McClurg Co., 1925.
139. PETER, MISS R. (editor): *History of Medical Department of Transylvania University*. Louisville: John P. Morton & Co., 1905.
140. PHILLIPS, U. B.: *Life and Labor in the Old South*. Boston: Little, Brown & Co., 1929.
141. POORE, BEN PERLEY: *Reminiscences of Sixty Years in the National Metropolis*, Vol. II. Philadelphia: Hubbard Bros., 1886.
142. PORTER, HORACE: *Campaigning with Grant*. New York: Century Co., 1897.
143. PORTER, W. A.: "Life of General Andrew Porter," *Pennsylvania Magazine*, Vol. IV, No. 3, 1880.
144. POWER, J. C.: *History of Springfield, Illinois, Its Attractions as a Home and Advantages for Business*. Springfield, E. A. Wilson & Co., 1871. Published under auspices of Springfield Board of Trade. *Illinois State Journal* Print.

145. RANCK, G. W.: *Guide Book to Lexington*.
146. RANCK, G. W., *History of Lexington, Kentucky*. Chicago: O. L. Baskin & Co., 1882.
147. RANCK, G. W.: *History of Lexington, Kentucky*. Robert Clarke & Co., 1892.
148. RANKIN, HENRY B.: *Intimate Character Sketches of Abraham Lincoln*. Philadelphia: J. B. Lippincott Co., 1924.
149. RANKIN, HENRY B.: *Personal Recollections of Abraham Lincoln*. New York: G. P. Putnam's Sons, 1916.

150. REYNOLDS, JOHN: *The Pioneer History of Illinois*. Chicago: Fergus Printing Co., 1887.

151. RIDENBAUGH, MARY: *Biography of Ephraim McDowell*. New York, 1890.

152. SANDBURG, CARL: *Abraham Lincoln, The Prairie Years*. New York: Harcourt, Brace & Co., 1926.

153. Sangamon County, Illinois, Court Records, 1871, Probate Court Book of Inventories.

154. Sangamon County, Illinois, County Court Records, 1882–1884, L. H. Ticknor, Clerk.

155. SAXON, LYLE: *Old Louisiana*. New York: Century Co., 1929.

156. SCRIPPS, JOHN LOCKE: *Life of Abraham Lincoln, 1860 Campaign*. Peoria, Illinois: Edward J. Jacob, 1931. Foreword by M. L. HOUSER. Also Cranbrook Press, 1900.

157. SHANE, REV. JOHN D., Kentucky Manuscripts, Wisconsin Historical Society.

158. SHAW, ALBERT: *Abraham Lincoln, The Year of his Election*. 2 vols. New York: Review of Reviews Corp., 1929.

159. SHERMAN, W. T.: *Memoirs of General W. T. Sherman*. 2 vols. New York: D. Appleton & Co., 1887.

160. SINGLETON, ESTHER: *The Story of the White House*. New York: McClure Co., 1907.

161. SPEED, JOSHUA F.: *Reminiscences of Abraham Lincoln*. Louisville, Kentucky: John P. Morton & Co., 1884.

162. *Spirit of the Times*. Draper Collection, Wisconsin Historical Society.

163. *Spirit of Washington*. 1832.

164. Springfield, Massachusetts, *News*.

165. Springfield, Illinois, *Register*.

166. STOCKARD, C. R.: *Physical Basis of Personality*. New York: W. W. Norton Co., 1931.

167. STODDARD, W. O.: *Abraham Lincoln*. New York: Fords, Howard and Hulbert, 1884.

168. STODDARD, W. O.: *Inside the White House in War Time*. C. L. Webster & Co., 1890.

169. SWISSHEIM, JANE GRAY, Swissdale, Pennsylvania, Letters from, to Chicago *Tribune*, July 17 and 20, 1882.

170. TARBELL, IDA M.: *In the Footsteps of the Lincolns*. New York: Harper & Bros., 1924.

171. TARBELL, IDA M.: *The Life of Abraham Lincoln*. New York: S. S. McClure Co., 1895. Doubleday, McClure Co., 1900.

172. TARBELL, IDA M.: *The Life of Abraham Lincoln.* New York: Macmillan Co., 1923.

173. TODD, LEVI: "Chronological Narrative of Events in Kentucky." Draper Collection, Wisconsin Historical Society, Kentucky Papers.

174. TODD, ROBERT S., in Draper Collection, Wisconsin Historical Society, Kentucky Papers.

175. TOWNSEND, WILLIAM H.: *Abraham Lincoln, Defendant.* Boston: Houghton, Mifflin Co., 1923.

176. TOWNSEND, WILLIAM H.: *Lincoln and his Wife's Home Town.* Indianapolis: Bobbs-Merrill Co., 1929.

177. TOWNSEND, WILLIAM H.: *Lincoln, the Litigant.* Boston: Houghton, Mifflin Co., 1925.

178. *Transylvania College Bulletin,* Transylvania Library. Vol. XIII, No. 3, March 1922.

179. WAKEMAN: Letter about Mrs. Lincoln, Chicago *Tribune,* January 19, 1930.

180. WALLACE, JOSEPH: *Past and Present of the City of Springfield and Sangamon County, Illinois.* 2 vols. Chicago: S. J. Clarke Pub. Co., 1904.

181. WALLACE, MRS. FRANCES: *Lincoln's Marriage,* Newspaper interview, September 2, 1895. Privately printed, H. E. Barker, 1917.

182. WALLACE, MRS. WILLIAM: Statement given W. H. Herndon, Lamon Copy, Huntington Library and Art Gallery, Pasadena, California.

183. WARREN, L. A.: *Lincoln Lore.*

184. WARREN, L. A.: *Lincoln's Parentage and Childhood,* New York: Century Co., 1926.

185. *Webster's New International Dictionary.* Springfield, Mass.: G. & C. Merriam Co., 1927.

186. WEIK, J. W.: *The Real Lincoln: A Portrait.* Boston: Houghton, Mifflin Co., 1922.

187. WHALER, JAMES: *Green River.* New York: Harcourt, Brace & Co., 1931.

188. WHITE, HORACE: "Abraham Lincoln in 1854," *Transactions of the Illinois State Historical Society,* 1908.

189. WHITE, HORACE: Introduction to Herndon's and Weik's *Abraham Lincoln,* second edition. New York: D. Appleton & Co., 1892 (see 75 b).

190. WHITNEY, HENRY C.: *Abraham Lincoln.* Garden City: Doubleday, Page & Co., 1908.

191. WHITNEY, H. C.: *Life on the Circuit with Lincoln.* Boston: Estes & Lauriat, 1892.
192. *Williams' Springfield City Directory*, 1860.
193. WINN, MARY DAY: *Adam's Rib.* New York: Harcourt, Brace & Co., 1931.
194. *Wisconsin State Journal.*

Index

Index

Adams, Charles Francis, 182–3
Adams, J. McGregor, 214
Adams, John Quincy, 176
Alston, John, 201, 202
Angle, P. M., 18–19
Arnold, Charles, 130, 155
Arnold, I. N., 14, 22, 126, 144, 149, 150–1, 152, 214, 226, 236, 238, 277, 320, 349
Audubon, 93
Ayer, B. F., 214

Badeau, Adam, 210–11, 271, 297, 298, 351
Baker, Julia, 291
Barlow, Thomas Harris, 95
Barnes, Captain, 298
Barrett, Jennie, 292
Barrett, Oliver R., 82, 210, 237, 291, 294, 332
Barton, William E., 3–4, 9, 14, 18, 60, 86, 140, 146, 147, 154–5, 166, 183, 237, 253, 278, 293, 313, 324, 325, 329, 351
Bayne, Julia Taft, 24, 55, 59, 61, 69–70, 71, 104–5, 139, 165, 279, 300, 301
Beecher, Edward, 11
Bell, John, 48
Bennett, James Gordon, 172
Beveridge, A. J., 46, 85, 143, 145, 149–50, 154, 328, 330
Birchall, Miss, 142, 291
Bissell, William H., 142
Black, 13
Blaigue, Mme, 99
Blake, S. C., 214, 305
Blennerhassett, Harman, 95
Bleuler, 230, 272
Boggs, Mrs., 91–2
Boswell, Mrs., 92
Bradwell, J. B., 27, 224, 308
Brady, 275
Breckinridge, John C., 89, 147
Briggs, Jane, 34
Briggs, Samuel, 34
Brooks, N., 59, 60, 61, 247, 265
Brown, Dwight, 291
Brown, F. F., 320, 330
Brown, John, 95
Brown, Mary Edwards, 28, 46, 77, 78
Brown, Samuel, 41–2, 87, 93, 96
Browning, O. H., 22
Browning diary, 154
Brownlow, Senator, 206, 209
Bryant, William Cullen, 122
Buchanan, James, 176
Bunn, Jacob, 143, 201, 312, 324
Burgundy, Duke of, 350
Burke, Edmund, 350
Burr, Aaron, 95, 99
Butler, Samuel, 302

Caldwell, Professor, 99
Calhoun, John, 121
Calhoun, John C., 89
Cameron, D. R., 214
Cameron, Simon, 209, 254, 271

Carpenter, F. B., 300
Carpenter, Lulu Boone, 57–8, 59
Carr, Eliza Todd (Mrs. Charles M.), 56, 67, 77, 78
Cartwright, 124
Chandler, Mary G., 294, 325, 352
Chapin, C. A., 225
Chase, Salmon P., 332
Cigrand, B. J., 27
Clark, George Rogers, 32, 34, 96
Clark, James L., 327
Clay, Henry, 35, 88–9, 90, 93, 96, 98, 99, 103, 116, 127, 234, 288
Clay, Thomas H., 101
Clemmer, Mary Ames, 23, 177, 179–81
Cogswell, Thomas, 214
Cole, A. C., 252, 257
Colman, Edna M., 23, 174–5, 177
Conkling, 143
Conn, Senator, 204
Cooke, Professor, 100
Corbett, Senator, 208
Cordella, Professor, 100
Crittenden, John J., 87
Crooks, Mayor, of Springfield, 39
Cullom, Shelby M., 345
Cunningham, Mrs. H. C., 118

Dahl, H., 225
Danforth, Willis, 25, 194, 213, 215–16, 265, 305–6, 316, 339
Darling, Henry, 227
Davis, B. F., 196
Davis, David, 11, 25, 26, 59, 60, 61, 124, 125, 167, 210, 213, 217, 240, 241, 243, 244, 246, 310, 330, 331
Davis, Jefferson, 94, 183
Davis, N. S., 212, 215, 305, 306
Dawson, Elodie Todd, 51
Dawson, N. H. R., 51, 52
Douglas, Stephen A., 9, 44, 87, 88, 113, 122, 124, 125, 144, 146, 147, 148, 254, 255
Drake, Dan, 93, 96, 97, 100
Dresser, T. W., 229, 305, 306, 344
Drew, W. J., 225
Dudley, B. W., 87, 93, 94, 95, 101
Dunham, W. S., 225
Dunlap, Miss, 291
Durand, H. C., 214

Eames, C. M., 22
Eames, Mrs. Charles, 177, 182
Eaton, Polly, 177
Edmunds, Senator, 206, 207, 209
Edwards, Elizabeth (Mrs. N. W.), 21–2, 43–5, 65, 66, 67, 77, 78, 79, 81, 85–6, 100, 113, 114, 119, 130, 145, 163, 225, 226, 227, 228, 229, 230, 235, 291, 307, 308, 317, 345
Edwards, Ninian, 44, 81, 99, 122, 163
Edwards, Ninian Wirt, 43, 44, 78, 81, 99–100, 122, 163, 225–6, 233, 245, 246, 291
Ellett, Mrs. E. F., 23, 177, 178
Ellsworth, Ephraim E., 167

Farwell, Charles B., 214
Fearon, H. B., 90
Fell, Jesse, 9, 22, 146
Fenton, Senator, 208

Ferguson, W. J., 186
Ferron, V., 100
Fillmore, Millard, 128, 176
Fiske, Jim, 307
Fitzgerald, Mrs., 194, 213, 307, 319
Flint, Timothy, 90
Fordham, E. P., 90–1
Foy, Eddie, 194, 213, 307, 319
Frazier, Oliver, 95
Frémont, John Charles, 146, 253

Gage, Lyman J., 214
Garfield, James A., 228
Garfield, Lucretia Randolph, 228
Giron, M., 101
Givin, Mrs., 177
Gleason, Cyrus, 225
Glyndon, Howard, 350–1
Grant, Julia Dent, 297, 298
Grant, Ulysses S., 53, 203, 204, 205, 206, 255, 298
Gratz, Benjamin, 178
Greenhow, Mrs. Rose, 177
Griffin, Mrs., 297
Grigsby, Mrs., 138
Grimes, J. W., 150
Grimsley, Elizabeth Todd, 23, 46, 55, 58, 184, 237
Gunther, Charles F., 294, 295
Gurley, 143

Hambrecht, George F., 203
Hammond, W. A., 316
Hanks, Dennis, 326
Hanks, John, 326
Hanks, Nancy, *see* Lincoln, Nancy Hanks
Hardin, John J., 40, 327
Harlan, James, 195, 197, 209, 279
Harlan, Mary, *see* Lincoln, Mary Harlan
Harris, B. F., 122
Harrison, William Henry, 127, 176
Hart, Joel T., 95
Hay, John, 154, 330
Hay, Logan, 291
Hay, Milton, 149, 331
Heinl, Frank J., 122
Helm, B. H., 23, 51, 52, 175
Helm, Emilie Todd, 20, 21, 22, 23, 48, 51, 52, 65, 80, 102, 103, 143, 144, 151–2, 185, 253, 265, 270, 289–90, 291, 315, 316
Helm, Katherine, 19, 20, 21, 22, 65, 80, 82, 90, 94, 103, 104, 106, 107, 140, 275–6, 277, 279, 280, 289, 291, 310
Henry, Patrick, 32
Hemingway, 47
Henderson, C. M., 214
Herndon, William H., 9, 10–13, 14, 15–17, 18–19, 22, 24, 86, 117–18, 120, 129, 149, 152, 154, 155, 168, 185–6, 218, 236, 238, 293, 297, 325, 330, 331, 342
Herr, Katherine Todd, 48, 138
Herr, W. W., 51, 175
Herrick, Genevieve Forbes, 23, 176, 278
Holland, J. G., 10
Holloway, Laura C., 23, 174, 177, 229, 310, 319
Holly, Dr., 93
Hoover, Mrs., 177
Houser, M. L., 9
Howell, Senator, 208
Humphreys, Alexander, 86
Humphreys, Mrs. Alexander, 86–7

Humphreys, Charles, 97
Humphreys, Elizabeth, *see* Todd, Elizabeth Humphreys
Humphreys, Elizabeth (niece of Betsy Humphreys Todd), *see* Norris, Elizabeth Humphreys
Hunt, Henry H., 98
Hunt, J. W., 100
Hunt, Sallie Ward, 177, 178

Iles, Miss, 291
Isham, R. N., 214, 215, 305, 306

Jackson, Andrew, 89, 90, 99, 115–16, 176
Jackson, Mrs. Andrew, 351
Jayne, Julia, *see* Trumbull, Julia Jayne
Jefferson, Thomas, 95
Jeffry, Mrs., 177
Johnson, Andrew, 146, 181, 186, 255–6, 257, 258
Johnson, H. A., 212, 215, 305, 306
Jordan, David Starr, 93
Jouett, 93, 95, 98

Keckley, Elizabeth, 23, 24, 55, 59, 60, 140, 169–70, 175, 181, 194, 195, 198, 199, 201, 222, 239, 240, 242, 265, 278–9, 297, 300, 311, 324, 333
Kellogg, C. H., 51
Kellogg, Franklin Pierce, 51, 337
Kellogg, J. H., 329
Kellogg, Margaret Todd, 51
Keys, Mrs. Edward D., 28, 65
Kimball, D., 225
Knowles, S. F., 225
Knox, 22
Koehler, G., 18
Koerner, Gustav, 88, 91–2

Lafayette, 89, 95, 97, 98, 100
Lamon, Ward H., 13, 14, 293, 333
Lanphier, Mrs. John C., 77, 78
Lestant, 313–14
Lewis, Lloyd, 58, 59, 155, 319, 332
Lincoln, Abraham, 3; and his sons, 55–6, 58, 59, 165; and his wife's family, 48, 49; characteristics, 117–20; finances, 148–51, 168–9, 195–6, 209, 236–8, 241; illness with smallpox, 140–1; influence of Mrs. Lincoln on, 3, 4, 323–5, 326, 327–31, 332, 333, 334; influence on Mrs. Lincoln, 323–5; melancholia, 328–31; mentality, 324, 325–8, 334; opinion of his wife, 294–6, 314, 319, 333; political career: (1842–51) 127–8, 251–2; (1851–61) 145–8, 156, 157–8, 252–3, 254–5; (1861–5) 171–4, 195, 254–5; reunion plans, 255–7; sources of information about, 8–9, 10–19
Lincoln, Abraham (grandfather of the President), 26
Lincoln, Abraham (of Mass.), 147
Lincoln, Edward Baker, 55, 126, 130, 139–40, 185, 263, 264, 301, 313, 319
Lincoln, Mary (daughter of Robert T.), 53

Lincoln, Mary Harlan (Mrs. Robert T.), 69, 194, 195, 202, 217, 319, 340
Lincoln, Mary Todd (Mrs. Abraham):
achievement of objectives, 163–4
ancestry, 31–43, 61
and her sons, 52, 54, 56, 57, 60, 61, 126
and Lincoln's candidacy for the Senate, 145, 148
and Lincoln's death, 180, 185–6, 240, 265, 313, 318, 319
and Lincoln's election to the presidency, 115–16, 128, 157
and preventable diseases in her family, 139–41
and slavery, 253
and society, 87, 92, 107, 108, 113, 114, 129, 130, 131, 141–2, 164, 167, 174, 178–84, 195, 238, 239, 269–71, 272
and spiritualism, 193, 264–6, 315–16
appearance, 275; as a child, 275, 276; as a young woman, 275–7; as a wife, 276, 277–9; in later years, 279
artistic sense, 289, 302
as hostess, 142, 144, 151, 152, 156–7, 166, 270
as Mistress of the White House, 164–5, 166, 173–4, 178–84, 239, 312
as mother, 70, 131, 137–41, 143–4, 164, 165–6
as wife, 151–2, 153–4, 155, 165, 166, 287; *and see* home life, *and* influence on Lincoln
at Niagara Falls, 144
at the Batavia Sanatorium, 223–5
at the Lincoln-Douglas debate in Alton, 144
birth, 65
childhood, 65–9, 71, 72, 77–8, 83, 102–3, 235, 315
courtship, 117
death, 343–5
delusions, 216, 217, 225, 306, 307, 308–9, 318
dementia, 310, 317
diabetes, 337, 342, 344
discontent with Robert, 27, 53, 194
drugs, use of, 315, 341, 344
education, 78, 83–6, 107, 317
emotionalism, 71, 106, 126–7, 184, 186, 193, 195, 213, 218, 287, 293–4, 301, 313, 314, 317, 318, 333, 334
engagement to marry Lincoln, 78–9, 117, 120–1
ethical training, 67–9
extravagance, 238–9, 247, 309, 310, 311, 318; *and see* irresponsible purchases
fall, at Pau, and its consequences, 227–8, 311, 342
fearlessness, 104, 166
features, 280–4
final illness, 343–5
finances, 128–9, 148–51, 164, 167, 168–70, 195–210, 211, 217, 233–4, 310–13, 319
hallucinations, 185, 215, 306, 309, 315, 317–18, 320, 341, 350
headaches, 213, 338–9

health, 193–4, 211, 213, 229, 337–45
home life, 66–7, 79–81, 82, 130, 137, 139, 151–2, 331–2
house on Eighth Street, Springfield, 143
immediacy, 70, 71, 104–5
in Chicago, 25, 58, 144, 193, 194, 198–9, 211, 214, 216–17, 222, 271, 306–7
in Europe, 25, 210–11, 213, 227, 228, 246, 271, 272, 309, 317, 342
in Florida, 213, 214, 216, 271–2
influence of Lincoln upon, 323–5
influences upon, 138, 148, 157, 158, 299
influence upon Lincoln, 3, 4, 323–5, 326, 327–31, 332, 333, 334
inherited and transmitted traits, 31–62, 66, 71, 234
in Lexington, 20, 21, 65–9, 77–8, 79–81, 83–7, 90, 92, 94–5, 101, 102–4, 107, 113, 126, 150, 234, 235, 263
in London, 271
in New York, 158, 166, 180, 199, 227, 228, 238, 309, 310, 311, 317, 342–3
insanity, 194, 200, 214, 215–18, 221, 229, 230; beginning of, 158, 310, 318–20; type of, 305–18
in Springfield, 21, 22, 71, 78–9, 83, 113–17, 120–1, 126–7, 128–31, 137–40, 141–6, 147–9, 150–8, 225, 227, 228, 236–8, 263, 270, 271, 309–10, 318–19
in Washington, 23, 71, 126, 167–70, 171–5, 178–86, 263, 311, 314
in Waukesha, 271
irresponsible purchases, 158, 169–70, 184, 217, 230, 238–40, 245, 247, 306–7, 309, 311
jealousy, 297–9, 302
love of adornment, 35
marriage, 15, 79, 121, 145, 236
mentality, 245, 247, 277, 287, 289, 290, 301, 324
objectives: (1842–51) 127; (1861) 164; (1865) 195–6, 198, 202; (1875) 223–4
pension bill, 25, 146, 193, 202–10, 218, 243–4, 257–9, 271, 312
personality, 70, 218, 266, 287, 288; in youth, 71, 72, 80, 102–7, 108, 288–9; in womanhood, 151–2, 153–6, 166, 172, 174–5, 182, 233, 247, 289–302, 309, 317
pictures of, 94, 275, 276–7, 280–1, 283, 340–1
political aims, 195
political influences on personality, 90, 128, 148, 157, 158, 253–4
political judgment, 115, 116, 148, 155, 157, 171–2, 251, 252–3, 314, 323, 334
public opinion of, 4–5, 19, 345, 349–52
quoted, 43, 45–6, 69, 82, 142, 143, 170, 185, 186, 197–8, 201, 202–3, 204, 205–6, 210, 253, 291–2, 340
religion, 69, 126, 263–6
sanity trials, 25, 26, 31, 53,

214–18, 221, 225–6, 233, 306, 307, 316
sources of information about, 8–10, 14, 15–16, 18, 19–28
suicide, attempt at, 221–3
thyroid trouble, 340–1
travel, 193, 194, 316–17
"wanderlust," 224, 316–17
wardrobe sale, 25, 193, 198–201, 208, 218, 242–3, 257, 259
youth, 78–9, 83, 84, 85–7, 90, 92, 94–5, 107, 113
Lincoln, Nancy Hanks, 326
Lincoln, Robert Todd, 17, 18, 25, 26, 27, 35, 53–4, 59, 60, 61, 69, 126, 129, 137, 138, 144, 165, 194, 195, 197, 198, 211, 212–13, 214, 216–17, 218, 221, 222, 225, 226, 227, 233, 241, 244, 245, 246, 308, 310, 319, 345
Lincoln, Thomas (father of Abraham), 26, 326
Lincoln, Thomas (Tad), 12, 25, 26, 35, 57–61, 70, 71, 137, 138, 140, 141, 144, 165–6, 193, 194, 195, 198–9, 204, 210, 211, 213, 218, 241, 243, 244, 263, 265, 271, 306, 307, 313, 317, 318, 319, 340
Lincoln, William Wallace, 55–7, 58, 61, 70, 126, 137, 138, 140, 144, 165, 167, 168, 169, 181, 184, 185, 186, 213, 265, 266, 313, 319
Logan, John A., 228
Logan, Stephen T., 11, 42, 114, 327
Louis XIV, 84
Lovejoy, 11
Lyon, W. G., 225
Maginnis, Mrs., 291
Margaret of Anjou, 350
Marshall, H., 95
Marshall, Thomas A., 95
Mason, James A., 214
Masters, Edgar Lee, 129
Matheny, 330, 331
Mather family, 324–5
Matteson, Joel A., 143
Matteson, Mrs., 291
Maximilian, 351
McCarthy, C. H., 256, 257, 258
McClellan, George B., 36
McCollister, C. L., 317
McCormick, Cyrus, 95
McCoy, Dr., 60
McCreery, Senator, 206, 208, 209
McDowell, Ephraim, 94
Medill, Joseph, 255
Menefee, Richard H., 95
Menninger, Karl, 330
Mentelle, 84
Mentelle, Mme, 78, 84, 85, 86, 107
Mentelle, Mary, 101
Moore, S. M., 214
Morrill, Senator, 208, 209
Morris, M. M., 127
Morrow, Honoré Willsie, 19, 170, 183

Napoleon, 8, 89
Nevins, Allan, 256, 257, 258
Newton, J. F., 12–13, 16, 236, 237, 290, 330, 332–3, 351
Nicolay, John G., 128, 328–9, 330
Norris, Elizabeth Humphreys, 19, 20, 21, 57, 79, 80, 86, 90, 102–3, 106, 107, 251, 275, 276, 289

O'Bannon, H. L., 50
Oglesby, Richard J., 194
Oldham, William, 47, 97, 99
Orne, General, 204, 298
Orne, Mrs., 199, 203, 204, 298
Owens, Mary, 87, 118–19, 120, 329
Owsley, Katherine Bodley, 85, 87
Oxford, Earl of, 350

Paddock, R. M., 225, 305, 306
Palen, 98
Parker, Eliza (mother of Mrs. Lincoln), *see* Todd, Eliza Parker
Parker, Eliza Porter, 37–8, 67, 77, 78, 80, 81, 126, 150, 234, 235
Parker, John, 100–01
Parker, R. B., 101
Parker, Robert, 37, 39, 150, 234
Parkhurst, S. B., 214
Patterson, A. B., 49–50
Patterson, Martha, 181
Patterson, R. J., 26, 27, 224, 225, 305, 306, 307–8, 316, 317
Pease, T. C., 252
Peck, John Mason, 122
Peers, B. O., 99
Pepin, 98
Peter, R., 94
Phillips, U. B., 90, 91
Pickens, Mrs., 177
Pinch, Esther, 29
Poore, Ben Perley, 23, 170, 177, 179, 186, 278
Porter, Andrew, 36–7, 39, 40, 41
Porter, David Rittenhouse, 36
Porter, Eliza Parker, 36, 37
Porter, G. B., 36
Porter, Horace, 298
Porter, James Madison, 36
Porter, Joe, 49
Porter, John Ewing, 36–7, 40
Porter, Robert, 34
Porter, W. A., 36
Power, J. C., 22
Pratt, Senator, 206, 209
Preston, Colonel, 34

Rafinesque, 93–4
Ranck, G. W., 84, 92–3, 95
Randolph, Thomas Jefferson, 101
Rankin, Henry B., 14, 22, 152–4, 277, 333
Rawlins, Mrs., 202
Reed, Rev. Dr., 263
Reed, Walker, 101
Remann, Henry, 55, 56
Richardson, 101
Riddle, A. G., 320
Roberts, William, 225
Russell, W. H., 183
Rutledge, Ann, 10, 11, 14, 16, 17–18, 19, 87, 329, 330, 331, 333

Sandburg, Carl, 14
Santa Anna, Antonio Lopez, 95–6
Saulsbury, Senator, 208
Saxon, Lyle, 313
Sayre, Lewis A., 227–8, 311, 342–3
Schaffer, 96
Schurz, Carl, 206, 209
Scott, —, 291–2
Scott, Winfield, 147
Scripps, John L., 9, 22

Seward, William Henry, 255
Shakspere, 5
Shaw, Albert, 107, 172–4
Sheriff, Patrick, 122
Sherman, William Tecumseh, 255, 298
Shields duel episode, 328, 329
Shipman, Mrs., 340
Shipman, P. L., 210
Singleton, Esther, 23
Slidell, Mrs. Alexander, 177
Smith, Ann Todd (Mrs. C. M.), 43, 44, 45–7, 49, 65, 66, 82, 130, 144, 163
Smith, Byrd, 96
Smith, C. M., 44, 45–6, 130, 163, 169, 238
Smith, Charles Gilman, 212, 215, 306, 319
Smith, Ed, 337
Speed, J. F., 120
Spencer, Senator, 206, 209
Stanton, Edwin M., 255, 300, 332
Stanton, Mrs., 298
Stedman, 315
Stephens, Alexander H., 255
Stevens, Thaddeus, 255, 256, 258
Stewart, A. T., 169, 197
Stewart, William, 214
Stockard, C. R., 62, 70–1
Stoddard, W. O., 5, 14, 24, 140–1, 181–2, 271, 279, 299–300, 318, 350, 352
Stoneberger, B. F., 130, 155, 230, 279
Stuart, John T., 11, 42, 94, 114, 226, 327, 329
Stuart, Robert, 81, 94
Sumner, Charles, 183, 193, 203, 205, 206, 255
Swain, F., 308
Swett, Leonard, 149, 214, 225, 330
Swissheim, Jane Gray, 319

Taft, Mrs., 300–1
Tarbell, Ida M., 14–15, 153, 328
Taylor, Zachary, 127–8, 146, 176
Terman, Lewis M., 327
Thompson, Mrs. Jacob, 178
Thurman, Senator, 208
Tipton, Senator, 206, 207, 208, 209, 243
Todd, Alexander H., 48, 51, 79, 185
Todd, Ann, *see* Smith, Ann Todd
Todd, Betsy Humphreys, *see* Todd, Elizabeth Humphreys
Todd, David, 32
Todd, David (son of Levi), 34, 42
Todd, David H. (half-brother of Mrs. Lincoln), 48, 51, 52
Todd, Eliza, 38
Todd, Eliza (aunt of Mrs. Lincoln), *see* Carr, Eliza Todd
Todd, Elizabeth (sister of Mrs. Lincoln), *see* Edwards, Elizabeth Todd
Todd, Elizabeth Humphreys, 20, 38, 41, 42, 48, 49, 51, 56, 67, 77, 78, 79, 80, 81, 82, 83, 85, 86, 90, 94, 106, 113, 263
Todd, Eliza Parker, 38, 43, 48, 49, 51, 65–6, 67–8, 69, 77, 85, 138, 235
Todd, Elodie, *see* Dawson, Elodie Todd

Todd, Emilie P., *see* Helm, Emilie Todd
Todd, Frances, *see* Wallace, Frances Todd
Todd, George (son of G. R. C.), 49, 50
Todd, George Rogers Clark, 37, 40–1, 43, 47, 49–50, 82, 175
Todd, John (great-uncle of Mrs. Lincoln), 32, 33, 35, 39, 40, 41, 42, 327
Todd, Rev. John, 32, 35, 41
Todd, Katherine B., *see* Herr, Katherine Todd
Todd, Levi (grandfather of Mrs. Lincoln), 32, 33, 34, 35, 39, 40, 41, 42, 234
Todd, Levi O., 42, 43, 47–8, 65, 66, 79, 82, 126, 144, 175–6
Todd, Louisa, 47, 48
Todd, Margaret, *see* Kellogg, Margaret Todd
Todd, Martha K., *see* White, Martha Todd
Todd, Mary, *see* Lincoln, Mary Todd
Todd, Robert (great-uncle of Mrs. Lincoln), 32, 33, 34, 35, 39, 40, 42
Todd, Robert P., 65
Todd, Robert S., 33, 34–5, 38, 39, 40, 41, 42, 43, 48, 49, 51, 65, 66, 77, 78, 79, 80, 81, 82, 83, 87, 88, 90, 96–7, 98, 99, 100, 101–2, 103, 106, 126, 130, 144, 149, 150, 234, 235
Todd, Sam (uncle of Mrs. Lincoln), 39–40
Todd, Samuel B., 48, 51
Torrey, John, 93
Town, 102
Townsend, William H., 20, 22, 38, 47, 48, 65, 84, 85, 118, 253, 277, 289
Trumbull, Julia Jayne, 145, 146, 163
Trumbull, Lyman, 145, 163, 208
Tyler, John, 36, 127, 176

Vincent, T., 101

Wade, Benjamin, 205
Wallace, Frances Todd (Mrs. William), 21–2, 43, 44, 45, 65, 66, 79, 81–2, 113, 117, 128–9, 130, 151, 152, 163, 175, 226, 229, 235, 236, 289, 291
Wallace, Joseph, 22
Wallace, M. R. M., 214, 225, 226
Wallace, William, 44, 45, 163
Ward, Dr., 84, 86, 102
Warren, Colonel, 142, 291
Washburne, E. B., 14, 277
Washington, George, 12, 36
Weatherhead, D. J., 225
Weber, Jessie Palmer, 46
Webster, Daniel, 89
Weed, Thurlow, 199–200, 201
Weems, Mason Locke, 12
Weik, J. W., 13, 18, 154, 293, 331–2
Whaler, James, 93–4, 108
White, Clement, 51, 52
White, Horace, 12
White, Hugh M., 89
White, Martha Todd, 48, 51, 52, 210
Whitney, H. C., 149, 238, 320, 330, 333
Wickliffe, Robert, 97, 99, 100
Wild, R. F., 225

Williams, 22
Williamson, 196–7, 242
Williamson, Mrs., 51
Willis, N. P., 55
Winn, Mary Day, 87–8, 327
Woodbury, Mrs., 177

Xampis, 100

Yates, Senator, 208, 209

A NOTE ON THE TYPE IN WHICH THIS BOOK IS SET

THIS book has been set in a modern adaptation of a type designed by William Caslon, the first (1692–1766), who, it is generally conceded, brought the old-style letter to its highest perfection.

An artistic, easily-read type, Caslon has had two centuries of ever-increasing popularity in our own country—it is of interest to note that the first copies of the Declaration of Independence and the first paper currency distributed to the citizens of the new-born nation were printed in this type face.